Language and Cultural Diversity in U.S. Schools

LANGUAGE AND CULTURAL DIVERSITY IN U.S. SCHOOLS
Democratic Principles in Action

Edited by Terry A. Osborn

Educate US
David Gerwin and Terry A. Osborn, Series Editors

Westport, Connecticut
London

Library of Congress Cataloging-in-Publication Data

Language and cultural diversity in U.S. schools : democratic principles in action / edited
    by Terry A. Osborn.
        p. cm.—(Educate US, ISSN 1551-0425)
    Includes bibliographical references and index.
    ISBN 0-275-98202-5 (alk. paper)
    1. Multicultural education—United States.   2. Language arts—Social aspects—United
States. 3. Sociolinguistics—United States.   I. Osborn, Terry A.
LC1099.3.L37   2005
370.117'0973—dc22   2005013516

British Library Cataloguing in Publication Data is available.

Library of Congress Catalog Card Number: 2005013516

ISBN: 0-275-98202-5
ISSN: 1551-0425

First published in 2005

Praeger Publishers, 88 Post Road West, Westport, CT 06881
An imprint of Greenwood Publishing Group, Inc.
www.praeger.com

Printed in the United States of America

The paper used in this book complies with the
Permanent Paper Standard issued by the National
Information Standards Organization (Z39.48-1984).

10 9 8 7 6 5 4 3 2 1

For Joshua and Juliana

In gratitude for their laughter.

Contents

Series Foreword

It is a rare week in which an issue in education fails to make headlines in the United States. Parents, policy makers, educators, and taxpayers have a stake in the developments regarding schools and schooling. Though the public is increasingly sophisticated in its understanding of the intricacies of education, however, popular media venues offer little opportunity for an in-depth treatment of the relevant points related to the vital decisions that are made in boardrooms, classrooms, homes, and voting booths. *Educate US* is a series presenting a comprehensive discussion of issues in a forum that minimizes technical jargon as it explores the various facets of the problems and potential in U.S. education. The authors and contributors to this series are those whose concerns about the health and welfare of education in the United States are translated into activism. Scholarship is not merely about the gaining of expertise; it includes an inherent component of advocacy. The nature of education in a democracy requires one to take a well-advised position and then to let one's voice be heard. This activity is at least as important as—in many ways so much more vital than—the technical aspects of the scholar's craft.

Language and culture are at the heart of the educational process in a democracy. Equity and justice in education necessitate a full understanding of the nature of language, cultural mediation, and schooling. The authors in this text, therefore, introduce the reader to some of the pressing issues of today.

The contributors help in fulfilling the more ambitious goals of the series, expanding the dialogue to include all of us who, as participants in a democracy, must make reasoned choices when we elect officials, support causes, and together shape the future of public education. Make no mistake, the world of public schooling, as is true for our democracy, is not a fait accompli. We make and remake our future collectively every day.

To participate in a meaningful and beneficial way, therefore, we all must recognize that deeper than questions of election year politics, accountability, and slogans, many decisions regarding education are essentially moral in nature. Choices that seem expedient or fit ideologically charged models designed to appeal to the masses may nevertheless be harmful to our society, and ultimately our children. If *Educate US* convinces series readers to weigh choices in that vein, it will have achieved its purpose. Living in a time of daily concerns related to homeland security and prosecuting numerous wars, we would do well to remember the words of Mark Twain, "It is curious—curious that physical courage should be so common in the world, and moral courage so rare." Curious, indeed.

Professor Terry A. Osborn, Series Editor

Acknowledgments

It is said that editing a text is like herding cats. I would dispute that description in that I have nothing but praise for a most professional group of scholars who have contributed to this text and have found cats to be much less cooperative. Beyond the contributors themselves, I would like to thank Elizabeth Potenza and Marie Ellen Larcada at Praeger for their patience and helpfulness. My colleagues in the Department of Curriculum and Instruction, Neag School of Education, continue to be a most supportive and dedicated community of scholars with whom it is an honor to work. Finally, Dina, Joshua, and Juliana keep it all in perspective.

Introduction: Participating in Democracy Means Participating in Schools

Terry A. Osborn and Dina C. Osborn

. . . dedicated to the proposition that all men are created equal . . .

These words penned by Abraham Lincoln almost two centuries ago continue to be relevant in public (meaning *of the people*) schools today. In a democracy such as the United States, we are obligated to consider the concept of equality and to identify and eradicate elements in education that may hinder equality. Over the years we realized that for democracy to function, men could not mean merely some men; it had to mean all men. Thus, slavery was inconsistent with democracy. Sometime later we recognized that *men* left out a large section of the population. We recognized that sexism was a threat to democracy. But these realizations evolved over time. They were not immediately grasped at the birth of the country.

As the twenty-first century begins to roll by, the hindrances to equality must be examined again. This time, the focus must shift to equality in terms of language and culture. This is the point of this text. As professors of education, our colleagues have dedicated large portions of their lives to the study of schools. We examine the roles of teachers, students, curricula, and other factors in schools. But perhaps more importantly, we examine the role of schools in shaping (and being shaped by) society. With this backdrop, let us begin our examination.

In this chapter we need to consider the meaning of three concepts: language, culture, and democratic education. We need to understand how these concepts relate to one another, and how they relate to a pursuit of equality for all men and women, of all colors, speaking all varieties of language and sharing all cultures. Finally, we will need to explore the reasons educational issues related to embracing diversity should be sought after and celebrated.

Language. We all use it. We all know at least one. It is what sets us apart from the animals, some say. But if we try to specifically define a language, the commonalities begin to fade. Language can be defined as a primarily aural/oral system of communication that humans use. It is creative in nature, and can be used to generate an infinite number of communications. But what is a language?

Some would answer this question with examples—perhaps "English, German, French, and so on." Yet this answer complicates the matter even more. Language originates in humans. Certainly, many faiths in the world ascribe the primary origin of language to God, as shown in this passage from Genesis 1:1–9:

> *Now the whole world had one language and a common speech. As men moved eastward, they found a plain in Shinar and settled there. They said to each other, "Come, let's make bricks and bake them thoroughly." They used brick instead of stone, and tar for mortar. Then they said, "Come, let us build ourselves a city, with a tower that reaches to the heavens, so that we may make a name for ourselves and not be scattered over the face of the whole earth." But the LORD came down to see the city and the tower that the men were building. The LORD said, "If as one people speaking the same language they have begun to do this, then nothing they plan to do will be impossible for them. Come, let us go down and confuse their language so they will not understand each other." So the LORD scattered them from there over all the earth, and they stopped building the city. That is why it was called Babel— because there the LORD confused the language of the whole world. From there the LORD scattered them over the face of the whole earth. (NIV)*

Regardless of its origin, in contemporary society language is transmitted culturally, from one person to another. In other words, language is a social phenomenon.

Each of us utilizes language as a way of expressing things we want to share. Each region of the country has, for example, its own words or unique expressions. In New England, one may eat a grinder, called a hoagie or submarine sandwich in other parts of the country. Perhaps I will drink a pop, a fizz, a soda, or simply a Coke with my sandwich. If one is not in the part of the country where those terms are *shared*, one may find puzzled expressions on the faces of the listeners.

Each family also shares certain aspects of language. We went on vacation together and celebrated holidays together, so we can say to other members of our family something like "He's acting just like Uncle Charley," and they will understand what we mean. Outside that small family circle, would such a sentence be understood? Unlikely. Yet, we still claim we all speak "English."

Each human being has his or her own language called an *idiolect*. This individual language shares in common many words and rules with the idiolects of others. In some cases we group these commonalities in a bigger concept called English. This is, in fact, English—a consensus or agreed upon set of idiolects. We also share similarities with other "languages." Cognates such as *Radio*, *Kindergarten*, and *Wiener* are "German" words similar to English words. So why do we not think of German and English as one language?

Linguists use a criterion called "mutual unintelligibility," or the inability of speakers to understand each other, to define when two languages are separate. In other settings, such a criterion is not used. Certainly a person from Mississippi, one from Maine, and one from California may all speak "English" and yet may be wholly unable to communicate with one another. So why do we not call these different languages?

Simply put, the definition of "language" is a political one. We share certain political ideas and objectives and thus we say we speak "English." We speak the same language merely because we say we do and we can back it up by compelling others to accept that idea. We compel them to accept it by suggesting that "English" is a thing separate from the people who use it. But as we have discussed, such a claim is groundless. English exists only because of its speakers' shared experiences. In treating a language as something one can separate from its speaker, however, equality begins to be threatened. More on that in a moment.

Culture is a word that is used a lot these days. A "cultural difference" or cultural "diversity" is a way of exploring differences among people, at the same time showing that people are the same. We all have a "culture" and we share that culture with others. But my culture may be different from your culture, and that makes them diverse. My culture shares certain experiences and perspectives, as does yours. But not all cultures enjoy the same level of influence in society. Some cultures are predominant (having higher levels of power) and others are subordinate (having relatively less power). If all are created equal in a democracy, we encounter once again a threat to that equality—differing levels of power.

Schools, so it is said, impart knowledge. But how do they do that? Primarily, knowledge in schools is taught through language. Mathematics is a language; science is teaching us new (or old) words for things and processes; physical education teaches us about our bodies, games we can play, and so on. Teachers use language, in part, to teach us these things.

Let us begin to shape the picture of schools presented here. Schools teach knowledge that is defined by the dominant culture as important. The dominant culture by definition is in power, and public schools by definition are ruled by elected officials who are also in power. Schools teach that knowledge in a language or languages. The language used in schools does not exist independent of its speakers; therefore, language in schools reflects the views, attitudes, and perspectives of those in power. At the same time, language in schools by definition serves to marginalize, or remove power from, members of subordinate cultures.

The premise of this book is that democratic schools today need to look at the role of language and cultural diversity in hindering equality. How do our educational practices result in the voices of some people being left out of the discussion? Perhaps even more important, how can schools work to improve the situation? We no longer have legal slavery in the United States. Sexism is viewed as a negative thing, though it may still be practiced. Discrimination based on gender or color is now seen as incompatible with a democratic school system. Separate is inherently not equal.

The time has come for language and cultural diversity to be seen through the same lens. Language is a basic human right, and the opportunity to learn from other "cultures" is fundamental to an education in a democratic society. We learn from one another as we all participate in schools, in the formation and communication of knowledge, regardless of our culture or language. We can be equal only if we all take part in, and have our shared experiences and perspectives expressed through, the educative process. Hopefully, that is a language we can all learn to understand.

Emergent Possibilities for Diversity in Reading and the Language Arts

Cara Mulcahy

Exposing students to a wide range of literature allows them to live vicariously through the experiences of others and begin to view life from a perspective that they might not otherwise be exposed to.[1] Literature can allow students to become more aware of their own language and culture as well as the language and culture of others. Children's literature written in the dialects of various cultural groups is an effective strategy for introducing linguistic diversity because it raises students' awareness of dialects and the differences among them.[2] As Marlene Carter discovered with her students, exposing them to literature written in Black dialect proved to be "a valuable tool for helping both Black dialect speakers and nondialect speakers value and respect Black dialect in literature and in America today."[3] Carter also makes the case for the importance of teaching Black dialect speakers standard English because it is the "language of power." If we want to empower students and have them succeed in college, in job interviews, and in advancing their chosen careers, then it follows that we must teach them the language that they need to succeed. In doing so, however, "we must respect the community language."[4] To do this effectively, however, literature by Black (and other) minority authors would need to be included in the curriculum throughout the year and not just during Black History month or when we are doing a unit on Black or minority writers, as is too often the case.[5]

Sadly, multicultural education is often little more than a superficial add-on to the standard curriculum. Although schools and districts acknowledge the importance of multicultural education in their mission statements, official policies, and curricula, in reality, these translate into superficial practices in the classroom. We see pictures of Native Americans, Africans, and the natives of other cultures, mostly European, attired in traditional costumes decorating school classrooms, libraries, and hallways. In language arts classrooms there is an attempt to broaden the traditional canon, so as to expose students to literature by people other than dead, white, European males. In science and math classrooms we might catch a glimpse of women who have been pioneers in these fields. As Sonia Nieto states in *Affirming Diversity*, however:

> *Open up almost any literature anthology used in the high schools and you will find a list of European and European American authors, almost exclusively male sometimes with a smattering of women and people of color for "balance." In art history, courses rarely leave France, Italy, and sometimes England in considering the "great" artists. What is called "classical" music is classical only in Europe, not in Africa, Asia, or Latin America. This same ethnocentrism is found in our history books, which place Europeans and European Americans as the actors and all others as the recipients, bystander, or bit players of history.*[6]

That we have to dedicate certain months in order to recognize and acknowledge certain groups is evidence that very little has changed when it comes to representing and including a diversity of cultures, societies, traditions, lifestyles, and perspectives in the standard curriculum.

Adding to concerns of this kind are the voices of language arts educators who continue to complain about the lack of interest shown by students in reading and writing. They wonder why students do not choose to read outside of school or why they whine and complain about having nothing to say when it comes time for them to write in school.[7] One well-acknowledged reason for such resistance is that students feel "their cultural identities have no place in the classroom" and therefore they "often reject the curriculum."[8] There is a large population of students that continue to feel unmotivated, dissatisfied, and disconnected from what they are taught in school.[9] This gap between "in-school literary functions" and "out-of-school discourse functions"[10] will continue to grow unless multicultural education is viewed as a foundation from which we build educational practices so as to provide young people with an education that is "meaningful and responsive to their needs."[11]

Alongside weaknesses of the kind mentioned in the preceding paragraphs in regard to how well cultural and student diversity are accommodated in the curriculum, there also exist culturally exclusivist tendencies such as those commonly associated with the concept of cultural literacy propounded by E. D. Hirsch[12] in which he calls for an emphasis on introducing all students to the dominant Western culture. This thrust toward uniformity found in Hirsch is not new in American education or in the teaching of reading, however. Historically, it was a quest for uniformity rather than diversity that guided educational policies in the teaching of reading as well as other areas of the curriculum. At different crucial points in the evolution of education in America dating back to the earliest of colonial times, the teaching of reading and literacy was considered a central task of schooling. In sixteenth-century New England, for example, the goals of schooling were considered to be almost exclusively bound with the teaching of reading. The purpose for such an emphasis was also clear: it was to teach religion—a uniform religion—to enable the young to succeed in battle with the old deluder Satan, as a notable law from 1647 put it.

Within a hundred years the primary emphasis on the teaching of reading for religious purposes was to give way to a different focus, but the aspiration to uniformity that one associates with the education laws introduced in the 1600s once again emerged strongly as Americanizing the youth of the nation became a major concern. Here, ironically, the price of liberty—the ideal of the new republic—was, once again, uniformity. While Thomas Jefferson and others offered their own educational responses to this, the response of Noah Webster stands out in the area of reading and the language arts. Webster's answer was to focus on reading and language as the key to bringing about a form of patriotic uniformity. Hence his dictionary, his spelling book, and his school texts all aimed at promoting such uniformity and nationalistic spirit.

As we entered the closing decades of the twentieth century, the emphasis on promoting civic uniformity through reading and the language arts would give way to a combination of both economic and cultural uniformity. This time the quest for uniformity would be propelled and instituted by the rallying cry of standards. While the scope of the curriculum measures invoked to promote this ideal would range well beyond reading and the language arts, reading was to find a special place of prominence in the designs of lawmakers, as is evident in the No Child Left Behind Act of 2002.

THE WORKSHOP APPROACH

While a conspicuous feature of the reading and language arts curriculum over the years has been the aspiration to promote not diversity but uniformity, a group of scholars and practitioners have developed and advocated an approach that holds out the promise of a new direction. Known as the readers and writers workshop, this is a challenging approach that accommodates the consideration of a range of pressing issues in regard to reading and cultural diversity. This approach opens up possibilities to allow for diversity rather than to deny it. We must question, however, if this approach makes the most of the possibilities for diversity as it has been developed to date.

The workshop approach, with its roots in progressive education and whole language theory, and its similarities to constructivism, deserves serious consideration when discussing issues of multiculturalism and diversity in the language arts classroom. Because of its theoretical and philosophical roots, the workshop approach to teaching acknowledges that language is influenced by the context, culture, and community in which it is used. It can thus be said that people will interpret language differently depending on their background knowledge and life experiences. Language is socially determined by the community in which one functions, and "the meanings for texts (for language, actually) are not in the text or even in the language. Language can only mean what its community of users know—the meanings users have attached to the experiences they have had."[13] Language, therefore, is understood not merely as a "tool for description and a medium of communication (the conventional view), but as social practice, as a way of doing things."[14]

Accepting the need to allow for the child's own experiences, proponents of the workshop do not view the students as empty vessels needing to be filled with knowledge imparted by the teacher, but as individuals with rich cultural backgrounds and a deep understanding of the world around them. Important to this approach is Louise Rosenblatt's transactional reading theory, which argues that both the text and the reader are active participants in the act of reading.[15] The text is acted upon by the reader, who brings his or her own background knowledge to the text and interprets the text from this perspective. Similarly, as readers interact with the text, they are affected by it because it adds new information to their background knowledge which may cause them to reflect upon what they already know and modify it to include new information. Therefore, both parties are altered by the experience. Neither the text nor the readers are passive participants in the event. What Timothy G. Reagan and Terry A. Osborn have to say of constructivism is pertinent: "constructivism assumes not only that learning is constructed, but also that the learning process is a personal and individual one, that learning is an active process, that learning is collaborative in nature, and that all learning is situated."[16]

Also important to the workshop approach is that by giving students time, choice, and positive responses, it is more likely that they will develop a positive attitude to reading and writing and ultimately learning. Reading and writing, accordingly, should not be taught in such a way that they become disjointed from the students' home life. Instead, students need to engage in reading and writing activities in meaningful and purposeful ways.[17] If not, students will not associate the activities they engage in at school with the rest of their lives. Quoting John Dewey, Nancie Atwell writes that "from the standpoint of the child, the great waste in school comes from his inability to utilize the experiences he gets outside of school in any complete and free way; while on the other hand, he is unable to apply to daily life what he is learning in school."[18] Linda Rief, too, is sensitive to these concerns. As she tells us, "I want students to see learning as connected to situations beyond our classroom walls. I want them to listen to, think about and interact with people outside the classroom about real issues."[19] Students need to "find work 'less and less of a school project, and more of a challenge to get real feelings out,' then we will all stand open-mouthed, silent, losing our words to surprise, over the extraordinary things kids can do."[20]

CULTURAL DIVERSITY AND THE WORKSHOP APPROACH

How do major authors associated with the writers workshop accommodate the demands of cultural diversity in their approach? Writers workshop has grown out of the work of Donald Graves and is now closely associated with the writings and practical projects advanced by Lucy Calkins, Nancie Atwell, and Linda Rief. Drawing primarily on Nancie Atwell's book *In the Middle* (1998), Lucy Calkins' book *The Art of Teaching Writing* (1994), and Linda Rief's book *Seeking Diversity* (1992), which describes the readers and writers workshop approach, one can identify the key features of the approach. These include creating an atmosphere of community and collaboration among students, purposeful evaluation through the use of portfolios, the publication of student work, fostering a desire for a lifelong love of reading and writing, and teacher modeling. This chapter focuses on a number of features of the workshop approach that are particularly helpful in examining it from the perspective of cultural diversity.

TIME, CHOICE, RESPONSE

Time, choice, and response are the underpinnings for everything that takes place in the workshop classroom. By giving students time, choice, and positive responses, Rief is able to hear the diverse voices of her students more clearly. This allows teachers to see students as individuals, and it enables teachers to be responsive to the individual needs of the students.[21] If one of the goals of the workshop approach is to enable students to experience the purposefulness and the joy of writing and reading, then it is crucial that they are given class time to engage in these activities. As Douglas Kaufman states, "Time is not a luxury for students, but a necessity. Time allows students' thought to ripen from the superficial to the profound."[22] Devoting class time to reading and writing reinforces the genuine importance of these acts as well as reinforcing the whole language belief that students learn to read and write through authentic engagement in these activities.

Providing students the opportunity to choose individualizes the focus of their work and develops intrinsic motivation. Through freedom of choice, reading and writing become more purposeful and less contrived, thereby avoiding meaningless tasks that "are merely masquerading as writing."[23] Similarly, when responding to students, whether through the use of response journals, conferences, or portfolios, the feedback ought to be positive and encouraging so as to continually motivate students and move them forward. Of equal importance is that the feedback be immediate so that students can immediately apply any ideas or suggestions to their reading or writing. Atwell reminds us that "After-the-fact response from a teacher comes too late; it assumes students will not only hold a teacher's advice in their heads until the next writing occasion and apply it to a new context, but that they actually read the teacher's written comments."[24]

A WELL-ORGANIZED AND HIGHLY STRUCTURED CLASSROOM

On first entering a classroom that adheres to the workshop model, a person might think that it has little order or structure. In reality, however, for such a classroom to run smoothly and efficiently a great deal of organization is required on the part of the teacher. In his book *Writing: Teachers and Children at Work*,[25] Donald Graves describes one of the classrooms he observes: "The surface order suggested no structure at all since the children were not consulting the teacher for next steps, nor was the teacher, Mr. Bangs, stopping and starting one activity after another. But three days' observation in the room revealed an important, underlying organizational structure. Mr. Bangs' plans were so well designed that they didn't show in the work the children were doing."[26]

This organization enables students to become independent learners and the "curriculum" to become more individualized and diverse. When observing Rief, Kaufman noted "she takes an extraordinary amount of time at the beginning of the year to focus on organizational and procedural matters until students follow them *independently*."[27]

THE WORKSHOP STRUCTURE

Reading and writing workshops adhere to a similar sequence of activities. The workshop begins with a 5–20 minute minilesson during which students are introduced to a new skill, strategy, procedure, or concept. Minilessons can be a time for students to share what they know, or a time for the class to discuss or analyze a piece of writing together. The content of a minilesson should be driven by the students' interests, projects, and intentions rather than the teachers and should "support the less able youngsters while also celebrating and raising the upper level of what children are doing."[28]

Following the minilesson, students have the opportunity to work independently on their reading or writing. A "status-of-the-class," which allows the students to quickly update the teacher as to where they are with their work and what they hope to accomplish that day, is usually conducted during this portion of the day. Following this, teachers begin conferring with students. This allows for greater teacher mobility and more immediate feedback from the teacher. Students may also be engaged in peer conferences at this time. In keeping with the ideals of progressive education, peer conferences provide time for student interaction, foster student independence, and aid in the development of student voice.[29]

Through this process, students learn how to question and critique themselves as they write. The powerful thing here is that as they are "working with word," they are "really working with thoughts."[30] Rief points out that when the questions are pushed back on the writers, this forces them to "make evaluative judgments."[31] This in turn leads them to be more independent readers and writers, which ultimately is the goal of the workshop.

The final portion of the class is a time when students may work in response groups to share and discuss their work with one another, complete their response journals, or partake in a whole class share.

STUDENT VOICE

When a teacher asks students to write, many classrooms explode with a chorus of student complaints: "I have nothing to write about," "Nothing ever happens to me."[32] This reaction may be triggered because the students have not yet found their voices and they are not used to choosing self-selected topics. For Graves, finding one's voice is central to the writing process and in collaboration with time, choice, and positive response; voice ignites student motivation and energy. Student choice allows students to develop the link between "voice and subject." This connection allows students to realize they have something to say. Over time the students refine the writing process to limit or narrow the topic about which they are writing so that whether imaginary or real, it is "filled with voice."[33]

As workshop teachers strive toward helping students discover voice, teachers become listeners. When conferring with students, Calkins, for example, suggests to ask: "Tell me what you know"; "Tell me what you wonder." Such questions prompt students to verbally express what they wish to communicate in their writing, which allows both students and teacher to better understand the students' intentions and to recognize their voice.[34] Throughout this process the teacher allows students to develop their own piece of writing, their own voice, as much as possible without the help of the teacher. It is by finding one's voice that a writer brings a piece of writing to life. If we interfere, it is no longer is the student's voice we are hearing. Rief explains that "Good conferences seem to be confirmations of what the students already know and have to hear themselves say. I will certainly make suggestions but only when I feel they are ready for them."[35]

The teacher has the tenuous responsibility then of understanding and locating the delicate balance between providing feedback, "nudging" writers forward while at the same time allowing them the space to realize their voice. A teacher who achieves this balance feeds the "voice ego" yet allows writers to "see the problem afresh in light of living up to internal demands of excellence and the original reason for writing in the first place."[36]

STUDENT-CENTERED LEARNING AND STUDENT INTERACTION

A workshop classroom may, at first, appear chaotic because of the constant student interaction. This student-centered, socially interactive environment which allows for student movement is unique to the workshop approach. "Here adolescents' social relations can serve scholarly ends. Kids can be active, talking and moving as part of their activity as engaged writers and readers."[37] Conversation is an integral element of the workshop. Through conversation students have the opportunity to express their points of view, which helps them understand what is being learned as well as provides teachers with the opportunity to gain an insight to the students' thinking. Because literacy is a social process, and language a social function, conversation affords students time to find and listen to their voices and to the voices of their peers, to respond to one another, and to hear the perspectives of others and learn about the life experiences of others. The importance of this, according to Dan Rothermel, is twofold: it contributes to the "growth of students as literate beings," and it moves students "beyond the rote, the routine, and obedient behaviors in the classroom."[38]

As students work in this atmosphere, there appears to be what Kaufman refers to as a constant buzz: "A successful workshop classroom . . . buzzes as participants maneuver through the room, guided by unique agendas, and it may seem to the inexperienced eye that chaos reigns."[39] Students are talking to each other about what they are reading and writing, they are peer conferencing, and they are conferring with their teacher. Atwell advocates for student interaction because "learning is also more likely when students can be involved and active and when they can learn from and with other students."[40] Similarly, "literary talk with a teacher and peers is crucial to kids' development as readers."[41] In *Conferences and Conversations*, Kaufman concurs, "education is a social process" and "when students converse, explore, and work together they develop multiple perspective and a 'social imagination' that gives them the ability to read others in the community better."[42] One way to foster multicultural education and a diversity of perspectives can be realized through this type of interaction.

The emphasis on student interaction often promotes an atmosphere of collaboration and community in the workshop classroom. Atwell and Rief both place an importance on building a sense of community in their classrooms, and many of the classrooms visited by Calkins also exhibit a community spirit. Such an atmosphere creates a more effective learning environment when students feel they can trust each other and their teacher. In Rief's experience she has found "that the better the students know me and trust me, the more honest they are."[43] They also "need to know and trust each other," but it takes time to build this collaborative atmosphere.[44] This community atmosphere is also important because instead of students competing with one another, as is what often happens, in a workshop classroom the aim is to help one another become the best reader and writer possible.[45]

PURPOSEFUL EVALUATION, OFTEN DONE THROUGH THE USE OF PORTFOLIOS

In *The Art of Teaching Writing*, Calkins describes the "current scene in assessment" as one where many teachers of language arts still fraction the curriculum "into an array of little skills, which they teach in a frontal teacher-led fashion with pretest, post-test, short lectures, work on the chalkboard, exercises, and activities." This practice, she continues, is reinforced by standardized tests and by the "practice of accumulating lots of little scores in gradebooks."[46] Many traditional approaches to assessment, including standardized tests, engage students in isolated reading and writing tasks that have little connection to their lives. Such forms of assessment tell us very little about student effort, improvement over time, or the process itself. Furthermore, seldom do they take into account students' backgrounds, culture, economic factors, or language. Unlike teachers who use the traditional approaches, teachers who use the workshop approach strive to move students toward independence and believe students should have a say and some control over how they are assessed and on what they are assessed.

In an attempt to address these issues, many workshop teachers have turned to the use of portfolios as a method of evaluation. Through the use of portfolios, students include writing pieces which they believe demonstrate their best work, reflect upon and evaluate their writing process, and set future goals for themselves—all of which lead them to become independent learners and to develop ownership of their reading, writing, and learning. Portfolios are representative of the work a student has done over a period of time and should, therefore, show how the student has grown.

Although there is no set of requirements for what should be included in a portfolio at Atwell's school, "students collect lists of books read and pieces written, personal spelling lists, individual proofreading lists, individual math computation records, photos that the teachers have taken of students at work and of the work itself, examples of work produced in each discipline and each major unit of study, and students' self-evaluation questionnaires."[47] Rief allows her students to include reading and writing from other disciplines "if they think their efforts are some of their best."[48]

Most important, portfolios allow for integration among process, product, and content. Because portfolios encourage students to evaluate their own writing, students become more aware of the importance of the writing process and are not concerned only with the end product. As such they are more aware and more critical of their writing throughout the process which makes their writing better. Rief acknowledges the importance of self-evaluation in the writing process because "the evaluative process helps them make their writing better" and because "the evaluation of writing in progress is as important if not more important, than the final product."[49] Similarly, the decisions that they make during the writing process improve their writing. In both Rief's and Atwell's experiences, "If kids can be taught how to detect and diagnose strengths and weaknesses and how to come up with strategies for dealing with those problems through conferences, questions and suggestions then we have taught them not only how to become better writers, but how to be independent writers along the way."[50]

MEETING INDIVIDUALS' NEEDS

Because of the characteristics discussed above, it is evident that this approach lends itself to individualized instruction. Differentiation of instruction continues to become more necessary and important to the success of all students. Through the workshop "we see our students as individuals and teach to the needs and intentions of each."[51] Similarly, students are assessed on an individual basis.

Everything about the workshop is geared toward what is in the best interests of the students. Beginning with time, choice, and response, students become the center of the curriculum. Conferences with either their peers or their teachers allow the students to focus on the specific areas where they seek guidance and assistance. Because of this, students do not have to wait until the teacher decides the class is ready to learn about a certain writing style, technique, or convention before they begin to experiment with it in their reading and writing. Students, through this approach, are challenged at their individual instructional levels instead of at a level that is trying to accommodate for everybody in the class regardless of learning style, ability, readiness, or interest. Rief states, "It doesn't matter what level these students appear to be. My job is to guide them beyond what they can already do, to challenge them to challenge themselves."[52]

Students usually are responsible for recording books they have read, pieces they have written, vocabulary words they have studied, and the techniques and conventions they have learned since the beginning of the year. This in combination with portfolio assessment and the reader-writer notebooks enables the students to receive credit for their progress and effort. This strategy allows the students, the parents, and the teachers to acknowledge where the students started from and how far they have developed over time. This assessment of students' progress is overlooked by standardized tests, end-of-unit exams, and other such assessments that measure only the final product.

TOWARD A CRITIQUE

Turning to a critique of the workshop approach, what can one now say of the extent to which this approach to the teaching of reading and language arts provides for cultural diversity or holds out either the promise or unlikelihood of doing so? The workshop structure provides considerable potential for addressing diversity and multiculturalism. Because the workshop approach claims to have the students at the heart of the curriculum, it is students' interests that ought to drive the curriculum. Before one considers this point, however, one must acknowledge that the workshop approach has some strikingly disappointing features for any advocate of cultural diversity and other progressive elements in the curriculum.

One such feature relates to the range of literature referenced by advocates of the workshop approach. When one examines diversity and multiculturalism, it is difficult to argue that Atwell does not attempt to open up and broaden the traditional canon. Thus she writes, "the term literature embraces more than the prescribed secondary-school canon of second-rate Dickens' Tales (*A Tale of Two Cities*), second-rate Steinbeck (*The Red Pony*), second-rate

Twain (*The Prince and the Pauper*), and second-rate Hemingway (*The Old Man and the Sea*)."[53] She then proceeds to introduce Black authors such as Maya Angelou, Walter Dean Myers, and Toni Morrison. This said, however, on closer inspection, one finds an interesting binary opposition in Atwell's approach. She extols the importance of broadening the canon, yet one is left to wonder how much of this is for "balance."

In her book *In the Middle*, Atwell not only cites few if any authors drawn from minority cultures but also appears to favor those drawn from the traditional canon. When studying poetry for Atwell, students study what Atwell names her "Big Six" American poets. The "Big Six" are E. E. Cummings, Emily Dickinson, Robert Frost, Langston Hughes, Walt Whitman, and William Carlos Williams. With the exception of Hughes, all are white European Americans. When teaching literature, she refers largely to units on Shakespeare, Arthurian legend and Greek mythology, and philosophy. Thus, while in some ways Atwell attempts to go beyond the traditional canon, in other more subtle ways she continues to reinforce the idea that the "classics" as we have always known them continue to be the "classics" and other literature is a stepping stone in our literacy growth to be able to appreciate the more sophisticated literature.

Atwell also appears to create a hierarchy of literature, which undermines certain kinds of literature, including adolescent literature and series novels. In so doing, she also undermines student choice. Not only does Atwell create a hierarchy of literature regardless of one's interest, age, and cultural and social background, she also uses her position of authority and power to influence student choices. In the following quotation from Atwell, for example, one may ask if it is really any surprise that Joe, one of her students, agrees with Atwell, the teacher: "I explained that these were novelizations, added them to the list, and expressed my disdain for them. Joe [a student] agreed."[54]

It might be argued that Rief shows a greater awareness of the importance of meeting the developmental needs of students by exposing them to a variety of literature and literary experiences even if the range of literature she draws upon is still limited in regard to cultural diversity. The descriptions she provides on her units of study surrounding the elderly, World War II, and "The Art of Literature" demonstrate how these units expose students to the perspectives and life experiences of others and draw their awareness toward issues of social injustice and issues of prejudice. The unit on World War II enables students to understand that issues of prejudice are not unique to Nazi Germany but are still prevalent today, all of which may lead to critical thought and dialogue among the students. One of her students, in response to *The*

Hiding Place, wrote, "Today, in America, we think we are way above and be-yond anything like that happening [the holocaust], or thinking of that sort. There are still people who are prejudiced, because they know no better. We deny it, but it's there."[55] The elective entitled "The Art of Literature," which Rief offers through a schoolwide activity block, demonstrates ways that teach-ers can broaden the definition of literacy and move toward incorporating the multiple literacies into their teaching. As Rief explains, "I look for ways in my classroom to allow students to respond to their works in ways other than just 'the word.' Writing is extremely important. But it is not the only way for liter-ate human beings to show what they know."[56]

In addition to its failure to give more play to a diverse range of literature— and while clearly accepting the importance of the point as is evident in its openness to accepting student viewpoint and input as well as community con-text and collaboration—the workshop also fails to develop as fully as it might important connections between what is read in school and what is happening in the broader society. This is important for the reasons that Bob Peterson points out when he writes that we must "help our students understand how their lives connect to the broader society, which so often limits them. We need to get students' asking the big 'why' questions about what they don't like and about what needs to change so that they can live fuller lives. When we do more than offer student-centered classrooms, when we connect students' ex-periences to social issues, our teaching becomes critical."[57]

Although the workshop approach does classify language as a social func-tion, it does not appear to consider how standard English can deny access to certain groups and marginalize people. It is important that through reading and writing students be made aware of ways they can empower themselves while remaining true to their dialect and social and cultural ways of commu-nicating with one another. Of course, the workshop approach does foster a spirit of collaboration and community, but it does not always do so for the pur-pose of demonstrating the power of a community of voices and what can be accomplished when we cooperate with one another to bring about social change. Although some students in the examples provided in works by advo-cates of the workshop approach considered here do voice their opinions or raise awareness about certain issues, it seems more an offshoot as opposed to one of the desired outcomes for the workshop. Students do not appear to learn that they have the power both collectively and individually to make change. Related to this, neither does the workshop approach challenge the sta-tus quo. According to Patrick Finn, "You can scour the several books and ar-ticles written on the topic by Nancie Atwell, for example, and not find a hint that she sees challenges to the status quo as a desirable, likely or even possible outcome of her approach."[58]

Clearly, there is less use of culturally diverse authors and less emphasis on critical mindedness than there could be in the workshop approach. On a positive note, however, this may be perceived as an easily remediable condition, and for good reason: it is clear from looking at the central features of the workshop approach that many of the principles and procedures upon which it depends are rich with possibilities for diversity and critical mindedness. This is clearly evident in the emphasis laid upon student voice and building the student's writing upon his or her own experience. If these two principles are accepted, the workshop approach provides students the opportunity to dictate both the kinds of experience they wish to call upon, thereby allowing the opportunity for diversity not possible when aspirations toward uniformity dominate. This interpretation draws support from the ideas of Paulo Freire.

Acknowledging the oppression to which many of his students, who were largely peasants, were accustomed and the life experiences to which they were conditioned, Freire believed he could not simply impose an external literacy curriculum on them and expect them to embrace literacy. To create real life connections and meanings through literacy, Freire situated students' learning within their spheres of knowledge and experience. This he did through the use of generative themes.[59] By listening to the workers and peasants talking with one another about different topics, Freire observed that certain generative themes emerged. Students' literacy learning was then tied directly to the themes that had been generated through their earlier discussions. As Ira Shor explains, and as is true of the workshop approach, through this approach "community research by teachers, with students as coinvestigators, established a student-centered, democratic process through which a literacy program was built from the bottom up rather than from the top down. Student subjectivity was the starting point but not the end."[60]

In addition to locating learning in the student's sphere of experience, Freire also "aimed to develop critical thought and action around themes identified in everyday life, so that by learning to read and write the students would also be gaining the power to critique and act on their conditions."[61] The combination of situated learning and critical thought is crucial. Raising awareness of one's circumstances without developing critical thought and reflection by which one can become empowered to act upon and change his or her circumstances may have a negative, despair-inducing effect on students.

Teaching for critical literacy, as Freire did, aims to "empower people to criticize and to emancipate themselves from oppressive social or economic conditions."[62] Because "literacy may enable some parts of society to control others," it is important that students be taught how to think and act reflectively about what they read in order to recognize how power relations operate in our society and to be able to understand and act against the social relations of oppression.[63] Freire strongly believed critical literacy means not just processing the ability to read words but the ability to understand the world and to act in ways to then change the social relations of oppression.

While the concern to promote critical thought found in Freire and his followers is not emphasized at all in the workshop approach, the possibility for doing so is implicit. Because it is the students who are said to drive the curriculum in a classroom adhering to the workshop approach, learning could easily be situated within the students' sphere of knowledge and experience. This, however, is often overlooked as it continues to be the teachers who choose the focus of the thematic units implemented.[64] Furthermore, teachers appear to recycle the units from year to year, which reinforces the fact that it is not the students' interests that are driving the inquiry. Linda Rief studies the elderly and World War II, and while she provides solid rationales for doing so, one has to imagine that student-generated topics might equally lend themselves to social awareness and the perspectives of others.

CONCLUSION

It may be said that as it has been developed to this point, the readers and writers workshop approach to the teaching of reading and the language arts has not highlighted cultural diversity. Just as important, however, the readers and writers workshop approach does contain in its guiding principles very considerable possibilities to do so. The dual influences of progressive or Deweyan philosophy and of whole language open up possibilities for cultural diversity in the teaching of reading and language arts in a manner that was not possible in other eras when educational goals shaped by aspirations to social uniformity held sway. By opening up the possibility for the individual student to have an input into the content of his or her own curriculum in reading and the language arts, the child-centered emphasis in these philosophies opens possibilities for adopting a rich cultural diversity that does not exist in other philosophies of reading and language arts. In so doing, this approach stands in sharp contrast to approaches to the teaching of reading and the language arts in which the emphasis was on promoting a socially imposed uniformity—be it to promote religious goals or civic goals in the seventeenth and eighteenth centuries or in a quest for a socially imposed uniformity based on a conservative concept of cultural literacy that emerged in the late twentieth century. Similarly, without exploring them, this approach opens up possibilities for developing a way of teaching that is more open to advancing critical literacy and the aspirations associated with ideals of social justice.

NOTES

1. Nancie Atwell, *In the middle: New understandings about writing, reading, and learning* (Portsmouth, NH: Heinemann, 1998); Linda Rief, *Seeking diversity: Language arts with adolescents* (Portsmouth, NH: Heinemann, 1992).

2. Lisa Delpit, "Language diversity and learning," in *Beyond heroes and holidays: A practical guide to K–12 anti-racist, multicultural education and staff development*, ed. Enid Lee, Deborah Menkart, and Margo Okazawa-Rey (Washington, DC: Teaching for Change, 1998), 154–65.

3. Marlene Carter, "The best of both worlds," in *Beyond heroes and holidays: A practical guide to K–12 anti-racist, multicultural education and staff development*, ed. Enid Lee, Deborah Menkart, and Margo Okazawa-Rey (Washington, DC: Teaching for Change, 1998), 146–53.

4. Carter, "Best of both worlds," 152.

5. Carter, "Best of both worlds," 152.

6. Sonia Nieto, *Affirming diversity: The sociopolitical context of multicultural education* (Boston: Pearson Education, 1992), 212.

7. Lucy Calkins, *The art of teaching writing* (New York: Longman, 1994), 12.

8. S. Kaser and K. G. Short, "Exploring culture through children's connections," *Language Arts* 75 (3) (1998): 191.

9. Kaser and Short, "Exploring culture"; T. W. Bean, S. K. Bean, and K. F. Bean, "Intergenerational conversations and two adolescents' multiple literacies: Implications for redefining content area literacy," *Journal of Adolescent and Adult Literacy* 42 (6) (1999): 438–48; Nieto, *Affirming diversity*; Ira Shor, *Empowering education: Critical teaching for social change* (Chicago: University of Chicago Press, 1992); Ernest Morrell, "Toward a critical pedagogy of popular culture: Literacy development among urban youth," *Journal of Adolescent and Adult Literacy* 46 (September 2002): 72–77.

10. Bean, Bean, and Bean, "Intergenerational conversations," 447.

11. Nieto, *Affirming diversity*, 222.

12. E. D. Hirsch, *Cultural literacy: What every American needs to know* (New York: Vintage Books, 1988).

13. Carole Edelsky, Bess Altwerger, and Barbara Flores, *Whole language: What's the difference?* (Portsmouth, NH: Heinemann, 1991), 10.

14. L. A. Wood and R. O. Kroger, *Doing discourse analysis: Methods for studying action in talk and text* (Thousand Oaks, CA: Sage Publications, 2000), 4.

15. Louise M. Rosenblatt, *The reader, the text, the poem: The transactional theory of the literary work* (Carbondale: Southern Illinois University Press, 1978).

16. Timothy G. Reagan and Terry A. Osborn, *The foreign language educator in society: Toward a critical pedagogy* (Mahwah, NJ: Lawrence Erlbaum Associates, 2002), 58–59.

17. See Edelsky, Altwerger, and Flores, *Whole language*, 7–9.

18. John Dewey quoted in Atwell, *In the middle*, 85.

19. Rief, *Seeking diversity*, 71. See Bean, Bean, and Bean, "Intergenerational conversations," where the authors refer to the "sharp divide that exists between their [students'] lives outside school and inside school. If educators do not do something to bridge this gap we will lose the students' interest because they will see little purpose of the in-school literacy functions as they apply their out-of-school experiences" (440).

20. Rief, *Seeking diversity*, 164.

21. Rief, *Seeking diversity*, 2.

22. Douglas Kaufman, *Conferences and conversations: Listening to the literate classroom* (Portsmouth, NH: Heinemann, 2000), 17.

23. Edelsky, Altwerger, and Flores, *Whole language*, 23.

24. Atwell, *In the middle*, 220.

25. Donald Graves, *Writing: Teachers and children at work* (Portsmouth, NH: Heinemann, 1983).

26. Graves, *Writing*, 33.

27. Douglas Kaufman, "Organizing and managing the language arts workshop: A Matter of motion," *Language Arts* 79 (November 2001): 117.

28. Calkins, *Art of teaching writing*, 202.

29. Atwell, *In the middle*; D. Graves, *Balance the basics: Let them write* (New York: Ford Foundation, 1978); Rief, *Seeking diversity*.

30. Calkins, *Art of teaching writing*, 222.

31. Rief, *Seeking diversity*, 125.

32. Calkins, *Art of teaching writing*, 12.

33. Graves, *Writing*, 21; Kaufman, "Organizing and managing."

34. Calkins, *Art of teaching writing*, 238.

35. Rief, *Seeking diversity*, 123.

36. Graves, *Writing*, 245.

37. Atwell, *In the middle*, 85.

38. Dan Rothermel, "It's conversation that drives the bus in the writing workshop," *The NERA Journal* 40 (2004), 31.

39. Kaufman, "Organizing and managing," 115.

40. Atwell, *In the middle*, 69.

41. Atwell, *In the middle*, 40.

42. Kaufman, *Conferences and conversations*, 15.

43. Rief, *Seeking diversity*, 49.

44. Rief, *Seeking diversity*, 37.

45. Barry Kanpol, *Critical pedagogy: An introduction* (Westport, CT: Bergin and Garvey, 1994), 29.

46. Calkins, *Art of teaching writing*, 311.

47. Atwell, *In the middle*, 301.

48. Rief, *Seeking diversity*, 134.

49. Rief, *Seeking diversity*, 122.

50. Rief, *Seeking diversity*, 125.

51. Atwell, *In the middle*, 72.

52. Rief, *Seeking diversity*, 98.

53. Atwell, *In the middle*, 36.

54. Atwell, *In the middle*, 170.

55. Rief, *Seeking diversity*, 108.

56. Rief, *Seeking diversity*, 149.

57. Bob Peterson, "My journey as a critical teacher: Creating schools as laboratories for social justice," in *Education is politics: Critical teaching across differences, K–12*, ed. Ira Shor and Caroline Pari (Portsmouth, NH: Heinemann, 1999), xiii.

58. Patrick Finn, *Literacy with an attitude: Educating working-class children in their own self-interest* (Albany: State University of New York Press, 1999), 148.

59. See, for example, Finn, *Literacy with an attitude*, 156–67.

60. Ira Shor, *Empowering education*, 47.

61. Ira Shor, *Empowering education*, 47.

62. Steven E. Tozer, Paul Violas, and Guy Senese, *School and society: Historical and contemporary perspectives* (Boston: McGraw-Hill, 2002), 248.

63. Tozer, Violas, and Senese, *School and society*, 259.

64. See, for example, Calkins, *Art of teaching writing*, 463–65.

Bilingual Education: Good for U.S.?

Mileidis Gort

One of the most debated and misunderstood educational topics today is bilingual education and its role in the academic achievement of English language learners (second-language learners of English) in U.S. schools. Although a growing body of research points to the educational, social, and psychological benefits associated with educating bilingual learners[1] in their native language as they develop skills in English, bilingual education continues to receive criticism in the national media. Much of the debate and criticisms are politically founded and based on misconceptions that run counter to research findings. These misconceptions are generally related to the goals and practices of bilingual education, the process of second-language acquisition and development, and even the threat to English as *the* language of the United States. This chapter will explain the rationale underlying quality bilingual education programs, address and clarify some of the myths and misconceptions surrounding bilingual education in U.S. schools, and present a case for bilingual education as fundamental to educational equity and full participation in a democratic society. The chapter will conclude with a discussion of the potential of bilingual/multilingual education for the development of an internationally competitive and globally competent citizenry.

Before describing what bilingual education is and what it is not, one must provide a context for the student population that is served by these programs. Bilingualism, both individual and societal, has historically been a fact of life in the United States and promises to remain so for generations to come. Presently, there are bilingual students in most classrooms in most schools throughout the fifty states, Pacific territories, and Puerto Rico. The numbers speak for themselves: one in four U.S. students lives in a household where a language other than English is reportedly spoken; the number of "limited-English-proficient" school-age children grew to 3.9 million in 2000–2001, or more than 8 percent of K–12 enrollment. While three in four bilingual students speak Spanish as a native language, other languages spoken by bilingual school-age children include Vietnamese, Hmong, Cantonese, Korean, Haitian Creole, Arabic, Russian, Tagalog, Navajo, Khmer, Mandarin, Portuguese, Urdu, Serbo-Croatian, Lao, Japanese, Punjabi, Armenian, Polish, French, and Hindi.[2] These numbers make it clear that rapid changes are under way in the U.S. student population, yet the number of students participating in bilingual education is actually quite low. In fact, bilingual education serves only a minority of eligible students (for example, recent U.S. Department of Education figures indicate that only three in ten bilingual students received some type of native language instruction in 2000–2001, although not necessarily a full bilingual program) and the number of participating students are decreasing given recent antibilingual initiatives that have passed in California (1998), Arizona (2000), and Massachusetts (2002).[3] These voter-approved ballot initiatives drowned out minority voices and virtually outlawed the option of bilingual education in these three states.

So, what is the big deal about an educational program model that serves a relatively small portion of the population? Why all the media attention? And, what exactly is bilingual education? To begin to answer these questions, a brief history and working definition of bilingual education are appropriate here.

FOUNDATIONS OF BILINGUAL EDUCATION IN THE UNITED STATES

Thirty years ago, the U.S. Supreme Court made a landmark decision that set the stage for contemporary bilingual education. According to the Court judgment, the civil rights of 1,800 Chinese-speaking bilingual students were being violated when the San Francisco Unified School District took no steps to help them acquire the language of instruction (English). The Court recognized the link between native language rights and educational equity, and citing Title VI of the Civil Rights Act, it ruled:

There is no equality of treatment merely by providing students with the same facilities, textbooks, teachers, and curriculum; for students who do not understand English are effectively foreclosed from any meaningful education. Basic skills are at the very core of what these public schools teach. Imposition of a requirement that, before a child can effectively participate in the educational program he must already have acquired those basic skills is to make a mockery of public education. We know that those who do not understand English are certain to find their classroom experiences wholly incomprehensible and in no way meaningful.[4]

Although the Court did not specifically recommend bilingual education or any other particular program of instruction, it did require schools to take effective measures to meet the educational needs of students who are not proficient in English. Within a year, the Office of Civil Rights issued "The Lau Remedies," which essentially mandated transitional bilingual education programs as the solution.

The Equal Educational Opportunities Act (EEOA) of 1974 has also been instrumental in protecting the language rights of bilingual learners and in promoting bilingual education as a key strategy to counteract the language discrimination and lack of access to the curriculum many bilingual students face in our schools. This law requires educational agencies to "take appropriate action to overcome language barriers that impede equal participation by its students in educational programs"[5] and interprets any failure to do so as denial of equal educational opportunity.

Although often simplified (and misunderstood) as an educational program for students who are not proficient in English, bilingual education can mean many things for different student populations and teachers throughout U.S. classrooms. This is part of the beauty of bilingual education—being consistent in its basic tenets but flexible in design to accommodate different student needs—but also leads to much of the controversy surrounding it. The *Encyclopedia of Bilingualism and Bilingual Education* describes "bilingual education" as "a simple label for a complex phenomenon."[6] Bilingual education programs, in fact, can take a variety of forms depending on several factors, including: the characteristics of students being served, the languages of instruction, academic/linguistic/social goals of the program, teacher qualifications, pedagogical objectives, and even community aspirations. In the final version of the Bilingual Education Act of 1994, Congress provided the following description:

The term "bilingual education program" means an educational program for limited English proficient students that:

(a) *makes instructional use of both English and a student's native language;*

(b) *enables limited English proficient students to achieve English proficiency and academic mastery of subject matter content and higher order skills, including critical thinking, so as to meet age-appropriate grade-promotion and graduation standards in concert with the National Education Goals;*

(c) *may also develop the native language skills of limited English proficient students, or ancestral languages of American Indians, Alaska Natives, Native Hawaiians and native residents of the outlying areas; and*

(d) *may include participation of English-proficient students if such program is designed to enable all enrolled students to become proficient in English and a second language.*

This broad definition allowed for a wide range of pedagogical approaches, ranging from those that aim for fluent bilingualism and biliteracy (reading and writing abilities in two languages) to those that focus on a rapid transition to the general English curriculum. Instruction in the native language to develop competency in the content areas was required under this definition, but certainly not a prominent component of most bilingual education program models.

Sonia Nieto offers a commonly accepted, and similarly broad, definition of bilingual education as "an educational program that involves the use of two languages of instruction at some point in a student's school career."[7] This simple definition, however, is not what most people have in mind when they think of bilingual education. Many people, critics in particular, miss the "bilingual" piece of the puzzle and think that bilingual education is instruction in the students' native language (not English) for most of the school day. Others believe that bilingual education consists of instruction in two languages that is equally distributed throughout the day. Schooling generally defined as bilingual education, however, actually comprises a dizzying array of program models or approaches. The most effective way to describe and differentiate bilingual education models is to look at several key features, including: program goals (i.e., bilingualism/biliteracy, English language development, etc.); student population served (i.e., language minority students only, language minority and native English-speaking students); language(s) in which literacy is developed; and language(s) of subject matter instruction. Depending on their structure and goals, bilingual programs can be characterized as either "weak" or "strong" forms of bilingual education. Weak forms are generally short term and transitional in nature, have English language development as their main (or only) goal, and only include students for whom English is a second language. Strong forms of bilingual education aim to develop full bilingualism and biliteracy, are comprehensive and longitudinal in nature, and usually integrate native English speakers with students for whom English is a second language in some way.[8]

Although there is no one-size-fits-all when it comes to educating bilingual learners, it is fair to say that some programs fit better than others. Program models vary significantly in their effectiveness, as documented by numerous comprehensive and longitudinal studies conducted throughout U.S. schools.[9] There is overwhelming evidence that bilingual education is generally more effective than other programs that mainly stress English development, not only for learning content through the native language but also for learning English. Even within the general umbrella of bilingual education, however, some approaches have been more successful than others. Specifically, those programs that stress native-language development and a gradual transition to English ("strong models") usually have proven superior in stimulating long-term achievement. Meanwhile, English-only programs have generally fared poorly when compared to bilingual programs. These apparently contradictory findings can be better understood if one considers the basic rationale underlying quality bilingual education programs in the United States.

HOW QUALITY BILINGUAL EDUCATION LEADS TO LITERACY DEVELOPMENT, SUBJECT MATTER UNDERSTANDING, AND ENGLISH LANGUAGE PROFICIENCY

Quality education in the native language provides bilingual children in U.S. schools opportunities to develop grade-level academic knowledge and literacy. It should be of no surprise that individuals most easily develop cognitive skills and master content material when they are taught in a familiar language. The knowledge that bilingual children gain through their native language helps make the English they hear and read more comprehensible. That is, using and developing the first language can help children acquire and develop English. This happens because a bilingual learner who has grade-level skills in math (or social studies or science), for example, gained through math instruction in her native language, will understand more in an English language–medium math class than a child who does not have a strong background in math. This leads to higher achievement in math *and* English language development.

Further, literacy developed in the native language transfers to the second language, English. This holds true for languages with similar writing systems (English and Spanish) as well as languages with different scripts (English and Chinese). The advantage to learning to read first in the native language is that individuals most easily develop literacy skills in a familiar language. That is, it is easier to learn to read in a language we understand. Once we can read in one language, we are literate and thus can read in general. All we have to do then is learn the idiosyncrasies of the new language,[10] English, but we do not have to learn to read all over again.

But, some people may ask, "if you want children to acquire English, then why not teach them English?" The development of English through instruction in English is indeed the third component of quality bilingual education. The combination of native language instruction in grade-level academic subjects and literacy development directly supports bilingual learners' development of English. Support for English language development comes through English as a second language (ESL) classes, and eventually through sheltered content classes[11] taught in English (appropriate for bilingual learners at intermediate levels of English proficiency). The best bilingual education programs include all of these characteristics: content and literacy instruction in the native language, ESL instruction, and eventually, sheltered content instruction in English.

MYTHS AND MISCONCEPTIONS SURROUNDING BILINGUAL EDUCATION IN U.S. SCHOOLS

Despite a strong research base supporting the benefits of long-term bilingual education, some common misconceptions prevail among the general public. These myths generally relate to the goals and practices of bilingual education, the process of second language acquisition, and the fear that English will lose ground to other languages in the United States. Probably the most common misconception of bilingual education is related to the goals of such an approach. Many people who have no direct connection to or experience with bilingual education seem to view it as a diversion from, rather than a means toward, learning English. If one accepts this as a factual premise, replacing these programs with more effective ways to teach English seems not merely reasonable, but beneficial to language-minority students (this was precisely the argument advanced by sponsors of the California, Arizona, and Massachusetts initiatives). But, as mentioned earlier, quality bilingual education has been shown to be the most effective way for nonnative English-speaking students to learn English while also learning grade-level content area and literacy skills. Unfortunately, a lack of awareness about the real issues related to bilingual education has been constant and pervasive among the general population.[12]

Another common myth surrounds the distribution of languages in bilingual programs and the belief that bilingual programs are, in fact, mainly native language programs that provide very little instruction in English. In reality, most bilingual education programs deliver a substantial portion of the curriculum in English, with secondary school students being less likely to receive any significant amount of native language instruction than elementary school students. A related myth is based on the number of languages used in bilingual programs. Rarely are there sufficient numbers of children in a given school district that speak the same language to make bilingual instruction practical for everyone. Even when there are enough children to create a bilingual program,[13] the shortage of qualified bilingual teachers typically makes it impossible. The majority of bilingual programs in the United States are Spanish/English programs, although programs incorporating other native languages also exist.

Other misconceptions are related to the process of language acquisition and the role that bilingual programs play in the rate of acquisition. Specifically, there is a myth surrounding the effectiveness of the "total immersion" ("sink or swim") method of learning English (that is, the best way to learn a language is through total immersion in the language being learned; no other language is used in instruction). There is no credible evidence to support this theory of language acquisition. On the contrary, research shows that it is not just the quantity of language exposure, but the quality of exposure. That is to say, if children are placed into English-only classrooms with little or no help in understanding the content of the lessons, they will not learn English or much of anything else. When children are provided with native language instruction that makes lessons meaningful, alongside English instruction specifically designed for second language learners, they will learn more English and more grade-level content material too.

Further, research has demonstrated that it takes children a long time to acquire full proficiency in a second language (that is to say, age-appropriate, grade-level proficiency). Although it may appear that they are fluent speakers of English because they are quick to learn the conversational English used on the playground and other social situations, second language learners normally need several years to acquire the cognitively demanding, decontextualized language required in academic settings.[14] Developmental bilingual education programs that emphasize a gradual transition to English-only instruction and offer quality, native language instruction in the content areas and literacy provide continuity in children's cognitive growth and lay the foundation for subsequent academic success in the second language. On the other hand, quick-exit bilingual programs or English-only approaches that try to rush the language learning process can interrupt that growth at a crucial stage in a bilingual child's development and may lead to negative effects on achievement.

Last, there is the myth that the power and prevalence of English as the national language of the United States is threatened by the promotion and acceptance of other languages and language groups. Could this be true? Could English really be losing ground to other languages in the United States? Reality could not be farther from this misleading claim and fear-producing strategy frequently adopted by English-only proponents. In the United States, heritage languages are lost over time both at the individual and community levels and typically die out within three generations. English has already been established as the dominant language among indigenous families in the United States. Language use among immigrant families shifts toward English in predictable patterns. For example, immigrant children are generally English-dominant by the time they reach adulthood; children born in the United States to first-generation immigrant families move quickly to English dominance once they begin school (if not earlier). Third-generation children are native English speakers and usually have very little, if any, heritage language skills. In fact, demographic evidence suggests that language shift to English in the United States has been speeding up, rather than slowing down. Thus, English is most certainly not losing ground in the United States. Ironically, the rest of the world fears exactly the opposite. Non-English-speaking countries see the international power of English and interest in American culture as a threat to their own languages and cultures.

BILINGUAL EDUCATION: GOOD FOR U.S.?

Why then the controversy surrounding bilingual education in the United States? Viewed from an educational perspective, the controversy may seem bizarre. After all, the main goals of quality bilingual education (academic achievement in the content areas, literacy development, and English language acquisition and development) are educationally sound expectations that are hard to argue against. An additional goal of some bilingual programs (i.e., developmental, or dual-language models) is the development of a second language. Knowledge of additional languages has historically been characteristic of educated and elite groups. Around the globe, virtually every educational system attempts to teach additional languages to its general student population (including the United States). In fact, most U.S. states mandate foreign language education programs and/or proficiency in a foreign language as a requirement for high school graduation. Even the No Child Left Behind Act (NCLB) of 2002 includes the study of foreign languages as a "core academic subject" and a prominent component of quality education. The current administration, through NCLB, regards the study of additional languages as crucial in educating American students for a global economy and recognizes it as a way to expand students' perspectives on other world cultures and ways of thinking. As the current national educational policy, NCLB evinces the importance of bilingualism for "educated" students:

> Foreign language instruction should be part of every child's education. A language is more than sounds and syntax: it is a culture, a way of thinking, and a perspective on the world. Each language is a precious resource that must be studied, used, and preserved precisely because a language opens the mind to new possibilities. The study of language is the study of life, literature, history, and thought. It is nothing less than the study of our world and ourselves. . . . Foreign language study is not expendable. It is not an add-on. It is essential for a 21st Century education.[15]

Yet, NCLB, which replaced the Bilingual Education Act in 2002, makes no mention of bilingual education as a way to achieve the goal of learning additional languages. In fact, bilingual education is not mentioned at all. In spite of its sound pedagogical basis and growing research support pointing to general academic benefits for language minority students (including competency in English and another language), bilingual education is left out of the NCLB conversation completely.

Thus, the bilingual education paradox emerges. While some legislation mandates foreign language education, other concurrent legislation virtually eliminates the use of ethnic languages in education for minority language speakers. In other words, English (or majority language) speakers are encouraged to learn Spanish (or any other foreign language from a small menu of offerings), but Spanish speakers (or native speakers of any other minority language) are forced to forget it. This is but one indicator that bilingual education is above all a political issue, not an educational one, because it is concerned with the relative power, or lack thereof, of various groups in the United States and the practice of equalizing the playing field for members of traditionally subordinate cultures. The question is not about providing quality education for minority language speakers, but about using a language other than English for instruction and thereby elevating its status as a worthy and viable language.

In debates about the effectiveness of bilingual education, both its proponents and opponents have recognized its potential for empowering traditionally powerless groups. That is, bilingual education provides students who historically have not been successful in U.S. schools the opportunity to learn and participate in the educative process through their native language (a basic human right), thereby rattling power structures and allowing new voices to emerge. Ironically, when middle-class, native English-speaking students participate in bilingual education programs (alongside language minority students) there is little controversy, if any. In fact, English speakers are congratulated on their accomplishments in learning a new language while their newly improved career options and enhanced earning potential are loudly and cheerfully discussed among parents, teachers, and administrators alike. Thus, bilingual education continues to be controversial not because it has not proven itself worthy as a pedagogical practice, but because it represents emancipatory and liberating education for traditionally subordinated groups whose voices have been silenced for too long. To advocate for bilingual education is to argue for the value of heterogeneity of viewpoints, histories, sociopolitical realities, and languages and to promote the intrinsic worth of diversity in general. In this way, bilingual education can be seen as fundamental to educational equity and full participation in a democratic society such as the United States.

THE POTENTIAL OF BILINGUAL/MULTILINGUAL
EDUCATION IN THE UNITED STATES

Although we have a long way to go in shifting the focus of the bilingual education debate from the politics surrounding bilingual education toward a conversation about quality education, current realities provide a window into the potential of bilingual/multilingual education for developing an internationally competitive and worldly educated citizenry. Given today's global economy and quickly expanding international market, the United States does not seem to be capitalizing on one of its most valuable resources: individuals with highly developed bilingual competencies for use in social, economic, diplomatic, and geographical arenas. The events of September 11, 2001, uncovered, among other things, a dire shortage of professionals with foreign language expertise. In fact, the need for individuals with highly developed language competencies in English and other languages has never been higher. Seen in this light, a strong argument *for* bilingual/multilingual education in the United States emerges.

The U.S. education system has generally been expected to address the nation's language needs, but the approach thus far can only be described as schizophrenic in orientation. A relatively small number of U.S. students receive long-term, quality instruction in any "foreign" language in their pre-K–12 education. Those who come to school with the gift of bilingualism (or the potential to develop bilingualism by maintaining the native language and adding English through quality bilingual education programs) are quickly moved into all-English programs where the native language, and thus the potential for bilingualism, is abandoned. Those students who come to school with English as a native language generally have to wait until high school to be exposed to a second language, and even then are only afforded minimal opportunities to develop any significant degree of proficiency in that second language. Colleges and universities are not doing any better: the number of students graduating with professional-level bilingual skills is minimal, including those who participate in study-abroad programs.

Clearly, the U.S. education system has made very little progress in developing the nation's language resources. Yet, the need for professional-level multilingual expertise is paramount and on the rise in our globalized, complex, and sometimes dangerous world. As growing numbers of English-speaking parents seek meaningful language-learning opportunities for their children, developmental bilingual education programs (dual-language models, in particular) are more popular than ever before.[16] Heritage language programs, designed to help minority-language students reclaim their ancestral languages, are also growing.[17] Over time, incremental developments such as these have the potential to revolutionize the way Americans perceive linguistic and cultural diversity, or at least open the door that allows alternative viewpoints to join the conversation.

NOTES

1. For the remainder of the chapter I use the term *bilingual* instead of other commonly used terms in the literature and legislation (i.e., English language learner, language minority student, limited English proficient student, etc.). Although many students enter U.S. schools as monolinguals in their native language, they are at the onset of bilingualism. Also, the other terms assume that language ability is measured by how much a person knows English and imply that only students who are not fluent in English can be considered bilingual.

2. Figures are based on reports for public schools in the fifty states and District of Columbia. See A. L. Kindler, *Survey of the states' limited English proficient students and available educational programs and services: 2000–2001 summary report* (Washington, DC: National Clearinghouse for English Language Acquisition, 2002).

3. For a comprehensive resource on language policy and the impact it has had on the education and academic achievement of bilingual learners, including the successful antibilingual education initiatives in California, Arizona, and Massachusetts and other recent developments in legislation in various states, see Jim Crawford's language policy Web site at http://ourworld.compuserve.com/homepages/JW CRAWFORD/ and the *Bilingual Research Journal* Special Issue on the Implementation of Proposition 227 at http://brj.asu.edu/v2412/abstractt.html.

4. *Lau v. Nichols*, 414 U.S. 563 (1974).

5. Equal Educational Opportunities Act of 1974, 20 U.S.C. 1703 (f).

6. For in-depth descriptions of the many bilingual education program models and their variations throughout the world, see Colin Baker and Sylvia Pris Jones, *Encyclopedia of bilingualism and bilingual education* (Clevedon, UK: Multilingual Matters, 1998).

7. S. Nieto, *Affirming diversity: The sociopolitical context of multicultural education*, 3rd ed. (New York: Longman, 2004).

8. For a more detailed description of bilingual program models found throughout the United States, see C. Baker, *Foundations of bilingual education and bilingualism*, 3rd ed. (Clevedon, UK: Multilingual Matters, 2001); C. Baker and S. P. Jones, *Encyclopedia of bilingualism and bilingual education* (Clevedon, UK: Multilingual Matters, 1998); M. E. Brisk, *Bilingual education: From Compensatory to quality education* (Mahwah, NJ: Lawrence Erlbaum, 1998); J. Crawford, *Educating English learners: Language diversity in the classroom*, 5th ed. (Los Angeles: Bilingual Educational Services,

2004); C. J. Faltis and S. J. Hudelson, *Bilingual education in elementary and secondary school communities: Toward understanding and caring* (Boston: Allyn and Bacon, 1998); S. Nieto, *Affirming diversity: The sociopolitical context of multicultural education*, 4th ed. (Boston: Allyn and Bacon, 2004); and C. J. Ovando, V. P. Collier, and M. C. Combs, *Bilingual and ESL classrooms: Teaching in multicultural contexts*, 3rd ed. (Boston: McGraw-Hill, 2003).

9. "Findings of effectiveness of bilingual education," *NABE News* (May 1, 1998): 5. See also Wayne Thomas and Virginia Collier, *National study of school effectiveness for language minority students' long-term academic achievement* (Santa Cruz, CA: Center for Research on Education, Diversity, and Excellence, 2003).

10. For languages with similar writing systems such as Spanish and English, this includes such things as new sounds for already known letters, new punctuation rules, new spelling patterns, and so on.

11. Sheltered content instruction was developed by Stephen Krashen in the mid-1980s as a way to provide English language learners (ELLs) with comprehensible content area instruction. Krashen wanted to "shelter" English learners from the potential learning problems they might experience from having to compete with native English speakers in a mixed language abilities classroom. Thus, sheltered classrooms are only appropriate for ELLs. The features of sheltered content instruction are: comprehensible language (English), focus on academic content, and ELLs with intermediate-level spoken and written English skills.

12. In a 1990 large-scale study (involving a national sample of non-Hispanic adults), Leonie Huddy and David Sears found that 68 percent of Anglo respondents were unable to provide a "substantially accurate" description of bilingual education and 55 percent reported giving little or no thought to the issue.

13. States that mandate bilingual education usually require at least twenty students of the same language background in a given district to create a program.

14. For a detailed explanation of the difference between social language and academic language and the time it takes to develop each, see Wayne Thomas' and Virginia Collier's large-scale, five-year study of the academic achievement patterns of bilingual learners in the United States: W. P. Thomas and V. P. Collier, *A national study of school effectiveness for language minority students' long-term academic achievement* (Santa Cruz, CA: Center for Research on Education, Diversity and Excellence, 2002).

15. Remarks of Education Secretary Rod Paige at the annual conference of the American Council on the Teaching of Foreign Languages, November 21, 2003, Philadelphia, Pennsylvania. To read the entire speech, go to http://www.actfl.org/i4a/pages/index.cfm?pageid=3397.

16. The Center for Applied Linguistics reports a total of 297 dual-language programs throughout twenty-five U.S. states as of May 2003. For more information, go to http://www.cal.org/twi/directory.

17. The Center for Applied Linguistics and the National Foreign Language Center are collaborating on an initiative to recognize and develop the nation's heritage language resources. For more information on the Heritage Languages Initiative, go to http://www.cal.org/heritage.

3

Accents and Dialects: Ebonics and Beyond

Timothy Reagan

Language, as we have seen in the previous chapters, is one of the key elements of understanding and responding appropriately to diversity in educational settings. Language variation and diversity exist not only with respect to different distinct languages, as in the cases of bilingual education and foreign language education, but also in terms of variation *within* particular languages. An important aspect of linguistic diversity, and one that is of considerable significance for classroom practice, is the variation that exists among different varieties of English. In this chapter, we will explore the differences between languages, dialects, and accents, both in general and in the particular case of English, and will then discuss the concept of linguistic legitimacy as it impacts educational practice. Finally, we will examine the case of Ebonics, or African American Vernacular English, as a powerful example of language variation that has significant educational implications for contemporary U.S. public schools.

LANGUAGES, DIALECTS, AND ACCENTS

The terms *language* and *dialect* are often used in ways that suggest or imply a difference in terms of the value, quality, or legitimacy of a particular language variety. *Language* is the term of preference when we are discussing a standard language,[1] while *dialect* is used to describe nonstandard language varieties. Thus, we distinguish between English (which could in fact be a number of different standard language varieties—American English, British English, Australian English, South African English, and so on)[2]—and "Southern American English" or "Appalachian English." The distinction is a fairly complex one, though: some varieties of Southern American English are in fact regional standard languages, while others are clearly nonstandard. The same challenge exists in other languages as well, of course: there are numerous varieties of Standard Spanish (Castilian, Mexican, Argentine, and so on),[3] as well as varieties that are perceived to be dialects ("Tex-Mex" or "Pachuco" in the Southwest, for instance).

Perhaps the most common way of distinguishing languages from dialects in everyday language is by using the criterion of mutual intelligibility.[4] In essence, if two speakers understand each other, we assume that they are speaking the same language, albeit perhaps different dialects, while if they do not understand each other, we say that they are speaking different languages. Mutual intelligibility works much of the time: it allows us to distinguish, for instance, among Russian, Spanish, and English as distinct languages. However, there are numerous examples of different language varieties where mutual intelligibility does not accurately distinguish what are believed to be languages from dialects. For instance, Norwegian, Swedish, and Danish share a high degree of mutual intelligibility, but they are generally viewed, both by their speakers and by others, as distinct languages. At the same time, there are varieties of German that are mutually unintelligible to a significant degree (just as there are varieties of English that are mutually unintelligible),[5] and yet, there would seem to be consensus that both German and English are unified, single languages, albeit perhaps characterized by significant internal variation.

In fact, the distinction between languages and dialects is really not an objective distinction at all; rather, the terms are used to express unarticulated, although clearly implied, status differences. As the linguist Max Weinreich once commented, "The difference between a language and a dialect is who's got the army and navy." In other words, the distinction between a language and a dialect is merely where a society wishes to draw it, based on social, political, economic, and even military factors. Even with respect to languages where one might expect greater clarity in this regard, we are often faced with complex and less than satisfying answers. For example, in response to the question, "How many Romance languages are there?" Rebecca Posner has commented, "An answer to this question that has been slightingly labeled *sancta simplicitas* is that there is only one: the languages are all alike enough to be deemed dialects of the same language. Another equally disingenuous answer might be 'thousands'—of distinctive local varieties—or 'millions'—of individual idiolects."[6] In short, the terms *language* and *dialect* are generally used in an ad hoc manner which has little to do with linguistics or with linguistic criteria. The question, "Is such-and-such a language or a dialect?" is simply not answerable from any body of the linguistic data. The answer, instead, must rely on non- and extralinguistic factors, and must be made not by linguists but by the speakers of the language variety at issue and the wider community. From the perspective solely of linguistics, as Ronelle Alexander has noted, "Each dialect, in fact, is actually a separate language, with its own internally consistent system."[7]

And what about the term *accent*? When we talk about someone speaking with an accent, we can actually mean any of three distinct things. First, the term can mean "a variety of speech differing phonetically from other varieties,"[8] which would mean that each of us speaks with an accent, regardless of whether the variety of language we speak is a standard or a nonstandard or regional variety. This usage is most appropriate from a linguistic perspective. Second, and more narrowly, accent is often used to identify any nonstandard or regional language variation—hence, we talk about a "Southern" accent or a "Bostonian" accent. Finally, the term *accent* is also, somewhat misleadingly, used to refer to the pronunciation of a language by a nonnative speaker of the language, as in "Paul speaks English with a French accent." In fact, what holds all of the meanings together to some extent is that in each case what is being focused upon are phonological differences within a particular language variety, which may be either the result of social, regional, or ethnic differences or the result of interference from a speaker's native language.[9] The important point with respect to accent is, as George Yule has commented, "Whether or not you think you speak Standard English, you will certainly speak with an accent. It is a myth that some speakers have accents while others do not. Some speakers may have particularly strong or easily recognized types of accent while others do not, but every language-user speaks with an accent."[10]

THE MYTH OF LINGUISTIC LEGITIMACY: WHY DOES IT MATTER?

Language is at the heart of virtually every aspect of education, and indeed, of social life in general. Language serves as the primary medium through which much learning takes place, and the acquisition of socially and academically appropriate language forms (both oral and written) is generally seen as one of the principal goals for the educational experience.[11] In addition, it is quite common for individual academic problems to be blamed on, or at least explained by, language differences. Underlying the educational discourse dealing with issues of language are a number of common assumptions about the nature of language, language structure, language difference, and so on, that tend to be shared by educators, parents, the general public, and indeed by students themselves. Perhaps the most powerful of these assumptions is that concerning what counts as a "real" language, and, even more important, what does *not* count as a "real" language.[12] What is at issue here is what can be called linguistic legitimacy: which language varieties are deemed by the society to be legitimate, and which are not. The idea that some language varieties are not "real" languages is a powerful and dangerous one. It is an idea that emerges, most commonly, in response to some perceived threat or challenge to a socially dominant language variety.[13] The concept of linguistic legitimacy is an important one for educators because it touches on issues of social class, ethnicity, and culture, as well as being embedded in relations of dominance and power.[14] Linguistic legitimacy as a construct is also important with respect to the implications that it has for the development and implementation of educational policy, as well as for its direct consequences for classroom practice.

THE CASE OF EBONICS

Very few debates about language are capable of producing the kind of heat, passion, and even outright anger engendered by discussions of Ebonics, or, as it is more accurately identified by linguists, African American Vernacular English, especially with respect to educational issues. In 1979, the *Martin Luther King Junior Elementary School Children v. Ann Arbor School District* decision led to a widespread public debate about the nature and status of African American Vernacular English,[15] not unlike that which recently took place with respect to the decision of the Board of Education in Oakland, California, to recognize African American Vernacular English as the primary language of a significant proportion of students in the school district.[16] In both instances, strong emotions on both sides of the debate all too often drowned out more moderate voices, and in both cases the public debate obscured the linguistic and educational issues that really needed to be addressed. Typical of much of the debate that surrounded that decision was Roger Hernandez's critical assertion that "The notion that black English is a language and that black kids are actually bilingual is ludicrous and patronizing. Ebonics is ungrammatical English. What students who speak Ebonics need to learn is that they are speaking substandard English and that substandard English brands them as uneducated."[17] Such an argument is no doubt a common one, even in educational settings and among educators. Nevertheless, it is also a deeply flawed argument, grounded not only in a misunderstanding of both language and linguistics in general but also of African American Vernacular English in particular.

Many well-meaning individuals, educators and noneducators alike, have raised grave reservations and concerns about both *King* and the Oakland policy with respect to African American Vernacular English. The concerns that have been articulated most commonly include doubts about the nature and origins of African American Vernacular English, its recognition in educational settings, and, perhaps most important, its effects on student learning and student achievement. Also raised have been fears about the implications of identifying speakers of African American Vernacular English as non–English speakers, as well as concerns about the social and economic language needs of speakers of African American Vernacular English. Echoing the concerns voiced by Roger Hernandez, Bill Maxwell, a well-respected African American columnist, wrote: "Oakland, like many other districts nationwide, is failing in part because grown-ups there lack the courage to call Ebonics what it is: a bastardization that has few redeeming elements. . . . Ebonics is acceptable in rap, poetry and fiction. But it has precious few redeeming qualities in the real world and, therefore, must be avoided in public."[18] Although the underlying concerns such views raise are certainly very real and legitimate ones, they are, as we shall see, nevertheless ill-informed and misleading. While a complete treatment of the social, linguistic, and educational aspects of African American Vernacular English is obviously not possible here, it may be useful to present a basic overview of what is actually known about the nature and origins of African American Vernacular English, as well as a brief discussion of possible educationally sound responses to the presence of large numbers of speakers of African American Vernacular English in the schools, and it is to this overview that we now turn.[19]

A good place to begin this discussion is with the labels used to refer to African American Vernacular English. Among the expressions and terms that have been, and in some cases continue to be, used in the literature to refer to African American Vernacular English are "nonstandard Negro English," "Black English Vernacular," simply "Black English," and, mostly in the popular literature, "Ebonics." Each of these labels has its own problems and limitations, as indeed does the phrase "African American Vernacular English." All of these labels share the common problem that they imply that we are talking about a single language variety, that this variety is simply a variant of English, and that it is spoken by Blacks. Each of these assumptions is actually quite misleading at best. First, there is no single language variety that constitutes African American Vernacular English; in fact, there are a series of related language varieties (distinguished by both geographic variables and those of age, gender, social class, etc.).[20] Second, the relationship of African American Vernacular English to Standard American English is itself an area subject to considerable debate, as, indeed, is the extent to which African American Vernacular English can be said to constitute a language distinct from English. In fact, one of the problems with all of these labels is that they seem to create a false dichotomy between "white English" and "black English" which is not only not reflective of linguistic reality,[21] but further, is in fact fundamentally racist in nature.[22] Finally, although the vast majority of speakers of African American Vernacular English are in fact African American, certainly not all African Americans use African American Vernacular English, nor are all native users of African American Vernacular English in fact Black.[23]

This having been said, the collection of language varieties that generally fall under the label African American Vernacular English do coexist with other varieties of American English, and are both notably similar to one another and different in significant ways from other varieties of American English.[24] What is perhaps most important to note with respect to the dilemma of what to call African American Vernacular English is that the debate itself is reflective of the very nonlinguistic and extralinguistic issues that color all aspects of the discourse about these language varieties. As Tom Trabasso and Deborah Harrison note with respect to the definition of "what is Black English":

> *It is a political question since language has served as an instrument of political and cultural control whenever two cultures meet. It is a social question since certain forms of speech are admired, prestigeful, codified and promulgated while others are accorded low esteem, stigmatized, ridiculed and avoided. It is an economic question since many feel that*

"speaking proper" or some variety of Standard English is required for
success in middle-class America.[25]

A much-discussed aspect of African American Vernacular English has to do
with how this collection of language varieties developed—that is, with what
the origins of the features discussed in the preceding text might be. Most linguists today would accept what is called the "decreolist view," which main-
tains that the differences between Standard American English and the varieties of African American Vernacular English can be best explained with
respect to the creole origins of African American Vernacular English.[26] As
Elizabeth Traugott has commented,

> *Viewed from the perspective of English-related pidgins and creoles, there*
> *seems to be no question that aspects of VBE [Vernacular Black English]*
> *can best be explained in the light of centuries of linguistic change, and*
> *development from a pidgin to a creole, through various stages of decre-*
> *olization, to a point where VBE, though largely assimilated into the*
> *various English vernaculars, still has features which clearly distinguish*
> *it from them. To claim that VBE derives from a creole, therefore, is to*
> *focus on its social and linguistic history, and on the relative autonomy*
> *of the Black community in America.*[27]

It should be noted, though, that recent research has suggested that in many
urban areas of the United States, this process of decreolization has not only
stopped, it may actually have been reversed. In other words, as the urban
Black population has been increasingly marginalized socially and economically, the language varieties that they speak may have begun to diverge from
the surrounding standard varieties of American English.[28] Among the linguistic features that may be developing in some contemporary African American Vernacular English varieties, for instance, is the use of the future resulta-
tive *be done* that has been documented by the sociolinguist John Baugh, as in
the sentence, "I'll be done killed that motherf**ker if he tries to lay a hand on
my kid again."[29]

The contemporary social and educational debates about African American
Vernacular English rest on two fundamental and distinct arguments.[30] The
first of these two arguments focuses on the nature of African American Vernacular English in general terms, and especially with respect to prescriptivist
judgments about what constitutes "proper English," and how such judgments

are related to the use of African American Vernacular English. The second argument concerns the relationship between African American Vernacular English and other varieties of American English, and is often presented in the terms of whether African American Vernacular English is really a distinctive language in its own right or whether it is simply a nonstandard variety of American English. Each of these arguments is important from both a linguistic and an educational standpoint, and each merits our attention here.

That the nature of African American Vernacular English as a language should be at issue in contemporary discussions, although perhaps understandable socially, politically, and educationally, is nevertheless a bit of a surprise, and even a puzzle, from a linguistic perspective. As Edgar Schneider has noted, "For more than twenty years, the dialect spoken by black Americans has been among the most salient topics of linguistic research in the United States,"[31] and there is a huge body of linguistic research dealing with various aspects of African American Vernacular English.[32] In fact, in modern sociolinguistics in the United States, the study of African American Vernacular English has provided a central framework for much contemporary research. In other words, from the perspective of linguistics, the status of African American Vernacular English is well established: African American Vernacular English is a series of related language varieties, spoken primarily by African Americans, which are rule-governed and which differ in significant ways from other varieties of American English.[33]

One often-cited example of how African American Vernacular English differs from Standard American English is the use of the "invariant *be*," which is used by African American Vernacular English speakers to identify the habitual aspect of a finite verb.[34] Thus, the meaning of the African American Vernacular English sentence, "She be around" is best conveyed by the Standard American English "She is usually around," while the African American Vernacular English "She around" would be best conveyed in Standard American English as, "She's around right now." The implications of this distinction in the classroom context are made clear in the following conversation between a teacher and an African American Vernacular English-speaking student reported by Shirley Brice Heath:

> *A teacher asked one day: "Where is Susan? Isn't she here today?" Lem answered "She ain't ride de bus." The teacher responded: "She doesn't ride the bus, Lem." Lem answered: "She do be ridin' de bus." The teacher frowned at Lem and turned away.*[35]

This is a powerful example of communication breakdown in the classroom context, and is due not to any deficiency on the part of the student, but rather to the linguistic limitations of the teacher. Lem responded accurately and appropriately to the teacher's question: he indicated that Susan had not ridden the bus on the day in question. The teacher, focusing on what she took to be an error in Standard English, attempted to correct Lem by rephrasing his answer. Lem not only understood the teacher's correction, but also recognized that she had not understood his point, and replied by using a form of the habitual aspect to emphasize that indeed Susan did *normally* ride the bus, but that she hadn't done so *on this particular day*. Even then, the teacher fails to understand Lem's point. The interesting feature of this miscommunicative event is that Lem is demonstrating considerably more metalinguistic knowledge and sophistication than is his teacher. As A. Warren and L. McCloskey have observed,

> *It appears that most Black English-speaking children understand more Standard English pronunciation and grammar than they use. . . . What aspects of Standard English they do not understand may be relatively superficial, at least from a linguistic standpoint (although perhaps not from a social one). The greater problem may be that their Standard English-speaking peers and teachers do not understand Black English.*[36]

The debate about African American Vernacular English is fundamentally an educational one, concerned with the most appropriate manner of meeting the needs of a particular group of students. Arguably the most important lesson to be learned with respect to the needs of African American Vernacular English speakers is that language *difference* does not in any way constitute language *deficit*. Although this has become something of a politically correct cliché in recent times, it is nonetheless worth emphasizing because while teachers and others may rhetorically accept the distinction between differences and deficits, all too often the distinction is not reflected in social and educational practice. Children in the public schools who are speakers of African American Vernacular English (as well as speakers of other nonstandard varieties of English) continue to be disproportionately misdiagnosed and mislabeled with respect to both cognitive and speech/language problems, and this alone would constitute a compelling justification for additional teacher preparation with respect to language differences, and specifically those differences commonly found in the language of African American Vernacular English speakers.[37]

Embedded in much contemporary educational discourse about African American Vernacular English are, in fact, strongly held views of linguistic inferiority. Such views are common not only in everyday discourse, but also, on occasion, in works that are in some sense "academic." Two recent works that demonstrate this point are Eleanor Wilson Orr's book *Twice as Less: Black English and the Performance of Black Students in Mathematics and Science*[38] and Sandra Stotsky's book *Losing Our Language: How Multicultural Classroom Instruction Is Undermining Our Children's Ability to Read, Write and Reason.*[39] In both instances, the position argued with respect to African American Vernacular English is one that is firmly grounded in a view known as "linguistic relativity." This view, which has its origins in the late eighteenth- and early nineteenth-century work of the German scholar William von Humboldt, was given its clearest and most popular articulation in the work of Edward Sapir and Benjamin Whorf, after whom it is commonly named as the Sapir-Whorf Hypothesis. In essence, the Sapir-Whorf Hypothesis is concerned with describing the relationship between the language that we speak and our thoughts and thought processes. As Whorf himself argued, "we dissect nature along lines laid down by our native languages . . . by the linguistic systems in our minds."[40] A more recent articulation of the fundamental premises of the Sapir-Whorf Hypothesis has been provided by Penny Lee, who suggests, "Although all observers may be confronted by the same physical evidence in the form of experiential data and although they may be capable of 'externally similar acts of observation', a person's 'picture of the universe' or 'view of the world' differs as a function of the particular language or languages that the person knows."[41] In its most extreme forms, which all too often include works dealing with the education of children from nonstandard language backgrounds, this view of the relationship between thought and language is actually deterministic in nature. Although there may well be elements of truth in a weak version of the Sapir-Whorf Hypothesis,[42] there is widespread agreement among linguists, psychologists, and educational researchers that a strong version of the Sapir-Whorf Hypothesis is simply not credible or defensible.

An especially interesting facet of the public discourse about the Oakland policy, and one which has not received the attention it merits in much of the mainstream press, was the body of supposedly humorous jokes and take-offs that became fairly widespread in the aftermath of the debate. The many jokes that were circulated, both orally and especially on the Internet, about the Oakland policy were generally based on flawed understandings of the nature of human language in general and African American Vernacular English in particular, and inevitably resulted in the trivialization of important educational questions. In addition, this body of "humor" was not only misguided and offensive, but was in many instances demonstratively racist.[43]

Basically, then, what the case of African American Vernacular English would seem to emphasize is that there is a fundamental distinction between what might be called "language-as-system" (that is, language as a linguistic phenomenon) and "language-as-social marker" (the sociological role of language). Further, in every society there is a hierarchy of linguistic variations, generally reflective of social class. This distinction helps us to understand why, in contemporary American society, African American Vernacular English and Standard American English can have the same *linguistic* status, while having markedly different *sociolinguistic* status.

CONCLUSION

The case of African American Vernacular English is, to be sure, an exceptional one, in part because of the complex history and structure of the language varieties involved, and in part because of the complicated nexus of language difference, race, class, and power that is involved. The issues raised in the case of African American Vernacular English are not unique, however—very similar challenges are associated with most, if not all, regional and nonstandard varieties of English in the United States. Rosina Lippi-Green, for instance, has forcefully and compellingly argued that Southern varieties of American English (in fact, both standard and nonstandard varieties) are stereotyped in ways that consistently result in assumptions about intelligence, as well as other social and cultural characteristics.[44] Lippi-Green argues,

> There is no doubt that in the delineation of the nation, we use accent
> as a cultural shorthand to talk about bundles of properties which we
> would rather not mention directly. When a northerner appropriates a
> pan-southern accent to make a joke or a point, he or she is drawing on
> a strategy of condescension and trivialization that cues into those stereo-
> types so carefully structured and nurtured: southerners who do not as-
> similate to northern norms are backward but friendly, racist but polite,
> obsessed with the past and unenamored of the finer points of higher ed-
> ucation. If they are women, they are sweet, pretty, and not very bright.[45]

What is really at issue here, of course, is language subordination, and it is such subordination, whether cultural or linguistic in nature, that continues to resist the embracing of diversity that is at the core of a socially and ethically defensible educational experience for all children.

NOTES

1. The term *standard language* refers to the particular variety of a language that is superimposed on the speech community as normative. In its linguistic sense, the term is merely descriptive, and does not imply any innate superiority of a "standard" variety over a "nonstandard" one. Some scholars prefer to use the terms *mainstream* and *non-mainstream* as less prone to be misunderstood as judgmental.

2. See, for instance, Peter Trudgill and Jean Hannah, *International English: A guide to the varieties of Standard English*, 3rd ed. (London: Edward Arnold, 1994).

3. For a discussion of language variation in contemporary Spanish, see Clare Mar-Molinero, *The Spanish-speaking world: A practical introduction to sociolinguistic issues* (New York: Routledge, 1997), 43–56.

4. See Aleksandra Steinbergs, "The classification of languages," in *Contemporary linguistic analysis: An introduction*, 3rd ed., ed. William O'Grady and Michael Dobrovolsky (Toronto: Copp Clark, 1996), 331–32.

5. See J. Chambers and Peter Trudgill, *Dialectology* (Cambridge, England: Cambridge University Press, 1980), 5. Also of interest here are H. Allen and M. Linn, eds., *Dialect and language variation* (Orlando, FL: Academic Press, 1986) and Suzanne Romaine, *Language in society: An introduction to sociolinguistics*, 2nd ed. (Oxford: Oxford University Press, 2000), 1–31.

6. Rebecca Posner, *The Romance languages* (Cambridge, England: Cambridge University Press, 1996), 189.

7. Ronelle Alexander, *Intensive Bulgarian: A textbook and reference grammar*, vol. 2 (Madison: University of Wisconsin Press, 2000), 316.

8. Peter Matthews, *The concise Oxford dictionary of linguistics* (Oxford: Oxford University Press, 1997), 4.

9. R. L. Trask, *Language: The basics*, 2nd ed. (New York: Routledge, 1999), 73–75.

10. George Yule, *The study of language* (Cambridge, England: Cambridge University Press, 1985), 181.

11. See, for instance, Ronald Wardhaugh, *Proper English: Myths and misunderstandings about language* (Oxford: Blackwell, 1999).

12. Timothy Reagan, "When is a language not a language? Challenges to 'linguistic legitimacy' in educational discourse," *Educational Foundations* 11, 5–28.

13. Timothy Reagan, "Objectification, positivism, and language studies: A reconsideration," *Critical Inquiry in Language Studies* 1 41–60.

14. See Timothy Reagan, *Language, education, and ideology: Mapping the linguistic landscape of U.S. schools* (Westport, CT: Praeger, 2002), 1–14.

15. See Geneva Smitherman, "What go round come round: *King* in perspective," *Harvard Educational Review* 51, 40–56.

16. For an excellent discussion of the Oakland controversy, see John Baugh, *Beyond Ebonics: Linguistic pride and racial prejudice* (New York: Oxford University Press, 2000). See also Carol L. Schmid, *The politics of language: Conflict, identity, and cultural pluralism in comparative perspective* (Oxford: Oxford University Press, 2001), 145–48.

17. Roger Hernandez, "Never mind teaching Ebonics: Teach proper English," *Hartford Courant*, December 26, 1996, A-21.

18. Bill Maxwell, "Miss Bonaparte wouldn't approve," *New Britain Herald*, January 2, 1997, B-2.

19. See John Baugh, *Out of the mouths of slaves: African American language and educational malpractice* (Austin: University of Texas Press, 1999); John McWhorter, *The word on the street: Fact and fable about American English* (New York: Plenum, 1998); S. Mufwene, J. Rickford, J. Bailey, and John Baugh, eds., *African-American English: Structure, history and use* (London: Routledge, 1998); T. Perry and Lisa Delpit, eds., *The real Ebonics debate: Power, language, and the education of African American children* (Boston: Beacon Press, 1998); J. Rickford and R. Rickford, *Spoken soul: The story of Black English* (New York: John Wiley & Sons, 2000); and Geneva Smitherman, *Talkin that talk: Language, culture, and education in African America* (London: Routledge, 2000).

20. See Walt Wolfram and Roger Fasold, *The study of social dialects in American English* (Englewood Cliffs, NJ: Prentice-Hall, 1974), 73–98.

21. See William Labov, *Language in the inner city: Studies in the Black English vernacular* (Philadelphia: University of Pennsylvania Press, 1972), xiii.

22. See S. Lanehart, "African American vernacular English," in *Handbook of language and ethnic identity*, ed. Joshua Fishman (Oxford: Oxford University Press, 1999), 211–25.

23. See Baugh, *Out of the mouths of slaves*; Baugh, *Beyond Ebonics*; McWhorter, *Word on the street*; Mufwene, Rickford, Bailey, and Baugh, *African-American English*; Perry and Delpit, *The real Ebonics debate;* Rickford and Rickford, *Spoken soul;* and Smitherman, *Talkin that talk.*

24. Labov, *Language in the inner city,* 36–37.

25. Tom Trabasso and Deborah Harrison, "Introduction," in *Black English*, ed. Tom Trabasso and Deborah Harrison (Hillsdale, NJ: Lawrence Erlbaum Associates, 1976), 2.

26. Peter Trudgill, *Sociolinguistics: An introduction to the study of language and society*, rev. ed. (Harmondsworth, Middlesex: Penguin, 1995), 50.

27. Elizabeth Traugott, "Pidgins, creoles and the origins of vernacular Black English," in *Black English*, ed. Trabasso and Harrison, 57–93.

28. See G. Bailey and N. Maynor, "Decreoloization?" *Language in Society* 16, 449–73.

29. Quoted in Trudgill, *Sociolinguistics*, 61.

30. See Edgar Schneider, *American earlier Black English: Morphological and syntactic variables* (Tuscaloosa: University of Alabama Press, 1989), 2–3.

31. Schneider, *American earlier Black English*, 1.

32. See Baugh, *Out of the mouths of slaves*; Baugh, *Beyond Ebonics*; McWhorter, *Word on the street*; Mufwene, Rickford, Bailey, and Baugh, *African-American English*; Perry and Delpit, *The real Ebonics debate*; Rickford and Rickford, *Spoken soul*; and Smitherman, *Talkin that talk.*

33. See Baugh, *Out of the mouths of slaves*; Baugh, *Beyond Ebonics*; McWhorter, *Word on the street*; Mufwene, Rickford, Bailey, and Baugh, *African-American English*; Perry and Delpit, *The real Ebonics debate*; Rickford and Rickford, *Spoken soul*; and Smitherman, *Talkin that talk.*

34. See William Labov, "Recognizing Black English in the classroom," in *Linguistics for teachers*, ed. L. Cleary and M. Linn (New York: McGraw-Hill, 1993), 149–73.

35. Shirley Brice Heath, *Ways with words: Language, life, and work in communities and classrooms* (Cambridge, England: Cambridge University Press, 1983), 277.

36. A. Warren and L. McCloskey, "Pragmatics: Language in social context," in *The development of language*, ed. J. Gleason (New York: Macmillan, 1993), 222.

37. See Timothy Reagan, "The case for applied linguistics in teacher education," *Journal of Teacher Education* 48, 185–95.

38. Eleanor Wilson Orr, *Twice as less: Black English and the performance of black students in mathematics and science* (New York: Norton, 1987).

39. Sandra Stotsky, *Losing our language: How multicultural classroom instruction is undermining our children's ability to read, write and reason* (New York: Free Press, 1999).

40. Quoted in David Crystal, *A dictionary of linguistics and phonetics,* 3rd ed. (Oxford: Basil Blackwell, 1991), 306.

41. Penny Lee, *The Whorf theory complex: A critical reconstruction* (Amsterdam: John Benjamins, 1996), 87.

42. See S. Elgin, *The language imperative* (Cambridge: Perseus, 2000), 49–71.

43. For an extended and powerful discussion of this point, see Baugh, *Beyond Ebonics,* 87–99.

44. Rosina Lippi-Green, *English with an accent: Language, ideology and discrimination in the United States* (New York: Routledge, 1997).

45. Lippi-Green, *English with an accent,* 215.

A Case Study in Cultural and Linguistic Difference: The DEAF-WORLD

Timothy Reagan

> *Lately . . . the deaf community has begun to speak for itself. To the surprise and bewilderment of outsiders, its message is utterly contrary to the wisdom of centuries: Deaf people, far from groaning under a heavy yoke, are not handicapped at all. Deafness is not a disability. Instead, many deaf people now proclaim, they are a subculture like any other. They are simply a linguistic minority (speaking American Sign Language) and are no more in need of a cure than are Haitians or Hispanics.*
> —*Edward Dolmick, "Deafness as Culture,"*
> The Atlantic 272 (3), 37

The idea that the Deaf[1] are a cultural and linguistic minority group—and, indeed, an oppressed cultural and linguistic minority group at that—is one that challenges many of our assumptions and preconceptions about both the nature of language and culture and of "disability." And yet, the view of Deaf people as a cultural community comparable in many ways to other cultural communities in our society is one that is gaining considerable support and credibility.[2] In this chapter, an overview of the nature of the Deaf cultural community will be provided, and the case will be made for advocating bilingual-bicultural education programs for Deaf students. Finally, the special challenge posed by the movement for inclusive education will be addressed.

It is important for us to note at the outset, however, that what is being discussed here is *cultural* Deafness, in contrast to what might be termed "audiological deafness." As Harlan Lane has cogently explained in his book *The Mask of Benevolence: Disabling the Deaf Community,*

> *Most Americans who have impaired hearing are not members of the American Deaf community. They were acculturated to hearing society, their first language was a spoken one, and they became hard of hearing or deaf in the course of their lives, often late in life. This book is not about them; it is about people who grow up Deaf, acculturated to the manual language and society of the Deaf community.*[3]

The same can be said for the arguments that follow in this chapter: they apply to the members and potential members of the Deaf cultural community alone. More precisely, the concern here is for children who are prelingually profoundly or severely deaf, and who will most likely spend their lives as members of the Deaf community.

AMERICAN SIGN LANGUAGE AND THE DEAF-WORLD

One of the intriguing aspects of any discussion of the Deaf as a cultural and linguistic community is the need to make a case that there really is such a thing as Deaf culture (or, as the concept is expressed in American Sign Language, the DEAF-WORLD) just as one sometimes needs to build a case for American Sign Language (ASL) being a "real" language.[4] The need for such discussions tells us a great deal already—not, perhaps, so much about the Deaf as about the stereotypes and biases of the hearing world, and about issues of power, paternalism, and cultural imperialism.[5] Central to any discussion of the culture and language of the Deaf must be a concern with the role of language in domination and power relations as these relate to Deaf-hearing interaction.[6] As Harlan Lane, speaking not only for himself but for many scholars concerned with the Deaf as a cultural community, has argued:

> *I maintain that the vocabulary and conceptual framework our society has customarily used with regard to deaf people, based as it is on infirmity, serves us and the members of the deaf community less well than a vocabulary and framework of cultural relativity. I want to replace the normativeness of medicine with the curiosity of ethnography.*[7]

Further, the language of pathology that is used to discuss the Deaf has encouraged an essentially paternalistic view of the Deaf. As Harlan Hahn has argued with respect to paternalism toward disabled people in general,

> Paternalism enables the dominant elements of a society to express profound and sincere sympathy for the members of a minority group while, at the same time, keeping them in a position of social and economic subordination. It has allowed the nondisabled to act as the protectors, guides, leaders, role-models, and intermediaries for disabled individuals who, like children, are often assumed to be helpless, dependent, asexual, economically unproductive, physically limited, emotionally immature, and acceptable only when they are unobtrusive. . . . Politically, disabled people usually have been neither seen nor heard. Paternalistic attitudes, therefore, may be primarily responsible both for the ironic invisibility of disabled persons and for the prior tendency to ignore this important area of public policy.[8]

This analysis of paternalism toward the disabled is especially powerful and vivid in the case of the deaf, as Lane notes:

> Like the paternalism of the colonizers, hearing paternalism begins with defective perception, because it superimposes its image of the familiar world of hearing people on the unfamiliar world of deaf people. Hearing paternalism likewise sees its task as "civilizing" its charges: restoring deaf people to society. And hearing paternalism fails to understand the structure and values of deaf society. The hearing people who control the affairs of deaf children and adults commonly do not know deaf people and do not want to. Since they cannot see deaf people as they really are, they make up imaginary deaf people of their own, in accord with their own experiences and needs. Paternalism deals in such stereotypes.[9]

In order to avoid such paternalism, writers on Deaf culture have attempted to deal with the world of the Deaf from what is basically an anthropological perspective, focusing on the ways in which Deaf people themselves see their world. No one has done this more effectively than Carol Padden and Tom Humphries, the Deaf authors of *Deaf in America: Voices from a Culture,* who describe their own undertaking as follows:

> The traditional way of writing about Deaf people is to focus on the fact of their condition—that they do not hear—and to interpret all other

aspects of their lives as consequences of this fact. . . . In contrast to the long history of writings that treat them as medical cases, or as people with "disabilities," who "compensate" for the deafness by using sign language, we want to portray the lives they live, their art and performances, their everyday talk, their shared myths, and the lessons they teach one another. We have always felt that the attention given to the physical condition of not hearing has obscured far more interesting facets of Deaf people's lives.[10]

In short, what Padden and Humphries and others[11] have compellingly argued is that the DEAF-WORLD is characterized by the same kinds of elements that characterize any other cultural community, among which are:

- a common, shared language
- a shared awareness of cultural identity
- distinctive behavioral norms and patterns
- cultural artifacts
- endogamous marital patterns
- a shared historical knowledge and awareness
- a network of voluntary, in-group social organizations

The single most significant component of Deaf cultural identity in the United States is competence in ASL, the community's vernacular language as well as a powerful marker of group solidarity.[12] It is important to note here, though, that this applies only to ASL; other types of signing that are commonly used, including both the pidgin sign language normally employed by hearing signers and the artificially constructed manual sign codes for English often used in educational settings, fulfill very different functions and are viewed very differently by the Deaf community.[13] Without going into unnecessary detail here, pidgin sign is generally seen by the Deaf as an appropriate means of communication with hearing individuals, while manual sign codes are widely rejected by the Deaf community as awkward efforts to impose the structures of a spoken language on sign.[14]

There is among the Deaf a very strong sense of cultural identity. Members of the DEAF-WORLD identify themselves as socially and culturally *Deaf*, maintaining a clear-cut distinction between audiological deafness and cultural Deafness.[15] From the perspective of the culturally Deaf, the fact of audiological deafness is neither a necessary nor a sufficient condition for cultural Deafness. Hearing children of Deaf people, who grow up with ASL as their first language, are (at least to some extent) members of the Deaf culture,[16] just as older hearing people who lose their hearing are, under normal circumstances, decidedly not Deaf—they are, rather, "hearing people who can no longer hear." It is interesting to note that in ASL there is actually a sign used to denigrate a deaf person who "thinks like a hearing person," roughly comparable in use to the term "Uncle Tom" among African Americans.

An important aspect of the cultural identity of Deafness is the rejection of a deficit view of what it means to be deaf. In a recent interview, when asked whether he would like to have his hearing restored, I. King Jordan, the President of Gallaudet University, replied, "That's almost like asking a black person if he would rather be white. . . . I don't think of myself as missing something or as incomplete. . . . It's a common fallacy if you don't know Deaf people or Deaf issues. You think it's a limitation."[17] This is seen most clearly, perhaps, in the widespread rejection within the DEAF-WORLD of cochlear implants, which are seen by the Deaf as a rejection of ASL as a legitimate language and the culture of Deafness as a legitimate and viable culture.[18] Thus, such attempts to medically "cure" or "remediate" audiological deafness are seen as not merely misguided, but culturally oppressive as well. As Lane notes, the perspective of the culturally Deaf toward such a medicalization of deafness is basically that:

> If the birth of a Deaf child is a priceless gift, then there is only cause for rejoicing, as at the birth of a black child, or an Indian one. Medical intervention is inappropriate, even if a perfect "cure" were available. Invasive surgery on healthy children is morally wrong. We know that, as members of a stigmatized minority, these children's lives will be full of challenge but, by the same token, they have a special contribution to make to their own community and the larger society.[19]

Not surprisingly, there are some significant differences with respect to behavioral norms between the hearing world and the DEAF-WORLD. Most notable in this regard are differences in eye contact patterns, rules governing the permissibility of physical contact of various sorts (including touching to gain attention), the use of facial expressions, gesturing, and so on.[20] From such differences cultural conflicts inevitably arise, of course, and when this happens, each culture tends to see the other as exhibiting rude and insensitive behavior.

The artifacts of the DEAF-WORLD are, for the most part, the technological devices that have been developed in recent years to facilitate the ability of the deaf to function in the hearing world. The key difference between the audiologically deaf and culturally Deaf with respect to the use of such technologies may be that there is a reluctance on the part of many culturally Deaf people to utilize technological devices (such as hearing aids) that focus primarily or exclusively on *hearing*, while audiologically deaf people are generally quite happy to use such devices. Technological innovations, such as telecommunication devices for the deaf (TDD/TTYs), which allow the Deaf person to use the telephone, television decoders for closed-captioned programs, doorbells and alarms tied to lights, and so on, on the other hand, are widely used, accepted and appreciated by the Deaf.

A common facet of cultural identity for most cultural groups is the presence and maintenance of endogamous marital patterns, and the same is true in the case of the culturally Deaf. There are strong cultural pressures supporting endogamous marriage in the Deaf community, and the rate of such marriages has been estimated to be as high as 90 percent—a remarkably high rate in contemporary American society. This high rate of in-group marriage is certainly facilitated by the role of the residential schools for the deaf, but is also tied to the common, shared language and culture of the DEAF-WORLD.

Members of the DEAF-WORLD have a strong sense of the history of their community, and this awareness has been passed from generation to generation, often as folklore, largely through oral (i.e., signed) means in the past.[21] However, the 1981 publication of Jack Gannon's *Deaf Heritage: A Narrative History of Deaf America* has contributed to ensuring a wider access to the historical awareness of the DEAF-WORLD.[22]

Finally, there is an extensive voluntary network of social organizations serving the Deaf, which helps to support the cohesiveness of the Deaf community and provides, to a significant extent, for the companionship needs of group members. This network includes local deaf clubs, the state and national organizations of the deaf (such as the National Association of the Deaf), sports associations, the National Theatre of the Deaf, and so on.

In short, there is a strong and compelling argument favoring the view of the Deaf as a distinct and vibrant cultural community in contemporary American society, and this argument has clear and significant implications for the education of Deaf children, as we shall see in the next section of this chapter.

THE CASE FOR BILINGUAL-BICULTURAL EDUCATION FOR THE DEAF

If one accepts the presence of Deaf culture, and the legitimacy of ASL, as suggested in the preceding section, then a number of fairly important educational implications have to be addressed. Current models and practices in deaf education, by and large, tend to assume a pathological view of deafness, in which the deaf are basically seen as deficient in significant ways when measured against a hearing norm. The acceptance of Deaf culture forces us to reconsider the norm against which the Deaf are to be measured, which in turn means that the kind of educational practice that is seen as appropriate looks very different from contemporary practice. Perhaps the greatest change to contemporary practice would be the altered status and role of ASL.[23] A growing number of educators of the deaf, as well as advocates for Deaf culture, have suggested that the most appropriate approach to the education of Deaf children is one that is essentially bilingual and bicultural in nature—utilizing ASL and English, and teaching children to function in both the hearing world and the DEAF-WORLD.

There is a substantial literature devoted to making an educational case for the use of ASL in the education of Deaf children.[24] Such arguments focus on the relative ease of acquisition of ASL for Deaf children, in contrast to that of either spoken English or manual codes for English, the fact that the acquisition of ASL parallels the normal acquisition of spoken language for the native language (L1) learner, the fact that ASL can be used effectively to teach both academic content and literacy skills in the spoken language, and finally, that early language acquisition is essential "for the continual development of cognitive skills and later acquisition of literacy skills in either a first or second language.[25]

Today, however, ASL is almost never used in formal educational settings; rather, where signing is employed, either Pidgin Sign English or one of the various artificially constructed manual sign codes for English is used.[26] In an educational environment based on a cultural model of Deafness, instruction would take place through ASL, and the goal for all students would be functional bilingualism in both ASL and English. Students would not only study the common curriculum shared with their hearing peers, but would also study the history of the Deaf culture and Deaf communities in other parts of the world. Thus, the goal for such a program would be students who would truly be both bilingual and bicultural, able to function competently and comfortably in the hearing world, while still at home in the world of the Deaf.[27] Such a program, of course, would almost certainly entail Deaf students studying together, in a setting not unlike that provided by residential schools, rather than in mainstreamed settings. This is an important point, since mainstreaming is almost universally seen as a good thing in our society. The problem is that for Deaf students, mainstreaming almost inevitably means a lack of contact with other deaf people. Instead of thinking about appropriate educational placement being based on the least restrictive environment, we might be better off (at least in the case of the Deaf) favoring the "most enabling environment"—a subtle distinction, but nevertheless an important one. It is important to note, though, that this does not automatically rule out the inclusion of hearing students in such an educational setting. Such students would be welcome, but only with the clear understanding that such a project rests on the rejection of the dominance of hearing cultural, behavioral, and linguistic norms. Further, an educational program grounded in a cultural model of Deafness would actively encourage Deaf children to be exposed to a wide variety of Deaf adults. In fact, given the importance attached to the use of ASL and familiarity with the DEAF-WORLD, such an educational program would generally favor the use of Deaf teachers—a radical departure from current educational practice. Finally, control of the educational program would rest, to a significant extent, in the hands of the local Deaf community, rather than in the hands of hearing experts on deafness and deaf education.[28]

THE CHALLENGE OF INCLUSIVE EDUCATION

There are a number of challenges that would have to be addressed if large-scale efforts were to be undertaken to provide Deaf children with bilingual, bicultural educational programs. None of these challenges are greater, however, than that posed by the growing popularity of the movement for inclusive education. The movement toward inclusive education in American education presents educators of the Deaf with unique challenges, and indeed is seen by some members of the Deaf community as threatening the very heart of the DEAF-WORLD. Jan Branson and Don Miller have suggested that mainstreaming, and by implication inclusive education, "is oriented not towards the educational needs of the Deaf but towards the reinforcement of the dominant ideology of equality of access to educational resources, an ideology which is in fact the foundation for the reproduction of structured inequalities."[29]

They term this phenomenon "epistemic violence of mainstreaming," and argue that:

> If Bourdieu and Passeron's analysis of Western educational systems revealed the hollowness of the rhetoric of equality of opportunity, revealing a hidden agenda, the reproduction of structured inequalities in terms of class, the power of the establishment in its most effective forms a symbolic power exercised through symbolic violence, such an analysis becomes even more devastating when applied to the hidden agenda shaping the education of the Deaf. The ideological denial of the structural importance of cultural difference serves to reproduce those differences as inequalities based in cultural and linguistic deprivation.[30]

In essence, what Branson and Miller are suggesting is that the pathological view of deafness and the Deaf is a kind of symbolic violence which denies personhood to the individual deaf person, as well as delegitimates the culture and language of the Deaf community. Insofar as this is true, efforts to address the educational needs of Deaf children that presuppose a hearing norm (whether linguistic or cultural in nature), especially by fully integrating such children in hearing environments separated from the culture and language of the DEAF-WORLD (whether through mainstreaming or inclusion), are not only inappropriate, but harmful. It is in this sense that one can speak of epistemic violence against the Deaf, in that such efforts entail the implicit rejection of the epistemological (as well as cultural and linguistic) world of the Deaf. In short, to return to Branson and Miller's argument, what such programs involve is a "distinctly imperial orientation, [in which] teachers, linguists and policy makers become the unwitting agents of an 'epistemic violence' that 'effaces the subject' . . . 'insidiously objectifying' the 'colonized' through a conceptual apparatus which robs them of their individual and cultural integrity, devaluing and distorting their differences."[31] Inclusive education, in short, whatever its benefits for many children, is no more a panacea than was mainstreaming, and, like mainstreaming before it, poses quite serious threats to the education of the Deaf as a cultural and linguistic minority.

CONCLUDING REFLECTIONS

At issue in the debate about the most appropriate way for the Deaf to be educated, ultimately, is the question of domination, power, and empowerment. The choice is between the hegemony of the hearing educational establishment, with its well-established power base and competing methodologies firmly planted in a view of the Deaf as deficient, and the DEAF-WORLD, with its pride in its own history, culture, language, and accomplishments. Although perhaps in new bottles, the debate is nonetheless "old wine," as the following quote from a 1912 letter to the principal of the New York School for the Deaf makes clear: "It is a lamentable fact that, in matters relating to the deaf, their education and well-being, few if any take the trouble to get the opinion of the very people most concerned—the deaf themselves."[32] In short, the debate is the same one that so many others in our society have had, and continue, to fight—the struggle for the recognition of their language and cultural rights.

NOTES

1. A common distinction made in writing about deafness is between "*deaf*" and "*Deaf*"; the former refers to deafness solely as an audiological condition, the latter to deafness as a cultural condition. The basic idea underlying this distinction is that when writing about cultural groups in general, capital letters are employed ("African American," "Hispanic," and so on). Thus, a person can be "deaf" without being "Deaf" (as in the case of an older person who gradually loses his or her hearing).

2. See Charlotte Baker and Robin Battison, *American Sign Language: A teacher's resource text on grammar and culture* (Silver Spring, MD: T. J. Publishers, 1980); Lois Bragg, ed., *DEAF-WORLD: A historical reader and sourcebook* (New York: New York University Press, 2001); Susan Gregory and Gillian Hartley, eds., *Constructing deafness* (London: Pinter Publishers, in association with the Open University, 1991); Harlan Lane, Robert Hoffmeister, and Den Bahan, *A journey into the DEAF-WORLD* (San Diego: DawnSign Press, 1996); Arden Neisser, *The other side of silence: Sign language and the deaf community in America* (New York: Alfred A. Knopf, 1983); Oliver Sacks, *Seeing voices: A journey into the world of the deaf* (Berkeley: University of California Press, 1989); Jerome Schein, *At home among strangers: Exploring the deaf community in the United States* (Washington, DC: Gallaudet University Press, 1989); and Sherman Wilcox, ed., *American deaf culture* (Burtonsville, MD: Linstok Press, 1989).

3. Harlan Lane, *The mask of benevolence: Disabling the deaf community* (New York: Alfred A. Knopf, 1992), xi.

4. In recent years, there have been ongoing debates in many parts of the country about whether ASL should be offered as a foreign language in secondary schools and in colleges and universities. Central to these debates has been the question of whether ASL is in some sense less "real" or "legitimate" than spoken languages—a position that ignores more than thirty years of linguistic research on the nature, structure, and uses of ASL. See Sherman Wilcox, ed., *Academic acceptance of American Sign Language (Special Issue of Sign Language Studies, No. 59)* and Sherman Wilcox and Phyllis Wilcox, *Learning to see: American Sign Language as a second language,* 2nd ed. (Washington, DC: Gallaudet University Press, 1997).

5. See Sherman Wilcox, "Breaking through the culture of silence," *Sign Language Studies* 55, 163–74.

6. See Michel Foucault, *The archeology of knowledge and the discourse on language* (New York: Harper & Row, 1972); and Stephen Ball, ed., *Foucault and education: Disciplines and knowledge* (London: Routledge, 1990).

7. Lane, *Mask of benevolence*, 19.

8. Harlan Hahn, "Public support for rehabilitation programs: The analysis of U.S. disability policy," *Disability, Handicap & Society* 1(2), 121–37.

9. Lane, *Mask of benevolence*, 37.

10. Carol Padden and Tom Humphries, *Deaf in America: Voices from a culture* (Cambridge, MA: Harvard University Press, 1988), 1.

11. See Baker and Battison, *American sign language*; Gregory and Hartley, *Constructing deafness*; Neisser, *Other side of silence*; Sacks, *Seeing voices*; Schein, *At home among strangers*; and Wilcox, *American deaf culture*.

12. It is important to note that just as ASL functions in this manner for the Deaf community in the United States and anglophone Canada, other natural sign languages serve similar functions in their societies.

13. See Ceil Lucas, ed., *The sociolinguistics of the deaf community* (San Diego: Academic Press, 1989); and Ceil Lucas and Clayton Valli, eds., *Language contact in the American deaf community* (San Diego: Academic Press, 1992).

14. See Claire Ramsey, "Language planning in deaf education," in *The sociolinguistics of the deaf community*, ed. Ceil Lucas (San Diego: Academic Press, 1989), 123–46. See also Timothy Reagan, "Language planning and policy," in *The sociolinguistics of sign languages*, ed. Ceil Lucas (Cambridge, England: Cambridge University Press, 2001), 145–80.

15. See V. Janesick and Donald Moores, "Ethnic and cultural considerations," in *Toward effective public school programs for deaf students: Context, process and outcomes*, ed. T. Kluwin, D. Moores, and M. Gaustad (New York: Teachers College Press, 1992), 49–65; Barbara Kannapell, *Language choice, language identity: A sociolinguistic study of deaf college students* (Burtonsville, MD: Linstok Press, 1993); and Timothy Reagan, "Cultural considerations in the education of deaf children," in *Educational and developmental aspects of deafness*, ed. Donald Moores and Kay Meadow-Orlans (Washington, DC: Gallaudet University Press, 1990), 73–84.

16. See R. Sidransky, *In silence: Growing up hearing in a deaf world* (New York: Ballantine Books, 1990).

17. Quoted in Harlan Lane, "Cochlear implants: Their cultural and historical meaning," in *Deaf history unveiled: Interpretations from the new scholarship*, ed. John Van Cleve (Washington, DC: Gallaudet University Press, 1993), 288.

18. Lane, *The mask of benevolence*.

19. Harlan Lane, "The medicalization of cultural deafness in historical perspective," in *Looking back: A reader on the history of deaf communities and their sign languages*, ed. Renate Fischer and Harlan Lane (Hamburg: Signum Press, 1993), 490–91.

20. See Carol Padden and H. Markowicz, "Cultural conflicts between hearing and deaf communities," in *Seventh Congress of the World Federation of the Deaf* (Silver Spring, MD: National Association of the Deaf, 1976), 407–11. See also Timothy Reagan, "Toward an 'archeology of deafness': Etic and emic constructions of identity in conflict," *Journal of Language, Identity and Education* 1(1), 41–66.

21. See Nancy Frishberg, "Signers of tales: The case for literacy status of an unwritten language," *Sign Language Studies* 59, 149–70; and S. Rutherford, *A study of American deaf folklore* (Silver Spring, MD: Linstok Press, 1993).

22. See Fischer and Lane, *Looking back*; Harlan Lane, *When the mind hears: A history of the deaf* (New York: Random House, 1984); and Van Cleve, *Deaf history unveiled*.

23. See P. Gutiérrez, "A preliminary study of deaf educational policy," *Bilingual Research Journal* 18(3/4), 85–113. See also Robert Hoffmeister, "ASL and its implications for education," in *Manual communication: Implications for education*, ed. Harry Bornstein (Washington, DC: Gallaudet University Press, 1990); Robert Johnson, Scott Liddell, and Carol Erting, *Unlocking the curriculum: Principles for achieving success in deaf education (Gallaudet Research Institute Working Paper 89/3)* (Washington, DC: Gallaudet University, 1989); Timothy Reagan, "The deaf as a linguistic minority: Educational considerations," in *Special education at the century's end: Evolution of theory and practice since 1970*, ed. Thomas Hehir and T. Latus (Cambridge, MA: Harvard Educational Review, 1992); and D. Stewart, "Toward effective classroom use of ASL," in *A free hand: Enfranchising the education of deaf children*, ed. M. Walworth, Donald Moores, and T. O'Rourke (Silver Spring, MD: T. J. Publishers, 1992), 89–118.

24. See, for example, M. Deuchar and H. James, "English as the second language of the deaf," *Language and Communication* 5(1), 45–51.

25. Peter Paul, *ASL to English: A bilingual minority language immersion program for deaf students* (Unpublished mss.), 2.

26. See H. Bornstein, *Manual communication*; see also Timothy Reagan, "Neither easy to understand nor pleasing to see: Manual sign codes as language planning activity," *Language Problems and Language Planning* 19(2), 133–50.

27. See François Grosjean, "The bilingual and bicultural person in the hearing and deaf world," *Sign Language Studies* 77, 307–20.

28. See Lane, *Mask of benevolence*.

29. Jan Branson and Don Miller, "Sign language, the deaf and the epistemic violence of mainstreaming," *Language and Education* 7(1), 21.

30. Branson and Miller, "Sign language," 37–38.

31. Branson and Miller, "Sign language," 23.

32. Quoted in Jack Gannon, *Deaf heritage: A narrative history of deaf America* (Silver Spring, MD: National Association of the Deaf, 1981), 363.

Foreign Language Education: It's Not Just for Conjugation Anymore

Terry A. Osborn

What are your memories of foreign language classes? If you are like most U.S. Americans, you may quickly retort with the oft heard refrain, "Well, I took Spanish (or French, Latin, or German) for two years, but I didn't learn anything." It is sad to admit, but most students who leave the foreign language classes of the United States are ill-prepared to do much except shake their heads in confusion or disgust at what they see as a colossal waste of time.

The reasons for this perception are multifaceted. Indeed, given two or even three years in the artificial environment of the foreign language classrooms of the United States, it is unlikely that anyone could walk out with any real skills in the language. This statement may seem dramatic, but the evidence is quite compelling. The Foreign Service Institute, responsible for training officers of the foreign affairs community such as diplomats, has developed guidelines for the number of hours of training necessary for the development of credible skills in language. The two years in the foreign language classrooms are insufficient.[1] Moreover, European countries start second language learning much earlier than the U.S. educational system, perhaps recognizing that any serious effort at multilingualism begins early in life.

Why, then, do we even have foreign language education in the United States? In this section, I wish to explore how foreign language education reflects an intellectual and social history in the United States related to diversity. To begin this analysis, it is likely helpful to consider two examples of *how* languages were taught, or methodologies: audiolingualism and suggestopedia. We will consider these methodologies in light of the sociohistorical background that framed their implementation.

Audiolingualism was a method popularized during the 1950s and 1960s, stemming from the need for trained linguists in World War II. It embraced a view of foreign language learning as the development of good habits, and was underpinned by beliefs about language learning rooted in behaviorism from theorists such as B. F. Skinner.

Suggestopedia is built around a theory of suggestology, and it attempts to understand how the world around us includes stimuli that are instructive. In the late 1970s, this method gained popularity as it stressed relaxation in terms of the psychological state of students and utilized bright pictures and baroque classical music as tools of language learning.

These methodological approaches demonstrate that language education does not occur in a vacuum. It is shaped by the social, political, cultural, and intellectual Zeitgeist, or spirit of the age. In the 1980s and 1990s, we began to move toward a more communicative emphasis, or looking at using foreign language to communicate with those who are native speakers of the language.

In order to fully facilitate this communication, it made sense to choose a number of themes that might often occur in interactions with native speakers. Weather, hobbies, school schedules, family members, professions, and similar themes formed the skeleton of language courses during those decades. However, since those who developed the language courses assumed that students might need this language when traveling abroad, they built communicative activities around situations that could (if one stretches credibility) occur in another country. Teenagers, however, think differently than adults— a claim that hardly surprises parents of teens.

High school students, in my experience, were not motivated to learn about talking to their counterparts in foreign countries about topics adults had chosen. Discussing the weather is the stuff of adult conversations, not those of teens. Further, in my experience both as a teen and a high school teacher I cannot recall a single conversation about hobbies, except perhaps within the confines of the foreign language classroom.

As the twentieth century closed, those of us in the field of foreign language began to consider the role of non-English languages in the fabric of contemporary U.S. life, rather than merely assuming all students would be motivated by preparing for a trip overseas most of them would never take.[2] In the national standards for foreign language learning, a document that guides the content of language classrooms in the United States expressed the struggle as follows:

> *To study another language and culture is to gain an especially rich preparation for the future. It is difficult to imagine a job, a profession, a career, or a leisure activity in the twenty-first century which will not be enhanced by the ability to communicate efficiently and sensitively with others. . . . Possession of the linguistic and cultural insights which come with foreign language study will be a requisite for life as a citizen in the worldwide neighborhood.*[3]

Many of us began to consider the analysis of foreign language education that was afforded by a critical, or power-related, view of language education. Language education not only teaches students about culture of foreign places, but also shapes present culture in the United States. But what *exactly* is culture? Lessow-Hurley has pointed out that:

> *Culture is something we all have but often find difficult to perceive. Culture, like language, is dynamic, changing to meet the needs of the people it serves. All cultures have coherent, shared systems of action and belief that allow people to function and survive.*[4]

Language teachers have often included discussions or activities related to "high-prestige" and "low-prestige" culture in language classrooms. At the same time, we recognize that foreign language classrooms seem to be another world, often having their own culture. All of these concepts of culture have underlying power relationships, most not always readily apparent, that have an impact on students' thinking and, as a result, their lives and the lives of their neighbors.

HIGH-PRESTIGE CULTURE

The works of Cervantes, Goethe, Moliére, and Dante are those many language educators herald as the greats of "foreign" literature. The artistic creations of Bach, Beethoven, Brahms, Louis Pasteur, Van Gogh, and Michelangelo are certainly worthy of note in a course that teaches languages. But let us consider how in contemporary society these unique individuals have become part of high-prestige culture.

Pointing to the canon, scholars have both affirmed and challenged the assumption that one can neutrally define a set of literary works that are inherently meritorious. Such appeals to intellectual traditionalism[5] are, in fact, rooted in cultural struggle. My purpose here is not to dismiss or challenge the contributions of the "greats." Instead, I would argue for a need to understand that there are no natural and neutral criteria for evaluating works of art, literature, or even science that make these contributors to high-prestige culture worthy of inclusion. Instead, it is because of the decisions of primarily academics and publishers that these works continue to take their place among recommended and required reading.

The issue for language courses is twofold: first, whose works, and thus their voices, are not being heard by our students because they fail to meet these inherently biased standards of "greatness," and second, what impression are we leaving with students about the process of selecting literature for inclusion? Are native speakers of the language in the United States who write given opportunities to become part of the language classroom if they are not part of the literary canon? If not, how can our students hear the voices of even their own neighbors in, for example, literature and art?

LOW-PRESTIGE CULTURE

What kind of greetings do speakers of a language give each other: a handshake, a kiss on the cheek, or a hug? When invited to dinner, should one bring some kind of gift? How many days of the week do speakers of the language in other countries go to school? These are many of the questions that can be asked and answered in a discussion of low-prestige culture in the foreign language classroom. And similar to the case of high-prestige culture, these items are not neutral or natural, but based on a social context.

Germans, for example, often bring a *Mitbringsel*, typically flowers, when invited to a meal at someone's house. Italian Americans likewise may bring the pastries—*cannoli* are usually a good choice. These cultural practices become part of a fabric of everyday life so much that many native speakers of the language associated with the practices neither question nor at times even understand them. Language students, on the other hand, for whom such practices *differ from their own*, are often first exposed to practices that seem "exotic" or foreign through blurbs in textbooks, usually in the form of a paragraph or two in some corner of a chapter.

We should question how the information is presented, that is, as chunks of virtual trivia to be stored away, and how the information is presented without regard to power relationships underlying the socially constructed meaning. Let us turn to the latter issue in the example of etiquette.

Etiquette, or any form of "social grace," tends to signal to other members of a culture a certain level of education or even "refinement." Usually, though, the fork to use for salad versus the one for seafood rarely is discussed in the language class. Instead, we present information on, for example, formal versus familiar forms of address (tú, Usted; du, Sie; and so on). These distinctions are important for our students to know, and often due to how the speaker would be perceived. But the distinctions are neither neutral nor natural. They are constructed both socially and historically to have symbolic meaning. Their usage, as a result, conveys social and symbolic messages about both speaker and hearer. How clumsy is the American who uses the wrong form of address for, by way of example, a mature woman or a dog? How is that person likely to be perceived?

One of my favorite illustrations of this issue relates to one of my students, who learned his lesson the hard way. As he entered a store in a small, psuedo-alpine village in northeast Georgia, he was ready to try out his German. Though in class after class I had stressed the importance of using the formal form of address, he was accustomed to the familiar form in practice with fellow students. He addressed the matronly German-speaking shop owner in the familiar, and received a blistering lecture that I imagine he remembers to this day.

To be frank, though, our students are not likely to actually practice the kind of etiquette or social forms taught in foreign language classes, or even discuss holidays, school routines, or anything else we teach as *culture*, since they are rarely called upon to interact with citizens of the "foreign" countries. Instead, their interactions with speakers of non-English languages are more likely to take place in the United States. Therefore, it makes sense to reevaluate the way we are teaching culture in all its forms. Further, since the information as presented in language classrooms most often highlights *differences from the students' own practices*, the cultural information tends to take on a feel of novelty, perhaps further creating divisions in the fabric of U.S. culture.

What I mean is that students begin to build a conceptual framework in this way of how the target culture's practices are different from, for lack of a better expression, "mainstream" U.S.-American practices. These chunks of knowledge lead to another cultural referent in U.S. society, that is, *foreignness*. Our education in language tends to reinforce the idea that you can tell differences in nationality on sight by practices, but also assumes that Americans could not, for example, follow "Hispanic" customs in regard to greeting or leave-taking. As a result, students who leave the foreign language classroom and see Latinos or others in their own towns who practice such behaviors might perceive those citizens as foreign, regardless of their place of birth.

This is not a new issue, though it is one that is often seen in the press. A century ago, the environment was similar in the United States as the world descended into war and many German Americans found their own loyalty to the United States, and their "foreignness," subject to scrutiny.

CLASSROOM CULTURE

Remembering that most students enter a mathematics or literature class with some limited knowledge of the subject, it is not at all uncommon for students to walk into a foreign language classroom with virtually no background knowledge in the subject of their study. They are virtually completely unable to communicate in the target language, and encounter a foreign language teacher. Dealing with behavioral issues becomes one of prime importance for the language teacher (and other teachers as well), for a variety of reasons beyond our discussion here.

The idea of a "culture" of a foreign language classroom is not different from that of other subjects in many ways.[6] The teacher serves as the "sage on the stage" in many courses. The subject matter being presented, however, does differ in terms of its sociological nature. Language is a marker of identity, an expression of culture in many forms, and a vehicle of personal expression in a way that biology or social studies are not. Even the fine arts, with their embodiment of a high level of personal expression, do not act as a ready-made identifier of large segments of the population in the way a language does.

By failing to address the sociological nature of language in both its nature and use, the foreign language classroom reinforces the myths surrounding the standard or "correct" form of all languages, especially English in the United States. Moreover, we fail to alert students that these distinctions are primarily political, not linguistic. As Rosina Lippi-Green states so well with regard to English:

> *What our schools do, for the most part, is to insist that some children forego the expressive power and consolation of speech in that variety of English which is the currency of their home communities. This gesture*

> *of denial and symbolic subordination is projected as a first and neces-*
> *sary step to becoming a good student and a good citizen.*[7]

If varieties of English such as southern or Brooklyn accents are subjected to this symbolic subordination, then certainly non-English languages used in the United States suffer a similar outcome.

WHAT IS THE FOREIGN LANGUAGE CLASS EXPERIENCE?

A metaphor used in describing contemporary language education is that of building bridges of understanding between cultures. It is certainly a pleasing and politically correct depiction, especially given the increasing attention to diversity in the United States, but in actuality aspects of language education may contribute to the maintenance of cultural divides. The lack of appropriate time commitments (i.e., we do not offer sufficient time for language learning) coupled with generally accepted, but time-dependent, potential advantages of language study (in other words, we suggest that language learning and language proficiency offer similar benefits) interact with an institutionally provided conceptualization of "otherness" I refer to as *foreignness* to cause this educational context to appear progressive, all the while perpetuating cultural misconceptions.

Benefits of foreign language study usually cited are directly tied to economic or status gain for speakers of English in the United States. Examples often include career benefits, such as increasing one's attractiveness to a prospective employer. Another point for high school students is that they fulfill a prerequisite of college admission, and even improve their ability to compete in a global marketplace. Curricula commonly mention the significance of foreign language education in increasing students' awareness or acceptance of cultural and linguistic diversity. Consistently absent from this part of the discussions, however, is the role that achieved language skill plays in fostering these desired positive attitudes.

Though mathematics education, for example, certainly provides some benefits to daily life, few would argue an awareness of numbers alone results in true understanding. It is, in fact, the ability to apply and use those concepts in meaningful ways on a regular basis to which mathematics provides its greatest benefits. Merely possessing an "awareness" of cultural differences, without a concomitant linguistic skill, could result only in defining boundaries with more certainty. In other words, it is likely that without the ability to actually *communicate* with members of the cultures represented by the languages of study, only an increased awareness of difference results, not a multicultural acceptance based on experience. Additionally, the benefits of foreign language study that are related to employment enhancement require considerable linguistic skill to actually be credibly attributed to language education.

In my own research, I have noted that a conceptualization of what can be termed *foreignness* is presented to students in multiple ways. Briefly, I would like to explore the examples of geographic fragmentation, English language/American synonymy, and language variety bias.

When a language teacher plans a foreign language lesson, he or she often includes information about the country or countries where the target language is spoken. Furthermore, cultural information in terms of both social routines and major accomplishments in the arts, for example, are regularly featured. Textbooks support this process by providing maps and cultural blurbs, and by pointing out significant cultural elements. However, when the instructional focus turns to speakers of the language in the United States, one traditionally begins to detect inconsistencies in the portrayals. One of the most conspicuous examples can be seen in maps.

In French, German, and Spanish textbooks, a map usually found in the front pages points to the countries or nations where French, German, and Spanish, as examples, are spoken as official languages. For the Spanish-speaking world, Spain, Puerto Rico, and most of the countries of Central and South America are depicted in a highlighted color. The continental United States, however, is routinely not highlighted, or only portions are noted: most commonly the states of California, New Mexico, Arizona, Texas, and Florida and the cities of New York and Chicago. In French textbooks, a similar pattern develops with Louisiana and New England, if any area of the United States, being highlighted. In German and Russian textbooks, though, rarely is anything in the United States highlighted.

Though such depictions may not be blatantly inaccurate, they are certainly misleading, by appearing to limit linguistic diversity to certain geographical areas in the United States and failing to carve analogous "holes" in countries where pockets of indigenous language speakers may live. In other words, the foreign language textbooks seem to fragment the United States alone into areas of significant linguistic diversity (e.g., part of the Spanish-speaking world). But by ignoring linguistic diversity found in every area of the United States, the impact may be even more significant, since native speakers of Spanish or other non-English languages who live in nonhighlighted areas (such as Washington, DC, and Hartford, CT, for example), would appear to be the "foreigners" among us.

I have argued, however, that geographical fragmentation is effective only to the extent "foreign" linguistic skills in these nonhighlighted areas are impoverished. If all English-speaking Americans were successfully educated to be bilingual speakers of English and a second language, geographical fragmentation would be meaningless in terms of where a "foreign" language is spoken in the United States. At this point, the concept is inaccurate, but nonetheless provides an effective image of *foreignness* if most English-speaking Americans remain monolingual. The implications of such a concept in the classrooms of urban environments should be especially disturbing.

In my view, the most pervasive indication of a conceptualization of *foreignness* found in the foreign language classroom seems to be treating the classification "American" and the English language as synonyms. As a result, logically, non-English utterances could seem, somehow, un-American.

The English language/American synonymy is, as in the case of geographic fragmentation, dependent on a broad-based failure of foreign language education programs to produce competent bilinguals or multilinguals. If all Americans were bilingual, this synonymy would be anachronistic. As long as monolingualism is the norm, then these embedded conflicts carry ideological weight and power, supported in commonsense linguistic assumptions of the "world" in which many U.S. citizens live.

An additional illustration of a way in which foreign language curricular documents and classroom activities contribute to the conceptualization of *foreignness* is related to the issue of language varieties. Though linguists have noted that the differences between a "language" and a "dialect" are primarily political, foreign language classes tend to favor one language variety, such as Parisian French, over others.

Yet, if most Americans were bilingual, though a pluralism of language status still might not be realized, a relative equality in the accessibility to power of speakers of all non-English languages would provide a structure which supports true self-empowerment. In other words, the status quo would not prevent such equal access simply by supporting a structural form of monolingualism, with the single language being English, as is currently the case. In short, for the self-proclaimed goals of foreign language education to be realized, specifically those of making cross-cultural connections and a linguistically pluralistic society, students in these classes would need, *at a minimum,* to reach levels of linguistic proficiency far beyond what the standard two-year requirement makes possible. Why does all this matter? Consider that a student walks into a classroom with a background, values, and ways of speaking, dressing, and acting that are embraced by those who are similar to the student. This form of culture varies and has been the root of misunderstandings in the educational setting, specifically as it relates to speakers of non-English languages. In certain regions of the country, for example, adding "sir" or "ma'am" to the response to a question by an adult is a sign of respect, and is thought to indicate, at a certain level, the quality of one's upbringing. But absence of these expressions in those who are from outside that region does not equate with disrespect or poor parenting. Likewise, when addressed by one in authority, in some cultures it is respectful to maintain eye contact with the speaker; in other cultures, maintaining eye contact is quite offensive.

The schools, notwithstanding perhaps the best intentions of some, are not neutral in regard to these cultural differences. Some are valued and supported, some are not. In the United States, for example, students who are talkative in the classroom regarding the subject matter at hand are generally viewed as active, engaged learners. This convention is grounded in those behaviors valued by the educators in *this* time and in *this* society. As a result, students whose cultural background may not reflect the same values may suffer in terms of evaluation of their academic performance on class participation. Lower grades may even mean fewer opportunities in terms of college admission or the corporate world.

At the same time, some common experiences, values, and behaviors are considered valuable and are expected in the places of privilege in society. At formal dinners, certainly, the forks beside one's plate are not interchangeable socially (though functionally they are) and the guest who knows no difference will likely be noticed. Though a faux pas may not result in discrimination, systematic devaluation of certain cultural expressions does, and it is this phenomenon that should be of concern.

Given that foreign language education is prerequisite to most college admissions, and secondary and tertiary graduations, but realistic expectations of proficiency are virtually nonexistent, then perhaps those who are successful in navigating the course requirements are actually only expected to recognize "foreignness" when they see it. That which is learned, I contend, has to do with those beliefs and attitudes regarding linguistic diversity that are valued, or held to be an expression of truth by this society in this time. Since the attitudes regarding language differences are inextricably intertwined with those regarding cultural differences, what is considered the "same" or "other" in terms of the values of Americans may well have its roots and be reflected in the mediation taking place between cultures in the foreign language classroom.

It then becomes an issue of great significance when the foreign language class creates in the minds of the college-bound and graduates of the U.S. society a cultural referent of what constitutes *foreignness*. When this educational context then takes on a role of primarily a "filter" course with no real expectation of the development of credible language skills, the very context that could strengthen democratic principles of equality in relation to linguistic and cultural differences finds itself operating to construct ideological frameworks diametrically oppositional. Beyond attitudes or conceptualizations of "American," foreignness, and the nature of language, though, the foreign language classroom contributes to a variety of sociocultural-conflict phenomena described by critical theorists.

In effect, by suggesting that all non-English languages are somehow related to that which is foreign, language educational endeavors reinforce a language identity by default. Though challenges to English as an official language are common, within the realm of commonsense, the national and official languages of the United States are both, and only, English. Non-English language speakers are thereby marginalized as the media of their expression take on a devalued position. A student who chooses to adopt the view of the dominant culture, therefore, is put in a position of assimilating linguistically. In addition, all historical evidence to the contrary, those students who speak American English as a native language are firm in their beliefs that English is *the* language of the United States.

Further analysis of curricula reveals assumptions about native speakers of non-English languages in the U.S. context. For example, if one took curriculum guides and textbooks available in the United States as a whole, American Sign Language, it would appear, both is and is not a foreign language. Similarly, Native American languages are not considered "foreign" in Oklahoma, but Native Alaskan languages would seem to be "foreign" in Fairbanks. Defining what foreignness is can, and often is, accomplished by default. In other words, the foreign language curricula and textbooks may create the framework of foreignness by showing what it is not.

In this chapter, I have not intended to levy an indictment against language educators, but I have attempted to point out that the concepts underlying an ideology supporting *foreignness* remain in place both within and beyond the term *foreign* itself. The task of language educators in the twenty-first century must shift to reflect activity greater than moving away from cultural "otherness." More than merely advocating the study of cultural similarities and differences, the critically aware language educator acknowledges a responsibility to point out to students how language, language policies, language planning, and language education are used in discriminatory ways.

NOTES

1. See A. O. Hadley, *Teaching language in context*, 3rd ed. (Boston: Heinle & Heinle, 2001); T. G. Reagan and T. A. Osborn, *The foreign language educator in society: Toward a critical pedagogy* (Mahwah, NJ: Lawrence Erlbaum Associates, 2002) for specific discussions. It is important to bear in mind that the hours of intensive Foreign Service Institute training are much more goal directed and include learners who are probably more motivated than those struggling through foreign language classes as a requirement in schools.

2. In fact, as most who have traveled to Europe can attest, it is rare that one cannot survive with skills only in English. This fact serves as a testimony both to the effectiveness of European language programs and the proliferation of English throughout the globe.

3. National Standards in Foreign Language Project, *Standards for foreign language learning in the 21st century* (Lawrence, KS: Allen Press, 1999), 12.

4. J. Lessow-Hurley, *The foundations of dual language instruction*, 2nd ed. (White Plains, NY: Longman, 1996), 95.

5. W. H. Schubert, "Perspectives on four curriculum traditions," *Educational Horizons* 74, 169–76.

6. For a more detailed discussion of the elements of power in a foreign language classroom, see T. Reagan and T. A. Osborn, "Power, authority, and domination in foreign language education," *Educational Foundations* 12(2), 45–62.

7. R. Lippi-Green, *English with an accent: Language, ideology, and discrimination in the United States* (London: Routledge, 1997), 132.

6

Multicultural Education Is Good for the United States Beyond Sensitivity Training

Wanda DeLeón and Xaé Alicia Reyes

From a universal standpoint, the notion of multicultural education should have been woven into the fabric of human behavior since the beginning of time. As we interact with those in our immediate surroundings, we develop responses and behaviors that will help us survive, coexist, and succeed. If we are unable to develop these, the opposite may happen: we may become fearful, isolated, and inept in our attempts to develop social networks that are essential for our survival.

Historical circumstances resulted in numerous opportunities for interactions between a variety of culturally and linguistically diverse groups, but rather than entertain the possibilities for equitable exchanges, generations of people from a variety of backgrounds positioned themselves as conquerors and established their cultural norms and linguistic forms as the dominant and acceptable norms and forms to succeed in this nation. Early settlers viewed themselves as civilized in comparison to the Native American populations and African slaves. Eventually, Anglo-Saxon Protestants imposed their hegemonic views on the Spanish- and French-speaking populations encountered through westward expansion.

Definitions and descriptions used through history to portray "Americans" reflect the struggle for social and political domination described in the preceding paragraph. John Jay, president of the Continental Congress and the first Chief Justice of the U.S. Supreme Court, wrote in 1787, "Providence has been pleased to give this one connected country, to one united people; a people descended from the same ancestors, speaking the same language."[1] Clearly this message conveyed the exclusion of nonwhite, non-Protestant, and non-English-speaking people. Jay excluded African Americans because they were considered property at this time in history; he ignored Native Americans because they did not speak English, practiced different religion, and were considered "heathen savages"; and he excluded the existence of large and economically important German colonies.

Centuries of damage done through hierarchical structures have been difficult to reconstruct through court decisions such as *Sheff v. O'Neill* and *Brown v. Board of Education* and the civil rights movement. The interpretations resulting from the enlightened but long overdue understanding of "liberty and justice for all" and that the acceptance that "separate but equal" do not represent equal practice, challenge the way our social institutions operate. These court decisions have connected the social, political, and economic implications of segregation and diversity to the structure of social inequalities. These understandings move us beyond the humanistic, individualistic, and behaviorist paradigms and position issues of diversity within a sociopolitical context.

Our need to reeducate ourselves to truly understand, respect, and practice inclusion in a pluralistic society has become both a societal and a curricular goal. Our schools and employers have engaged in staff development to rectify and restructure patterns of social interaction that diminish some and privilege others. The process of seeing others as our equals and acknowledging our inherent sameness has required interventions such as sensitivity training in workplaces and revisions to language and pictorial usage in printed material such as newspapers, government and other public documents, textbooks, and visual images that might offend, exclude, or stereotype any group. In this context and by moving beyond the descriptive and communicative function of language we review the successes of this impetus at different levels and promote an agenda of socioeconomic restructuring that is necessary for the success of any and all initiatives being implemented in the United States.

WHAT IS MULTICULTURAL EDUCATION?

Plurality is a condition needed in a democratic society, and two of its fundamental concepts are interdependence and equality.[2] The idea of multicultural education is part of the framework of American democratic values. It is shaped in the democratic ideas of freedom, justice, equality, equity, and human dignity. Multicultural education is conceived as an educational reform, as an idea, as a concept, and as a pedagogical practice.[3] An offspring of the civil rights movement, multicultural education "is grounded in the principles of social equality, personal liberation, critical democracy, and an acceptance of the political and partisan nature of knowledge, human learning, and the educational process."[4]

While many have ignored the value of multiculturalism, some appear to go along "with the program." Others have constructed a defensive stance toward cultural pluralism, concerned that focusing on cultural pluralism will divide the nation. There is no consensus on the definition of multicultural education. The notion of multicultural education of teachers, teacher educators, scholars, policy makers, and politicians takes different meanings. Over the past twenty years, many definitions have been proposed, and they have outlined practices and educational policies at all educational levels.[5] Some educators ascribe the diversity of definitions for multicultural education to one of semantics and not substance, and argue that the definitions are a reflection of the field and orientation of the individuals.

However, if there is one major barrier to an enlightened perspective on any issue, it is the unwillingness to entertain paradigms that differ from our own. The plurality of definitions and perceptions of multicultural education have been connected to different positions within the political spectrum and placed any discussion about multiculturalism, diversity, or multicultural education in an ideological context. Christine Sleeter's reviews of critiques to multicultural education concluded that all the critiques are based on political perceptions: conservative, liberal, or radical.[6]

While conservatives recognized the increase in diversity, they still advocated and emphasized individual rights and cultural commonalities. Their conceptualization of cultural diversity is only presented as part of their description of the United States as a nation of immigrants that came together under "the moral forces of American idea."[7] The central argument of conservative critics is that multicultural education is a radical political movement that focuses on changes in the curriculum that will result in national segregation. These critiques imply that this nation is unified and ignore the social struggle over the meaning and representation of freedom and equality.

On the other side of the political spectrum, critical educators argue that the field of multicultural education is not radical enough, that the mainstream liberal call for the "inclusion of diversity," as *the* solution for educational and social inequalities, ignores the tension between political democracy and economic inequalities.[8] They have argued that multicultural education is designed to fit into the curriculum and into the models of traditional schools and have portrayed it as a "modernistic attempt at equalizing educational opportunity," as an "ideological agenda that attempts to redress perceived social, economic, cultural and linguistic inequalities of the past."[9] They accused mainstream multicultural educators of depoliticizing the concept of "otherness" by deemphasizing educational and social inequalities that perpetuate the myth of schools as a social equalizer. Furthermore, it is claimed that mainstream multicultural education has ignored the role of schools in the process of social reproduction of inequalities.[10] Any transformative practice or movement in schools can only be seen as part of the "struggle for a radical shift in the current distribution of power and wealth." Many critical educators stressed the need to understand how economic and social structures in our society that distribute power and wealth have affected the relationship between schools and the economic development of our communities.[11] Mainstream multicultural educators have acknowledged that their emphasis on school practices tends to isolate schools from their socioeconomic and political context.[12]

RESISTANCE: AN ONGOING CHALLENGE

This diversity of perceptions has major implications not only for social interactions but also for the development and implementation of national policy and program development. The goal of creating a democratic society where all people are treated with equity and given equal access to resources and opportunities is accepted on the surface, but implementation seems to lag. As stakeholders and policy makers scramble to find strategies to foster inclusion and implement changes, there is a range of troublesome responses. The need to develop policies that enable the integration of different racial and cultural groups has been stated for many national and international scholars at the Kennedy School of Government at Harvard University. In response to the question of what kind of policies the president was elected in 2004 to pursue, Dr. Ron Ferguson, a senior research associate and a professor at the Wiener Center for Social Policy, stated:

> *Elected officials, and the President most of all, need to set a vision for the society: promote, reinforce, continually restate ... that we are headed toward becoming a society where no group is a majority, where every group needs to feel a part of the mainstream, where every group*

*needs to feel that they have access to and, in fact, a right to the oppor-
tunities that others enjoy.*[13]

Some individuals who opposed these recommendations have argued that
these initiatives are mere smoke-and-mirror schemes to create jobs at the expense of not addressing other needs. We do not deny that many of the resistance modalities to create a pluralistic democracy are the result of miseduca-
tion and its gaps and omissions in historical facts, but we stress the
importance of placing any discussion about multiculturalism, diversity, or
multicultural education in a sociopolitical context. Any serious attempt to
undo the damage that has plagued U.S. society for centuries and that has created numerous challenges in our educational settings cannot succeed if we
depoliticize the concept of "otherness" found in our texts and conversation
and ignore the tension between political democracy and socioeconomic inequalities.

Context, including time and space, is at the center of the process of understanding the effect and consequences of a particular group of events in society
and in our schools. This is not a linear or one-sided process. Framing complex
processes such as history, education, national identity, and multicultural education is not an easy task and will require the ability to see things from a variety of perspectives. Writings and conversations of people are not transparent
representations of reality. They are constructed and shaped by certain conventions and understandings of the social world. This notion about text and talks
moves us from the orthodox notion of language as an access to *reality* and
source of information to a multiperspective, a critical notion of language use,
to the social significance of language. The rhetoric of objectivity and neutrality
adopted by many "intellectuals" and fueled by their claims to authority have
been used to "justify" patterns of subordination of one group by another. This
exercise exposes the social and political implications behind writing and conversations and how they are used to reproduce and legitimize ideologies that
position individuals and structure societies in a hierarchical relationship of
power. Furthermore, it uncovers reaffirmations of tainted beliefs and inequitable environments that create an antagonistic climate for the desired re-
forms.

In the preceding example, we will examine the latest article by Samuel
Huntington, *One Nation, Out of Many,* published by One America in September 2004.[14] Huntington served in the White House as coordinator of security
planning for the National Security Council. Presently he is the director for
Strategic Studies and chairman of the Harvard Academy for International and

Area Studies in the Center for International Affairs and the author or editor of over a dozen books and ninety scholarly articles. Huntington is considered by the mainstream media as an authority in international affairs.

As we examine selected passages from Huntington's article, we encourage reflection and critical inquiry of the text and its effects on any attempts to meet the goals put forth by Ferguson. Ultimately, we want to convey that writing and conversation are shaped by certain conventions and understandings of the social world and therefore are social cultural and ideological artifacts and provide the spaces for contestation and resistance. Accordingly embedded in discourses that fuel hatred and domination of one group by another and the justification of privilege and superiority of a single homogeneous group is the obvious assertion that multicultural education *is* good for the United States, which begs the question: "Who benefits from the absence of a multicultural education agenda?"

ONE AMERICA: WHICH ONE?

Moving beyond the accuracy or inaccuracy of the events presented in Huntington's article, we found patterns of exclusion and omission that are relevant to the discussion of the benefits of multicultural education in a pluralistic and a democratic society. While the article is full of arguments that reflect the author's ideologies and sociocultural affiliations, we have paid particular attention to the representation of the United States as *a monocultural society—"America's core culture."* We have selected this representation because it is at the center of the rationale against multicultural education. By defining the national identity and the social function of education around what he defines as America's core culture, Huntington legitimizes the conservative arguments against multicultural education as "anti-Western ideology" and as a threat to national unity. However, it is within the assumptions, omissions, and contradictions of the article that we found spaces to question and contest Huntington's ethnocentric perspective of reality and history.

WHAT DO YOU MEAN BY AMERICA? OR, WHICH AMERICA?

In the title *One Nation, Out of Many,* Huntington brings in the idea of a monocultural society. While he is acknowledging the pluralistic composition of U.S. citizenry, he also introduces the concept of a common culture society.

This concept is better known as "melting pot" which suggests the assimilation of all of a society's citizens into a common culture. The "melting pot" has been used as a euphemism of the Americanization process, a process described by Sonia Nieto as *Angloization* because it goes beyond learning English or a culture; it requires all individuals to "eat, dress, talk, and even behave as European America."[15] However, for Huntington, the assimilation has to be to the Anglo-Saxon Protestant culture, and that is what defines an American: "Through our history, people who were not white, Anglo-Saxon protestants have become Americans by adopting America's Anglo-Protestant culture and political value. . . . 'A quarter or more of Hispanics have shifted from traditional Catholic faith to protestant evangelical churches,' unquestionably a significant manifestation of assimilation." The uses of the term *adopting* in the above passage suggest to the reader that this assimilation process was intentional and voluntary. Susan Dicker describes the assimilation or Americanization process of the seventeenth and eighteenth centuries as "a compulsory acculturation, a cultural genocide experienced by Native and Afro Americans."[16]

The use of the term *America* as the equivalent for the United States— "Americans' core culture has primarily been the culture of the seventeenth- and the eighteenth-century settlers who founded our nation"—and its citizens as "American" is a commonly shared conception by many. One might call this a simple accident of speech, for as immigrants flocked to the United States and spoke of coming to America, the misnomer took on a life of its own. It is, however, an important discussion to have when we consider the positionality of nations and continents within a hierarchical structure of a global economy. The world has come to know U.S. citizens as Americans, and all other citizens of the "Americas" are excluded from the label by default. From the text we can conclude that the cooption of the term *America* is part of the ethnocentric belief that Anglo-Saxon Protestant culture is superior and at the center of everything and all other cultures are measured up to and evaluated from it: "Would America be the America it is today if in the seventeenth and eighteenth centuries it had been settled not by British protestants but by French, Spanish, or Portuguese Catholics? The Answer is no. It would not be America; it would be Quebec, Mexico, or Brazil." The fact that "America" is a continent that included these among other countries is a point that was not made very often, if at all. Thus the talk of American education, politics, economics, and so on evokes the thought of United States–based contexts. Huntington's conceptions of America and Americans reproduce and legitimize cultural, economic, and political control of the dominant class.

"AMERICA'S CORE CULTURE"

Huntington links America's core culture to the early settlers who founded the nation. Although one cannot argue about the elements described being the predominant characteristics of the official discourse of the United States, an inclusive or a multiperspective description of the history would have acknowledged that the preeminence described by his discourse came through conquering and squelching other cultures and norms beginning with those of Native Americans and continuing with the cultures and languages of lands and peoples of Spanish and French ancestry through westward expansion. In other words, the "core culture" was imposed and upheld as the paradigm for success in this country at the expense of demoting all others. Huntington's perspective, as evidenced in the following list, not only reflects a high level of in-group identification but also signals what A. Mazama[17] has called "the pervasiveness of European evolutionary thinking," a Eurocentric discourse that conveys that certain innate and natural European qualities "lead to the universal path to the progress":

- The central elements of that culture are the Christian religion; Protestant values, including individualism, the work ethic, and moralism; the English language; British traditions of law, justice, and limits on government powers; and a legacy of European art, literature, and philosophy.

- It was, after all, Anglo-Protestant culture, values, institutions and the opportunities they created that attracted more immigrants. . . . Millions of immigrants and their children achieved wealth, power, and status in American society precisely because they assimilated themselves into the prevailing culture.

Huntington's claims about the elements of the Anglo culture seen as a catalyst for opportunities and the rationale for immigration again ignores that those very elements were secondary to the need for economic opportunities during the Irish potato famine and the need to escape war-torn countries throughout the world. In many cases, migration toward the United States has been the by-product of U.S. participation in those wars as "liberator." In addition, Huntington's text discounts the efforts made to lure labor from other countries under the guise of financial freedom and opportunity with many immigrants encountering exploitation and abuse upon their arrival in the United States. This representation of the "American core culture" mirrors the widely accepted idea that all the agents or actors in American history are Europeans, in this case British, while others are just spectators of history:

- Subsequent generations of immigrants were assimilated into the culture of the founding settlers and modified it, but did not change it fundamentally.

- Protestant beliefs, values, and assumptions, however, have been the core element (along with the English language) of America's settler culture, and they continue to pervade and shape American life, society, and thought.

Positionality does not seem to be the only implication of the above passages. The words *settler culture* themselves imply that the settlers brought a culture that was allowed to flourish in another context yet evolved into imposing itself. In a context where land was viewed as a space to be nurtured, venerated, respected, and shared, the new perspective was to own it, conquer it, and see it as an empowering asset. In this clash of ideologies, Huntington only acknowledges the latter approach as the legitimized perspective and now the norm.

Furthermore, Huntington imposes and upholds as the paradigm for success the European ethnic group experiences:

> *Throughout our history, people who were not white, Anglo-Saxon Protestants have become Americans by adopting America's Anglo-Protestant culture and political values. This benefited them, and it benefited the country. Millions of immigrants and their children achieved wealth, power, and status in American society precisely because they assimilated themselves into the prevailing culture.*

Following the line of thought in the preceding passage, one might argue that immigrant success stories are only possible through assimilation into this "core culture." Again, these remarks leave us with the questions: Who was part of Huntington's success paradigm? Native Americans, African slaves, Spanish, and Mexicans were all divested of their potential to access power by way of language policy, limited to no access to education. Layers of immigrant groups that followed were only able to succeed depending on the proximity of their phenotypical and cultural characteristics to those of the dominant class. Some were able to "pass" as members of the dominant culture and altered their names to protect themselves from the rejection and persecution suffered by those who were perceived as outsiders. Then whose successful assimilation of "people who were not white" was Huntington referring to? Who can be called Americans? Nieto has pointed out the label of American is usually reserved by whites; everyone else (Native, African, blacks, Spanish, Asians, and Mexicans) receives the hyphenated American. When will African-Americans or Mexican-Americans or Asian-Americans stop to be hyphenated Americans? If race is not part of America's cultural identity, how is it that all nonwhite, non-European residents of this land shared a history of social inequality and discrimination? Overtly, Huntington's claim ignores the presence of any form of inequalities in the system and a history of racial discrimination in this country. By claiming that all groups will advance socially in the same way that European immigrants did, Huntington legitimizes whose and what experience counts and uncovers their understanding of who can speak, when, and with what authority.[18]

If we accept the premise that those who founded America were predominantly Anglo-Saxon, Protestant English-speaking people, we would then consider Americanization as the process by which newcomers acquire the traits and attributes of the dominant culture. This is the way it was explained by Huntington:

> As immigrants poured in during the late eighteenth century, our forefathers saw the need to "make Americans" of the new arrivals on their shores. . . . The acquisition of American citizenship, the renunciation of foreign allegiances, and the rejection of dual loyalties and nationalities are key components of this process.

This really means that one can only be "American" by denying one's identity essence, which rests fundamentally on language and culture. Or what is worse, a dominant group has imposed their notion of what it means to be "American" based conveniently on those characteristics they possess. This provides them with a rationale to exclude and marginalize those whose characteristics and behavior depart from the norm the dominant group imposes.

The "rubric" established by this group is outlined by Huntington in a way that makes any differences appear damaging and prejudicial to the "good of the order." Thus any fostering of equal status to speakers of other languages and to those who espouse different religious beliefs is viewed as an assault to the national goals. Huntington asserts that public schools had been created in the nineteenth century and shaped in considerable part by the perceived need

to Americanize and Protestantize immigrants. These movements were re-
warded by an Americanizing trend that reached its peak during World War II
which described the 1950s, according to scholars cited by Huntington, as the
era of integration. We might argue that the integration of immigrants in the
fold of a united military front is not the image we think about when we use
the term *integration*. Efforts to produce the type of integration we think about
when we hear the term require the validation of differences in our society and
the equalization of characteristics and values of all citizens. A parallel discourse of resistance unfolds in the face of the imposed privilege of the dominant group.

THE SUPERFICIAL AND THE PROFOUND

This analysis meant to frame the discussion of the way we provide multicultural education. Resistance modalities cannot only be contextualized in
many of the behaviors encountered when sensitivity and diversity training are
required. They can be found in texts, institutions, social practices, and cultural forms that conceal the hidden structure. As multicultural educators, we
conceive culture and language as the two most significant factors in democratic societies. The notions of multiculturalism and multilingualism are
under attack constantly by those who argue for homogeneity in both language
and culture with English and Anglo culture as the dominant threads. For
Paulo Freire and other cultural workers, language symbolizes one of the most
important aspects of democratization of societies, and culture is conceived as
an interconnected system that "represents social processes that are intimately
linked to class, gender, sexual and racialized formation, upheld by particular
social structures, such as those which we find in public schools. . . . [There-
fore,] they are tied to the reproduction of power relations through social organizations."[19] With this, many of those who are uncertain about the path to
follow or who are part of the dominant group and enjoy the benefits of the system of privilege are persuaded to be oppositional and feel insecure with regard to diversity.

A DIALOGUE OF RESISTANCE

The possibility of embracing differences is not quite what Huntington con-
templates in the discussion of integration. In fact, the progressive thinking

behind the validation of differences and the inclusiveness of civil rights legislation and lobbying that would ensure access and opportunity to all who
wished to partake of the freedoms promised by the U.S. Constitution were
viewed as an assault on the ideology and policies, lamented by Huntington as:

> *the new popularity among liberal elites of the doctrines of "multicultur-
> alism" and "diversity," which elevate sub-national, racial, ethnic, cul-
> tural, gender, and other identities over national identity, and encourage
> immigrants to maintain dual identities, loyalties, and citizenships. Mul-
> ticulturalism is basically an anti-Western ideology. Multiculturalists
> argue that white Anglo America has suppressed other cultural alterna-
> tives, and that America in the future should not be a society with a single
> pervasive national culture, but instead should become a "tossed salad"
> of many starkly different ingredients.*

One can easily see a hierarchy that denies the possibilities of assigning any
positive attributes or value to characteristics and traits that fall outside the
rubric of American as equal to white, Anglo-Saxon, and Protestant. This de-
fies any notion of integration that equalizes and includes any of the original
inhabitants of this nation as well as immigrants of non-Anglo descent. The al-
leged glue that bound groups together in the 1950s era is based on the ap-
proximation of the newcomer immigrant groups to the markers of whiteness,
Protestantism, and Anglo-Saxon traits in addition to male dominance.

Clearly the significance and implication of the pattern of exclusions and
omissions that characterized Huntington's historical recollection increase
when we add the inconsistencies and contradictions within his arguments. To
accuse multiculturalists of promoting divisiveness and anti-Western ideologies is tantamount to ignoring the realities of our uniqueness as individuals
and the deliberate suppression of existing differences with historical movements such as slavery, westward expansion, Chinese internment, and ex-
ploitative labor recruitment for agriculture and industrial purposes. On the
other hand, mention is made of the practices that preceded multicultural
movements whereby Germans established their own schools to preserve their
language and traditions and Japanese and Jewish immigrants created Satur-
day and Hebrew schools, respectively, to coexist with Americanization efforts.
Most of these groups cherished the opportunity to belong to the American
fold but continued to nurture their valued cultural traditions in an effort to
strengthen their understanding of themselves and their histories. In fact, the
linguistic contributions and cultural meanings that abound throughout the

country are a result of the collage of contributions of the diverse groups that have coexisted in the United States in spite of the dominant paradigm imposed by the official discourse of privilege for some at the expense of the exclusion of many.

THE GREATER CONTEXT: OUR PLACE IN THE WORLD

The truth be told, all things American are exported throughout the world through media representations and marketing. Music and film have made icons of media figures, and America conjures images of U.S. celebrities that are not, in spite of Mr. Huntington, white, Anglo-Saxon, and Protestant. In fact there are the likes of P. Diddy, Beyonce, J Lo, Marc Anthony, and others who do not reflect the rubric. Lifestyles promoted by these rich and famous stars do not necessarily represent the values and traditions that are "basic tenets" of Americanization, although they too speak English and cherish the freedom that allowed them to pursue their dreams. The fact that two of the four celebrities just mentioned are able to perform in Spanish and relate to some of the cultural features and traditions of Puerto Rican culture only enhances their possibilities in the world. The realization of the power that this richness allows them could easily be a reflection of a more diversity-embracing society. Hence all U.S. citizens might benefit from an image in the world that speaks to multilingual and multicultural capabilities.

From a marketing and business-oriented perspective it makes no sense to try to limit the range of possibilities of a diverse citizenry by squelching the variety of perspectives that might contribute to a variety of ways to solve problems and address the needs of many different people.

International exchange and political conflict among world powers might have been addressed more effectively by leaders and a constituency that valued and was better informed about world affairs and perspectives. The tendency to center on one's own way of decision making and functioning is decidedly predicated on an ideology that is both ethnocentric and nationalistic, leading people to challenge even the simplest experiences while abroad. For example, during a recent trip to a foreign country, a U.S. citizen paid with dollars in a tourist shop and received some small change in the local currency. It was clearly an almost insignificant fraction of the equivalent in U.S. money, but the individual questioned the cashier about "why they were given change in local currency and demanded it in U.S. currency although there was no equivalent amount. To the question of why the change was not in U.S. currency, the cashier simply responded, "because you are not in the U.S." This episode is reminiscent of the attitudes labeled as chauvinistic and imperialistic in the 1960s and 1970s, which would be favored by those who propel single-minded Americanism based on a white, Anglo-Saxon prototype over the true reflection of U.S. demographics. In fact, this belief in a homogenous America permeates in the identity markers of many who cannot or will not respond to questions about their ethnic heritage and insist they are just "American" or "white"!

IN SEARCH OF A NEW FRAMEWORK

It seems that a more benevolent and embracing United States would make for a more "patriotic" society. The concept of patriotism has been shifting as if guided by knee-jerk reactions to immigration and events such as those of September 11, 2001. If indeed the notions of "liberty and justice for all" truly represent "American" ideology and patriotism, then the interpretation of "all" cannot be narrow. It must include all of those who are here constructing and contributing to the concept of a homeland they honor through their patriotism.

As people seek refuge and opportunity in a country which they perceive as a safer, more equitable environment, they develop a loyalty to this new homeland. Although some would argue that retaining one's cultural traits and language reflects a continuation and retention of an outsider identity, the truth is that the chosen new context shapes and defines people as well in a symbiotic relationship. How one arrives at this balance is closely linked to an educational stance that is open to a critique of the text and the context in which schooling takes place. This stance should also afford transformative possibilities for all participants in the teaching and learning process. Ultimately, our goal would be to improve the social conditions of *all* people in society. This cannot occur within a paradigm that reinforces the privilege of one group and fosters its superiority.

The framework suggested by Zeus Leonardo[20] combines Critical Social Theory (CST) and transformative knowledge, themselves frameworks resting on the rationale that quality education encourages students to become aware of, if not actively work against, social injustice. Thus an inquiry-based pedagogy would bring out knowledge about historical processes and policy development as they affect the potential of all members of society to access opportunity. Under this design, students would be able to ascertain the equity concerns that might or might not have informed policy concerns in terms of their impact on teaching and learning and eventually on society as a whole. Huntington's arguments favor a pedagogy that dictates the facts that are to be learned in a fashion that limits student engagement or questioning. His model seems to illustrate what Paulo Freire[21] called the "Banking" model in which students functioned as passive receptacles and their learning was comparable to depositing information and selected knowledge into vacant space. Students' prior experiences would not be relevant for synthesizing or questioning the selected knowledge. The mere regurgitation of these facts would suffice to participate in society. This, of course, would be possible for those who are educated in the context where the schemata of the privileged group prevailed.

Inequitable funding limits these possibilities, and the curriculum will be more aligned with these schemata in a locus where the socioeconomic conditions match those of the group that decides and constructs policy. Widespread economic inequity creates differential conditions of schooling that limit those possibilities for the majority of students in the United States.

BRIDGING SOCIOECONOMIC INEQUALITY

The opportunity to forge ahead in education is severely limited by the structures that condition educational funding to property taxes throughout this country. In his recent presentation for a group of organizations concerned with social justice and equity, David Rusk pointed to economic indicators that reflected an increasing gap between the small tax burden shared by the wealthiest in a number of states and the limited possibilities to increase economic access to fair housing and adequate education spending throughout the country. His proposal for mixed-income neighborhoods as the only or best way of integrating schools was extremely well received.

Multicultural educators challenge the belief that the schools are a social equalizer under the current structure of social and economic inequalities. They stress the importance of critically understanding the mode of hegemonic control that seems to separate educational "success" from the continuance of conditions that perpetuate privilege for only certain races and classes.[22] As a liberatory education, multicultural education calls for the eradication of all forms of human suffering and oppression, which will require a comprehensive analysis of oppression and the privilege system. As a counter-hegemonic movement, multicultural education must be able to constantly re-construct itself in the process of uncovering, and give meaning to different forms of, oppression and new realities. Thus it is essential to uncover and give meaning to realities. Grant and Sachs[23] argued that a critical view of the social meaning of language provides a different platform to analyze schools' prac-tices, the treatment of differences and otherness, and the distribution of cul-ture and power in a multicultural society. It is the tool to examine the dis-courses that deny access to institutional structures and obstruct the construction of alliance among oppressed groups.

The role of multicultural education is to develop a counter-hegemonic dis-course that calls for alliance and solidarity among all groups. It is important to understand that "the struggle against oppression [is] a human struggle in which we [have] to build solidarity across our differences."[24] In order to avoid fragmentation, one of the modes of hegemonic control, it is important to un-derstand any relationship of power[25] and the need to develop a praxis that works for the transformation of social consciousness and the reconstruction of social structures.

NOTES

1. *Concerning dangers from foreign force and influence. The Federalist: paper 2.*

2. G. Gay, "The relationship between multicultural and democratic education," *The Social Studies* 88(1) (1997), 5–12.

3. NAME (National Association Multicultural Education), (February 2003), *National Association for Multicultural Education: Resolutions and position papers.* Re-trieved October 2003 from the World Wide Web: www.name.org.

4. G. Gay, "Mirror images on common issues," in *Multicultural education, critical pedagogy and the politics of difference*, ed. C. E. Sleeter and P. McLaren (New York: State University of New York Press, 1995).

5. J. Banks and C. A. McGee-Banks, *Multicultural education: Issues and perspectives*, 3rd ed. (Needham Heights, MA: Allyn and Bacon, 1997); G. Gay, "Curriculum theory and multicultural education," in *Handbook of research on multicultural education*, 2001 ed., ed. C.A.M. Banks (San Francisco: Jossey-Bass), 25; S. Nieto, *Affirming diversity: The sociopolitical concept of multicultural education* (White Plains, NY: Longman, 2000); C. A. Grant and W. F. Tate, "Multicultural education through the lens of the multi-cultural education research literature," in *Handbook of research on multicultural edu-cation*, ed. J. Banks (San Francisco: Jossey-Bass, 2000).

6. C. E. Sleeter, "An analysis of the critiques of multicultural education," in *Handbook of research on multicultural education*, ed. J. Banks (San Francisco, CA: Jossey-Bass, 2000).

7. D. Ravitch, "Multiculturalism: e pluribus," *The American Scholar* 59(3) (1990), 337–57.

8. H. A. Giroux, *Theory and resistance in education* (New York: Bergin and Garvey, 1983); A. Darder, *Reinventing Paulo Freire: A pedagogy of love* (Boulder, CO: Westview Press, 2002); P. Freire and A. Faundez, *Learning to question: A pedagogy of liberation* (New York: Continuum, 1989); C. J. Ovando and P. McLaren, *The politics of multiculturalism and bilingual education* (Boston: McGraw-Hill, 2000); B. Kanpol and P. McLaren, eds., *Multicultural education and postmodernism* (Westport, CT: Bergin and Garvey, 1995); C. A. Grant and J. M. Sachs, "Multicultural education and postmodernism," in *Critical multiculturalism: Uncommon voices in a common struggle*, ed. B. Kanpol and P. McLaren (Westport, CT: Bergin and Garvey, 1995).

9. Ovando and McLaren, *Politics of Multiculturalism.*

10. M. Apple, *Education and power* (London: Routledge, 1995).

11. Darder, *Reinventing Paulo Freire.*

12. Sleeter, "An Analysis."

13. R. Ferguson, *Policy, potential and promise* (The Kennedy School, Harvard University, August 9, 2004). Retrieved December 2004 from the World Wide Web: http://www.ksg.harvard.edu/news/election2004/ron_ferguson_education.html.

14. S. Huntington, *One nation, out of many* (One America, 2004). Retrieved December 2004 from the World Wide Web: http://www.taemag.com/issues/articleID.18144/article_detail.asp.

15. Nieto, "Affirming Diversity."

16. S. J. Dicker, *Languages in America: A pluralist view (Bilingual education and bilingualism)*, 2nd ed. (Clarendon, UK: Multicultural Matters, 1996); G. Meyer, "Language right vs. English only: A question of democratic right," *Bilingual Review* 21(3) (1996), 282.

17. A. Mazama, "The Eurocentric discourse on writing: An exercise in self-glorification," *Journal of Black Studies* 29(1) (1998), 3(14).

18. M. Apple, *Education and power* (London: Routledge, 1995); A. Darder, *Culture and power in the classroom: A critical foundation for bicultural education* (New York: Bergin and Garvey, 1991); H. A. Giroux, *Theory and resistance in education* (New York: Bergin and Garvey, 1983); Darder et al., 2002.

19. Darder, *Culture and Power*, 128

20. Z. Leonardo, "Critical social theory and transformative knowledge," *Educational Researcher* 33(6) (2004), 11–18.

21. P. Freire, *Pedagogia del oprimido*, 25th ed. (Distrito Federal, Mexico: Siglo Veintiuno Editores, Sa., 1970).

22. P. McLaren and J. S. Munoz, "Contesting whiteness critical perspectives on the struggle for social justice," in *The politics of multiculturalism and bilingual education: Students and teachers caught in the cross fire*, ed. C. J. Ovando and P. McLaren (Boston: McGraw-Hill, 1997).

23. C. A. Grant and J. M. Sachs, "Multicultural education and postmodernism," in *Critical multiculturalism: Uncommon voices in a common struggle*, ed. B. Kanpol and P. McLaren (Westport, CT: Bergin and Garvey, 1995).

24. Darder, *Culture and Power.*

25. M. Apple, *The state and the politics of knowledge* (New York: Routledge Falmer, 2003); Apple, *Education and Power*; Darder, *Culture and Power.*

Policies for a Pluralistic Society

Casey Cobb and Sharon F. Rallis

Other cultures are not failed attempts at being you; they are unique manifestations of the human spirit.

—Wade Davis

Once called a melting pot, the United States is a conglomerate or composite nation, its parts coming from many sources. Immigrants arrived both escaping oppression and drawn to the dream of opportunity and abundant resources. Our national heritage proclaims us as a multicultural refuge and place of opportunity. The welcome inscribed on the Statue of Liberty calls for the world's tired and poor with the implication that we accept and honor diversity. The Declaration of Independence espouses for all the values of liberty, equality, and the pursuit of happiness. The Bill of Rights protects individual freedoms like speech and voting and protects against the establishment of a state religion. In the democratic ideal, each individual person has an equal right to achieve happiness and is free to pursue happiness in his or her own way, within certain reasonable bounds. We celebrate the richness of our plural society with people from many different backgrounds, cultures, and ethnicities, all who bring a variety of languages, holidays, and foods. One could expect then that our national policies be designed to ensure that these values are realized.

Yet, ensuring equity in these values is a challenge. Throughout our history, national policies have handled our diversity in different ways, some successful, some less so. Educational policy is one area where we see both ends of the spectrum. Many of our education policies historically appear to reflect these espoused values, for example, the free public education law, redistributional policies that establish equitable school finance formulas, and laws that promote equal educational opportunities for people with disabilities. Other policies, however, support practices that reflect the struggle of power and privilege[1] and enable social control by dominant ideologies. Ability grouping into categories such as college prep and vocational tracks is such a policy; it appears to group students for improved instruction but in truth may merely mask social Darwinism.[2]

Current education policies, such as the standards-based reform and accountability movements, actually belie democratic tenets that accept and value diversity. Policies that provide a narrow definition of what is important to know and of how to measure what is known run counter to the development and appreciation of individual differences and talents. These policies prescribe behaviors that result in inequitable treatment of students (e.g., the required use of multiple-choice standardized tests prevents some students from demonstrating their attainment of knowledge) that reinforces the belief that there is one size and that size fits all. The ultimate message is one of assimilation; if you are different, then you need to change to meet the standard.

This chapter explores the conflicting messages in U.S. educational policies. Specifically, we examine the standards and testing movement and its implications through the sweeping federal legislation of the No Child Left Behind Act (NCLB). We critique the act's narrowness and the narrowness of measures used to assess student learning. We also critique the act's effect on individuals who teach and learn in schools. Finally, we offer an alternative to the standardization of student outcomes—an alternative that values and embraces individual talents, interests, and backgrounds.

ONE SIZE FITS ALL

Many of today's education policies seek in our children a sameness. One such set of policies is related to the standards movement in education, which took root in the late 1980s following concerns over the performance of U.S. schoolchildren relative to their international peers. Although many of these concerns were misconstrued, standards-based reform initiatives were pushed onto the national agenda as a solution. Nearly all states have established a set of academic content and performance standards in specific disciplines at specific grade levels. For example, in its fourth-grade language arts standards, the state prescribes what every fourth grader should know and be able to do. State academic standards are used by districts as a blueprint for the curriculum that guides instruction. Thus standards-based instruction is very much a part of public schools. And why not? Standards-based instruction appeals to common sense. Defining what children should be able to know, do, or exhibit at specified grade levels provides schools with an articulated and common set of objectives. Absent academic standards, each school would be left to pursue its own aims.

Establishing a desired set of learning standards is a good idea in principle. However, the testing and accountability policies that have followed the standards craze have compromised the role of standards. In practice, standards have come to mean standardization. Furthermore, the press to document achievement of standards has led to an excessive focus on testing the masses en masse. This centralization of accountability has forced a reliance on economical and simplistic measures that are used in the same way across all students. Testing, then, becomes problematic when it places a disproportionate focus on only those standards that are readily measurable.

NATIONAL ACCOUNTABILITY

Arguably the most influential federal education policy to date—the No Child Left Behind Act—requires states to hold their schools accountable to annual performance objectives. Under NCLB, every state must assess the performance of its public schools against a common set of learning standards in the basic skill areas. States use a standardized assessment to measure student learning in these areas and to evaluate school performance. All students in all public schools are tested annually in reading/language arts and mathematics in grades 3–8 and at least once during high school. In 2006 learning in science also will be made accountable. Repeated failure of any school to meet annual performance objectives results in punitive consequences for the school and for those who work in them.

We argue the educational goals explicitly endorsed by NCLB are restrictfully narrow. Schools are asked to do and do much more for students than develop skills in the "three Rs." The reality is that education serves multiple, often competing, purposes—creating good citizens, preparing students for college and the workforce, socializing and developing lifelong learners, advancing the economic and labor needs of the nation—and typically reflects the unique characteristics of local cultures.

Under NCLB, performance is both narrowly defined and narrowly measured. NCLB returns to a basics-only approach. Nearly every state measures the performance of its schools (and students) against state academic standards using state assessments. These state standards assume there is only one credible way to read, write, and compute. They allow no room for discovery or the use of alternative constructs. So within an academic domain, who could argue against a common set of standards? While *standards* does not have to mean *standardization*, that is what has become of them. A one-size-fits-all approach makes today's standards measurable and attainable, but they are of only limited value. Many performance expectations relative to those standards have become watered down. While some states still strive for high expectations, at some point—even under the aggressive goals of NCLB—a more realistic strategy is to set performance standards at a level where a politically and economically acceptable proportion of students will fail to attain them. Nonetheless, the goal of performance standards and now especially accountability is for *all* students to achieve them.

THE TEST CRAZE

The primary vehicles for measuring performance are state assessments. Given the consequences surrounding the accountability goals of NCLB, it is no surprise that what is assessed is what most schools pay attention to. Some would even argue that the tests serve as a de facto state curriculum. Certainly this shaping of curriculum happens where high stakes or consequences are attached to the exams. Daniel Domenech, past president of the American Association of School Administrators and superintendent of the Fairfax County Public Schools, speaks to these unintended effects:

> *Much of the criticism against Virginia's Standards of Learning tests has to do with their emphasis on facts and recall. Teachers believe they spend an inordinate amount of time on drills leading to the memorization of facts rather than spending time on problem solving and the*

development of critical and analytical thinking skills. Teachers at the grade levels at which the test is given are particularly vulnerable to the pressure of teaching to the test.[3]

And he cautions, "A real danger exists in that the test will become the curriculum and that instruction will be narrow and focused on facts."[4]

State assessments are typically standardized tests administered annually in specific subjects at particular grade levels. The stringent accountability provisions associated with NCLB have placed considerable pressures on schools to perform well on these tests. Consequently, the test results have become the dominant focus of most schools across the country. Most pressured are those schools that have been performing below state averages. Many of these underperforming schools serve economically depressed communities in the inner cities, which are often home to large numbers of ethnically, racially, and linguistically diverse families.

Not all students can or are going to reach performance standards. This is, paradoxically, a necessity within a centralized and politicized accountability system that actually differentiates achievement. Consider that if all students indeed met the standard, the taxpaying public would likely consider the standard too easy to reach. Variation in achievement is not a skeptical view of all children's abilities, depressed expectations for some kids, or an allegiance to Spearman's *g*; rather, it is a realistic account of the variability in the manner in which children perform on a *common* assessment—*any* common assessment. Not every child can achieve at the highest level on any one assessment; children differ in their ability to demonstrate their knowledge and unique talents.

REALIZING CULTURAL AND LINGUISTIC CAPITAL

Anyone can find a reason why children learn and perform differently. However, one of the most visible reasons for differences in children today are their differences in culture and language. This diversity, however, brings to the classroom a cultural richness that should not be overlooked or disregarded by the narrowness of standards and testing.

Unfortunately, the accountability movement has forced schools to honor English-only approaches to educating language minority students. Although in many states there are standards that call for students to understand diverse cultures and languages, these are often drowned out by the enormous pressure to perform on those standards that are actually measured. Math and reading skills get top billing. Furthermore, the testing is done primarily in English, which in turn compels English-only instruction. Regrettably the norm in American schools is one of cultural isolation and linguistic repression. But there are examples of promising practices that value, honor, and share individual diversities.

Virginia Collier's extensive research on bilingual education points to the overwhelming benefits of dual language programs.[5] Dual language programs, also referred to as two-way immersion programs, deliberately integrate English language learners (ELLs) with native English speakers in the classroom. A balanced number of ELLs with a common first language (e.g., Spanish) and native English students receive content and literacy instruction in *both* languages. Such programs typically continue through the elementary grades. Dual language programs are considered to be an *additive* model of bilingual education.[6] The ELL learns English, while continuing to develop her native language and honor her native culture. Research indicates that both ELLs and native English speakers benefit academically, linguistically, cognitively, socially, and culturally.[7]

In contrast, many bilingual education policies promote a decidely *subtractive* model. Consider the passage of legislation in California, Arizona, and Massachusetts that forcefully promotes English-only instruction and communication.[8] With subtractive programs, ELLs learn to speak English virtually at the expense of their native language. Subtractive programs are at odds with the principles of multicultural education. They tend to (1) segregate ELLs from their native English-speaking peers (e.g., English as a Second Language pull-out programs) and/or (2) immerse ELLs in English-only classrooms. Both of these approaches fail to honor the linguistic and cultural diversity of ELLs and fail to take advantage of the linguistic and cultural richness of students from all backgrounds. The irony is that in the long run additive models actually serve *all* children better than English-only approaches. Our policies should be more additive than subtractive if we are to be true to our pluralistic values.

CONFLICTING PURPOSES OF SCHOOLING

National standards and accountability policies like NCLB highlight another challenge American public schools face: implementing the multiple and often conflicting purposes of schooling. Our public schools are expected to enable students to reach their potential as individuals at the same time they are expected to prepare them as good citizens who embody the nation's values and institutions. Benjamin Franklin attributed to schools the small task of providing wisdom, riches, strength, virtue, piety, welfare, and happiness. To achieve these purposes, what federal policies must be established? And what resources are to be committed to their implementation? While the rhetoric surrounding standards and the testing prescribed by federal law to ensure that all students meet these goals sounds supportive of these goals, such policies actually hinder the American ideal, especially in light of the diversity in our classrooms.

First, as we have established, standards become standardization. Let us assume that the mandated standards are both high and attainable. We still have a problem with the resulting classrooms and schools filled with look-alike students who fit the mold set by the standard. The individual loses importance. That some students have special abilities (often labeled disabilities) or bring alternative perspectives or ways of accessing the world becomes irrelevant when value is measured by performance on single assessments.

Focusing student effort toward attaining a defined goal and set of objectives obviates the achievement of unknown potentials. The human potential in classrooms with students from various cultures and communicating in multiple languages is enormous and untapped. We know that different languages draw on different parts of the brain; we know that certain ideas and emotions are best (or only) expressed in certain languages. *Corazon* means more than heart. We know that different cultures interpret artifacts and events in the world differently. Imagine the new ideas and perspectives that may be generated were students with linguistic and cultural diversity encouraged to pursue the American ideal of identifying their own strengths and abilities and defining their own views of happiness. Current accountability policies hamper this generative process in schools.

Moreover, these policies do not promote the development of a strong citizenry. Since we are a nation of immigrants, a conglomerate society, dominant culture or English-speaking students do need to respect and appreciate immigrant classmates if they are to promote collective goals. To do so, they must know and understand the cultures and backgrounds of their classmates. At the same time, their immigrant classmates need to develop fluency in our nation's history, values, and language in order to contribute to the growth and strength of their new home. The focus on narrow curriculum and test scores squeezes out important cultural aspects of the curriculum; the loss of art, music, and history weaken the prospects to forge strong citizenry with understanding and commitment to shared values thus preventing cultural exchange and growth.

Resources are directed to testing and teaching to the test, not to building individual opportunity or to creating knowledgeable citizens who contribute to the American ideal of reasoned democratic choices for the good of the whole of society.

INDIVIDUAL AGENCY AND RESPONSIBILITY

Perhaps one of the most discouraging effects of these accountability movements is their message about individual responsibility for one's own learning. On one hand, few of these policies include measures that can serve to build the individual teacher's instructional capacity or student's capacity to achieve. For example, little or no provisions for teachers' professional development are made so they can provide more assistive and alternative instruction; in fact, one of the most common responses to low test scores is to assign underachieving students to summer school sessions, throwing at them more of the same teaching that has failed them already. Students who are culturally or linguistically challenged to perform well on the tests do not receive adequate instruction to allow them to gain necessary skills to take the tests. Thus, the onus for improvement—or blame for failure—ultimately lies with the individual teacher and student.

On the other hand, NCLB and the standardized tests used to measure learning run counter to individual agency and responsibility. The expectations and outcomes are defined and immutable. Tools for measuring attainment are narrow and standardized. No room exists for alternative constructions or creativity. Teachers and students are disempowered. Teachers limit their scope, saying "I have to teach to the test. I have to be sure everyone will meet proficiency standards. I have no time for anything else." Similarly students might well ask: "With such defined end results, why should I bother to do anything else? Why should I push myself? I don't need to think for myself."

This disempowerment is evident in classroom visits we have made during the past two years for several research and evaluation projects we have been conducting. Teachers perform, following the script from their materials. Students sit quietly unengaged, responding only when called upon or given a directive. Students do not initiate interest or action. In one language arts class in a middle school filled with immigrants, migrants, and refugees, the teacher asked the students to locate metaphors and similes in a text about family vacations. Few if any students could locate the prescribed sentences, so they waited to be told the correct answers. We wondered why the teacher did not find and use a text the students might have found more relevant to their lives. Her response was that this was the text the curriculum called for and since the curriculum prepared the children to take the tests, following the curriculum was essential. We wondered why the students did not ask questions. They responded that they did not need to ask; they needed to listen for the answers. The persons in this class hardly exhibit any sense of agency or personal responsibility.

A BETTER WAY

Schools that honor and empower those who work and learn within them are not an idealistic dream. The prominent educational philosopher John Dewey described them years ago. They are schools that are learning-centered first, and that take children where they are and build on their strengths. They are schools that honor diversity by valuing individual talents and backgrounds through such practices as heterogeneous grouping and individualized education plans. They are schools that enrich students' lives by joining language minority and language majority students in the same classrooms to share cultures and languages. We need not hold students accountable to one way of talking, learning, or achieving. To do so runs counter to the pluralistic society to which America lays claim.

NOTES

1. P. L. McLaren and C. Lankshear, *Politics of liberation: Paths to Freire* (London: Routledge, 1994).

2. J. Oakes, *Keeping track: How schools structure inequality* (New Haven: Yale University Press, 1985).

3. "My stakes well done," *The School Administrator Web Edition*, December 2000. Available at http://www.aasa.org/publications/sa/2000_12/domenech.htm.

4. "My stakes well done."

5. See, for example, http://www.crede.ucsc.edu/research/llaa/1.1_final.html.

6. R. Landry, "Additive bilingualism, schooling and special education: A minority group perspective," *Canadian Journal for Exceptional Children* 3(4) (1987), 109–14.

7. Landry, "Additive bilingualism." See also additional research sponsored by the Center for Research on Education, Diversity, and Excellence (http://www.crede.ucsc.edu).

8. Specifically, California's Proposition 227, Arizona's Proposition 203, and Massachusetts' Question 2.

8

What September 11 Also Teaches Us

David Gerwin and Terry A. Osborn

December 7, 1941, is a day that will live in infamy. The words, familiar to most Americans, appear at the beginning of the speech President Franklin D. Roosevelt addressed to a joint session of Congress, requesting a declaration of war against Japan. During that war, with Roosevelt's permission and the agreement of the Supreme Court, the Department of War interned over 120,000 American citizens and residents from Japan or of Japanese ancestry. Internment took place on the West Coast of the United States, where the army believed the threat of a Japanese attack was great and suspected the Japanese citizens of a racial loyalty to Japan. Hawaii, the site of the Japanese attack on December 7, had a much larger Japanese population, but the Department of War did not undertake any such internment program there. Allowing Japanese Americans to continue their lives in Hawaii while rounding them up in the mainland was only one of the many internal contradictions of this racially based internment program, which also included drafting these "disloyal" citizens into the army directly from the internment camps.

September 11, 2001, will also live on in the American memory. No one has yet captured the moment in rhetoric approaching FDR in front of Congress, or Lincoln at Gettysburg. World War II and the Civil War pitted regular armies against each other over defined political and even ideological differences. Perhaps American society lacks a language to articulate and memorialize the murkier and nearly anonymous acts of twelve terrorists with box cutters who opposed specific American policies in the Middle East, sought to purify their own nations, and had an eschatological mission that Americans may not fully comprehend.

The War on Terrorism, declared by President Bush without the constitutional formality of a specific act in Congress, is open-ended and murky on many scores, but the enemy does have a face. The enemy is Muslim, the enemy is Middle Eastern, the enemy is an Arab. Yet the nation is not dotted with internment camps, and quite to the contrary the President and other public officials have been at pains to include an Imam next to a rabbi and a priest or minister at public ceremonies and to declare the Muslims are not the enemy, Islam is not the enemy, Arabs are not the enemy. Terrorists are the enemy, and guilt by association is not to be the stated policy of the day.

This improved response to a domestic attack owes something to the forces that created multicultural education, and even to the efforts of multicultural and critical language educators across the United States. The intolerance and cultural guilt-by-association that followed September 11 measure the distance between the attitudes multicultural and critical language educators seek to foster and the state of the nation today. The nature of the differences between the world multicultural educators envision and the national response to the terrorist attacks on the World Trade Center and the Pentagon can inform the particular lessons that critical educators emphasize in their classrooms.

Claiming some credit for multicultural education comes with a concomitant acceptance of responsibility for what has not changed yet. At the risk of confusing the impact of the broader social forces that gave rise to an organized movement for multicultural education with the more specific and modest accomplishments of multicultural education itself, this broad, societal assessment takes the commitments of critical educators seriously. The stakes are nothing less than social transformation, yet educational studies with careful controls and one-to-ten-scale responses typically measure attitudes or group behaviors before and after some course. Rarely do they measure life choices, such as buying a house in an interracial neighborhood or voting in response to the racial undertones of a political campaign. No one argues that a one-to-one correspondence exists between a world languages course and a decision to buy an apartment in a block with many Spanish speakers. After all of the caveats, transformative education seeks societal transformation, even as it proceeds class by class and student by student. The purpose of paying attention to language and culture in education, to repositioning "foreign" as modern language, to decentering a dominant culture and giving students tools to examine and appreciate many cultures while maintaining universal values, is to create a more humane society, in which people see themselves as global citizens, while still honoring their ties to a particular family, ethnicity, or country. Taking that ambition seriously means looking across decades and generations, using the historian's tools to compare the present with the past and to chart a course for the future.

Japan's attack on Pearl Harbor provides a compelling historical analogy for the September 11 attack itself, since the attack on Pearl Harbor was the last significant foreign attack before September 11 on U.S. soil. World War II, however, was a conventional war fought against the standing army of opposing nations. It began with formal declarations of war and concluded with peace treaties, quite unlike the current War on Terror that the United States is now waging and its two major military expressions, the attacks in Afghanistan and the war in Iraq. A more helpful yardstick for measuring the ability of Americans to wage war is the Spanish American War of 1898, and even more specifically the three-year battle to pacify the Philippines.

THE IRAQI WAR IN HISTORICAL PERSPECTIVE

When President Bush directed American forces to invade Iraq, subsequent to a Congressional resolution authorizing his use of armed force, he intended the invasion to oust Saddam Hussein from power. U.S. military action was aimed at installing a new regime, in some way representative of the Iraqi people. The liberation of Iraq has led to the occupation of Iraq by American forces, with no particular end in sight to the presence of U.S. troops. There is a government in Baghdad that works with the United States, there are rebel forces in many parts of the country, and there are hot zones where U.S. forces do not patrol. The challenge, from the perspective of multicultural educators, involves maintaining the distinction between terrorists, who attack the Iraqi civil population and U.S. forces, armed militias with political ends, and Iraqi civilians. For many members of the U.S. armed forces, and the American society at home, the challenge may be as simple as maintaining a distinction between Arabs and terrorists.

The U.S. invasion of Iraq occurred as a result of the Al Qaeda assault on the World Trade Center and the Pentagon. Some of the U.S. public believe that Saddam Hussein worked with Osama Bin Laden and bears some clear responsibility for the attack on September 11. Vice President Dick Cheney, in particular, emphasized an Al Qaeda–Iraq connection. The Bush administration highlighted the possibility that if Saddam Hussein possessed weapons of mass destruction and gave them to Al Qaeda operatives, the United States faced an imminent threat. The specific arguments about what vague contacts Hussein's government had and at what time and to what extent they involved active support are subtle (and rebutted by the September 11 commission report), but they did not convince the public. Arabs attacked America, and in going to Iraq the United States was, in some certain measure, fighting back against the Arabs. Prolonged fighting with Iraqis and a long-term U.S. military occupation of Iraq risk degenerating into a struggle with Arabs or into equating Arabs with terrorists.

One hundred years ago America faced a strikingly similar situation. Launching a war to liberate Cuba from Spain, the United States ended up with control of Cuba, Puerto Rico, Guam, and the Philippines. No one in Cuba, Guam, or Puerto Rico offered resistance. America granted Cuba formal independence, with significant limitations spelled out in the Platt Amendment. The American press and politicians changed their portrayal of the various peoples in these colonies from our peers, freedom lovers suffering under colonial rule, to childlike races unprepared to face democracy. Postwar cartoons depicted Uncle Sam as the teacher in a one-room schoolhouse giving lessons in democracy to unruly, childlike races of colored people. The acquisition of the Philippines in particular provides a grim warning of what might happen in Iraq if Americans cease to distinguish between the complicated Iraqi nation and those specific Iraqis taking up arms against the United States.

The war of liberation turned particularly sour when President McKinley decided to annex the Philippines as a territory of the United States, paying Spain $25 million as compensation for any property left on the island. The Filipino forces, led by General Emilo Aguinaldo, had been allies of the United States at the beginning of the war. Admiral Dewey transported Aguinaldo from Hong Kong to the Philippines and helped him assemble the Filipino troops. Yet when the Spanish were forced out of Manila, the Americans would not let Aguinaldo and his forces in. Despite the meeting of a constitutional convention, the United States also refused recognition to the new Philippine Republic, declared on January 1, 1899, and its president, Emilo Aguinaldo.

From February 4, 1899, to July 1902, Filipino forces resisted the American conquest, and this warfare soon turned into an indiscriminate battle against the civilian population. U.S. troops, whose commanders told them they were fighting savages, committed atrocities against fighters and civilians alike. When the fighting ended, the war had claimed the lives of more than 4,200 U.S. soldiers, 20,000 Filipino soldiers, and 200,000 Filipino civilians.[1] A U.S. Senate hearing that began on February 1, 1902, heard testimony of the widespread use of water torture, indiscriminate killing of any male ten years or older, and the wholesale burning of villages. The *Boston Herald* reported, on the basis of these hearings, that "Our troops in the Philippines . . . look upon all Filipinos as of one race and condition, and being dark men, they are therefore 'niggers,' and entitled to all the contempt and harsh treatment administered by white overlords to the most inferior races."[2]

Currently, U.S. military deaths in Iraq have topped 1,000, a count that does not include dozens of deaths sustained by other coalition armies, or the deaths of civilian contractors. A September 25, 2004, article in the *New York Times* reported that from April 2004 to the time of the article, 140 foreigners had been abducted, and that while most were freed, dozens had been killed.[3] Since Iraqi officials kept information about armed forces secret, no clear estimate of Iraqi military deaths in the invasion seems readily available. Prior to this report, only a statement about the lack of figures for Iraqi military casualties in the *Hamilton Spectator* (May 22, 2003) and a similar statement by General Richard B. Meyers, chairman of the Joint Chiefs of Staff, at an April 15, 2003, State Department briefing (Federal News Service) were widely available public record. No consensus exists over the number of Iraqi civilian deaths, although currently 10,000 dead seems to be the lowest figure, and most estimates appear to be in the range of 10,000–27,000 civilian deaths.[4]

The body count provides a rough measure of the war in the Philippines against the war in Iraq. Roughly forty-eight Filipino civilians died for every one U.S. soldier who died. Currently, civilians are not paying the same price in the Iraq that they paid in the Philippines. Using an estimate of 20,000 civilian casualties would yield a 20:1 ratio. Since many thousands of deaths occurred during the initial U.S. assault and efforts to capture the cities, unless sustained bombing reoccurs one can hope that the ratio of Iraqi civilian to U.S. military deaths should not reach anything like the figures seen in the Philippines. Unfortunately, the United States launched an air strike on Sadr City, a 2.2-million-person slum of Baghdad, as part of a campaign to stop the Mahdi Army, insurgents loyal to dissenting Muslim cleric Moktada al-Sadr. U.S. planes have also launched air strikes in Fallujah aimed at Al Qaeda cells under the command of Abu Musab Al-Zarqawi. These strikes have destroyed homes and other civilian structures, and caused civilian deaths. With American forces unable to control significant portions of Baghdad, the future of America's relationship with the 25 million Iraqis that live there cannot be predicted at this time. If the United States begins a sustained campaign of aerial bombing, the Iraqi death toll could dramatically escalate, and the civilian deaths might become comparable to those of 100 years ago in the Philippines, when a war of liberation became a war of conquest.

Still, at least as of September 2004, the American invasion of Iraq has not become a war upon the civilian population of Iraq. Americans have not leveled cities, or burned towns, or forced civilians to relocate en masse while burning a location to the ground. News stories, such as a *New York Times* article on arriving U.S. Marine Corps forces from December 12, 2003, reported intentions to win over civilians. Marine commanders stated that they were not planning to surround villages with barbed wire, demolish buildings, detain relatives of suspected guerillas, or risk civilian casualties by calling in bombing strikes. They stressed the need to win over Iraqis in order to obtain "indigenous intelligence reports" and that any other tactic would merely prolong the struggle with anti-American insurgents.

EDUCATIONAL PERSPECTIVES

Critical language educators or multicultural educators who opposed the U.S.-initiated war in Iraq may find all of these figures obscure apologies for the war. They are not. Rather, they measure the extent to which the war *in* Iraq has not become a war *on the people of* Iraq. To the extent that has not occurred, American forces retain an ability to distinguish among Iraqis, and not to treat the entire population as the enemy. Much of the credit for the existence of a military doctrine that can understand the strains on civilians and renounce specific strategies as more harmful than helpful comes from lessons learned in Vietnam. Should the entire country turn decisively against the American army in all forms, these distinctions will no longer be valid and the United States will have to admit failure and go home, or attempt to become an army of occupation. While the outcome is open, the ability to avoid treating an entire people as "other," a goal of critical foreign language and multicultural education, is the chief asset upon which all other hopes rest. The abuses at Abu Ghraib and other military prisons prove, among other things, the importance of having soldiers who can distinguish between friend and foe within Iraq.

According to Mr. Hirsch's article in the May 10, 2004, issue of *New Yorker* magazine, an investigation by General Taguba found that soldiers in the U.S. Army's 372nd Military Policy Company stationed at the American military–run Abu Ghraib prison were

> *Breaking chemical lights and pouring the phosphoric liquid on detainees; pouring cold water on naked detainees; beating detainees with a broom handle and a chair; threatening male detainees with rape; allowing a military police guard to stitch the wound of a detainee who was injured after being slammed against the wall in his cell; sodomizing a detainee with a chemical light and perhaps a broom stick, and using military working dogs to frighten and intimidate detainees with threats of attack, and in one instance actually biting a detainee.*

These actions presumed that all detainees were enemies. The widespread abuses in the prison contrast with what Americans have *not* done in towns and villages across Iraq. This may be cold comfort, but compared with the Philippines of 100 years ago, where torture and atrocities were standard procedure at all times, there is a measure of change. The war of liberation against Spain became a deadly war of conquest against the Filipinos. In the name of that conquest U.S. armed forces committed atrocities against fighters and civilians alike, and declared that all Filipinos were savages, outside the realm of civilized warfare. If the U.S. resists that attitude and wins Iraqi civilian support, or leaves when that support is no longer obtainable, then the U.S. soldiers and policy makers have demonstrated an increased ability to perceive humans with multiple, conflicting allegiances, whereas in the past (including Vietnam), many U.S. troops and policy makers merely saw "others." That recognition, as partial and painful as it may appear to those who opposed the war from the beginning, preserves the lives of Iraqi civilians. Measured against the suspicion that the United States went into Iraq because Arabs attacked on September 11 and these are Arabs, the gain seems minimal. Measured against the deaths and U.S. behavior in the Philippines during that war, the change seems significant.

MEASURING HOW FAR WE HAVE COME

Choosing a measuring stick for the domestic response to the September 11, 2001, attacks similarly determines how one assesses multicultural progress in the past century. For those who choose World War II as the basis for comparison, recognition that Japanese internment has not been duplicated provides grounds for subdued optimism. In World War II about 600,000 Italians, resident aliens, had to register with the FBI, were fingerprinted and photographed, and faced restrictions, curfews, and in the case of 2,100 Italians who were residents of America but not citizens, detention. Tens of thousands of these restricted residents-but-not-citizens had children serving in the American armed forces during World War II, even as their parents were detained.

Unlike the treatment accorded people of Japanese descent, people of Arab heritage in the United States, whether citizens or noncitizens, have not yet been gathered by the tens of thousands and placed in detention camps. July and August 2004 press reports about U.S. Census Bureau disclosures raised fears that the government was planning for such detentions. In 2002 and 2003, recent reports revealed, the U.S. Customs Service and then the Homeland Security Department requested and received from the Census Bureau two lists. One list contained cities with 1,000 or more Arab Americans. A second listed Arab Americans by zip code, broken down by country of origin, specifically Egyptian, Iraqi, Jordanian, Lebanese, Moroccan, Palestinian, Syrian, Arab/Arabic, and Other/Arab. Although the data are public and can be compiled by anyone from the Census Bureau Web site, civil liberties groups made explicit comparisons to the 1940s when the Census Bureau provided comparable information on Japanese Americans in support of internment.[5] As of October 2004, the U.S. government has not taken any further public steps that raise fears about an impending detention of the 1.2 million Arab Americans recorded by the U.S. Census Bureau.

However, the United States is following the practice pioneered during World War II of forcing tens of thousands of noncitizens who are residents in the United States to register and be photographed. Two specific programs, part of the USA PATRIOT Act legislation (including the "National Security Entry-Exit Registration System") mandated that males age sixteen or older with immigrant visas from twenty-one mostly Muslim countries and North Korea be fingerprinted, photographed, and interviewed or face criminal charges.

A series of deadlines stretched from 2002 to 2004. The first deadline, December 16, 2002, applied to visa holders from Iran, Iraq, Libya, Sudan, and Syria. When hundreds showed up to register in Southern California, hundreds were handcuffed and jailed, practices that were followed in some cases in other cities, including Houston and Cleveland. Though some detainees faced criminal charges, many had paperwork problems, often stemming from INS backlogs. In all, under these two September 11–related laws directed at specific, Arab, immigrant groups, 4,000 people have been detained in prison without charges for varying amounts of time. In addition, in the immediate aftermath of September 11, the FBI, acting under direction of Attorney General John Ashcroft, detained another 1,200 people. Many of these 5,200 people have been deported, but always for visa violations ranging from the most technical problems to actual criminal convictions. Not a single one of these 5,000 people has been convicted by any court or jury of an act of terrorism.[6]

The registration law recalls the World War II registration of "enemy aliens," but the sheer number of Arab Americans detained since September 11 resembles the U.S. government's actions in an earlier war. During World War I over 6,000 German and Austrian nationals were detained by the United States. These World War I detentions lasted longer than the average registration-related detention (although not all September 11 detainees have been released yet), but it is sobering to realize that in the post–September 11 world the United States has detained nearly the same number of residents who are not citizens as were detained (for a longer period) in World War I.

For multicultural and critical language educators, the most relevant point is that these restrictions are based only on country of origin. These regulations are not coupled with any personal action by an individual—they are not laws that apply to individuals, but to "Arabs" writ large. On October 31, 2001, the Department of Justice issued new regulations allowing the indefinite detention of any immigrant they consider a possible terrorist threat, even if an immigration judge has ordered that individual's release. Taken as a whole, these actions amount to a suspension of due process as a right for an entire class of people, based on their ethnicity and their lack of citizenship. Noncitizens resident in the United States, it appears, have only as much freedom as the Attorney General of the United States and the Secretary of Homeland Security are willing to grant.

World War I provides a final lesson in the curtailment of liberties. In the name of unity, the federal government silenced dissent. Part of this crackdown attacked the left in general and dealt a significant blow to antiwar movements and to labor organizing.

> *Congress passed the Espionage Act (1917) restricting freedom of speech during wartime through harsh penalties for antiwar activity and banning treasonous material from the mails. The law was strengthened the next year by the Sedition Act, which made it illegal to "utter, print, write or publish any disloyal, profane, scurrilous, or abusive language" about the government or the military. Thousands of pacifists and radicals who opposed the war (Eugene Debs among them) were arrested under these laws, which weakened the Left by censoring its press and prosecuting its leadership. . . . In the summer of 1917, the Post Office Department refused second-class mailing privileges to newspapers and magazines that were critical of the war, the draft, or even the way the war was being conducted. Socialist periodicals, with a combined prewar circulation exceeding half a million, were banned from the mails. Critics of the war were also silenced through arrest. Fifteen hundred people were put on trial for opposing the war or counseling draft resistance.[7]*

These laws restricted all citizens, and call to mind current provisions of the USA PATRIOT Act that allow the FBI to find out what materials patrons check out of the libraries, to search a person's home without letting the person know, or to investigate a person while making it a crime for that individual to let anyone know that he or she is under investigation. Any citizen designated as "aiding a terrorist organization" even unknowingly can end up economically quarantined. Other steps taken under this legislation warn that general legislation can be applied quite selectively.

In a similar vein years earlier:

> *the foreign-language press was closely watched: a federal law required that articles discussing the war or the government be submitted in translation for prior approval—a process so costly that many papers folded, and others adopted a pro-government stance in hopes of winning exemption from the rule.[8]*

The rich, multilingual heritage of America diminished markedly under that assault, most notably a significant bilingual German and English population, perhaps even contributing significantly to today's difficulties in teaching other languages to Americans whose first tongue is English.

Following World War I, and after the 1917 Russian revolution raised fears of a communist revolution in the United States, the 1920 Palmer Raids swept up thousands of workers. As has been the case in the post–September 11 atmosphere, many immigrants were deported without any judicial process for political associations that not only were legal but also would have been constitutionally protected for an American citizen.

WHAT CAN WE CONCLUDE?

The conclusion we reach after reviewing the historical comparisons offered is like the proverbial glass that is half full and half empty. The glass is half empty because the United States has detained approximately 5,000 people with little judicial oversight and deported many of them, and none have been shown in court to have any relationship to any terrorist enterprise. Had the September 11 attacks never occurred, these people would still be in the United States, working in their communities and contributing to the language and multicultural diversity that we recognize as a source of American strength and richness. The glass is half empty as well because those detained have overwhelmingly been either Arab or Muslim, most both, and were detained for reasons of nationality and religion rather than for any individual suspicious action. The assaults on September 11 detainees held at the New York Metropolitan Correction Center, like the assaults on detainees in Abu Ghraib, underscore the human capacity to abuse anyone singled out as a cultural "other" and an enemy. The glass is half empty because American troops are in Iraq based on spurious links between Saddam Hussein and Al Qaeda, because Iraq is an Arab country, and because the war against the terrorists teeters on the brink of a war against the civilian population, and whatever else you call it, that becomes a war to maintain an occupation rather than to liberate.

One can see the glass as half full because we have so far effectively distinguished, at least in rhetoric, among the terrorists, Arabs, Muslims, and U.S. citizens. Let us consider an application of cultural and language diversity around the world. One of this chapter's authors, Terry A. Osborn, has written extensively on the need to stress the lack of language uniformity in the United States. Gerwin concludes that we need to emphasize the language diversity of European countries, and the increasing complexity introduced by the movement between European Union countries, the spread of that union, and questions of citizenship and state ideas. The Muslim presence in Europe, from the crusades in Spain to current significant populations in England as a result of the Empire, or France, because of Afghanistan, are issues of diversity that can be dealt with in many venues of education, including language and multicultural education. The lesson that we learn is not a simple one of progress or the lack thereof, though it is in our responsibilities as scholar, historian, classroom teacher, student, and citizen that we have tried to make some of those judgments.

Political correctness, though it can be attacked from the right and the left at the same time, is a phenomenon that multicultural, diversity, and language awareness helped create and is not as negative as some would indicate. There is clearly a new line in society in what is acceptable in public utterance as evidenced by the fact that Senator Lott of Mississippi was forced to step down when he claimed that the world would have been better if Strom Thurmond had been elected president on an explicitly Dixiecrat segregationist platform. Endorsing segregation as public policy is no longer acceptable in the public remarks of a political leader, even in the context of a birthday party for a colleague. Thus, change *is* possible, if we courageously confront the issues that continue to divide the United States along the lines of language and cultural diversity.

NOTES

1. http://www.loc.gov/rr/hispanic/1898/chronphil.html.

2. Cited in Daniel B. Schirmer, "Republic or empire," in *Anti-imperialism in the United States, 1898–1935*, ed. Jim Zwick, http://www.boondocksnet.com/ai/dbs/re16c.html#N_42_. Retrieved April 27, 2005.

3. *New York Times*, Section A5, September 25, 2004.

4. Matthew Davis, "Counting the civilian cost" (British Broadcasting Company News On-line, September 22, 2004), http://news.bbc.co.uk/2/hi/middle_east/3672298.stm. Retrieved April 27, 2005.

5. *New York Times*, Section A11, August 26, 2004; Section A14, July 30, 2004.

6. Reported in an op-ed piece by David Coles, *Los Angeles Times*, September 20, 2004.

7. *Who built America? Working people and the nation's economy, politics, culture and society*, vol. 2 (New York: Pantheon, 1992), 30–31, 60.

8. *Who built America?*, 60.

Appendix

The level of language and cultural diversity in the United States is astounding. When one looks at Census Data, for example, it is clear that over 8 million Americans speak a language other than English at home. This appendix should serve as a reference for readers to see the extent of diversity within their own communities.

Language Spoken at Home for the Citizen Population 18 Years and Over Who Speak English Less Than "Very Well," for the United States, States, and Counties: 2000

State/Area	Area Name	Total	Speak Spanish or Spanish Creole	Speak other Indo European language	Speak Asian or Pacific Island language	Speak other language
US	United States	8079960	4521485	1702185	1582520	273775
AL	Alabama	26585	15110	6580	4175	720
AL	Autauga County	270	125	120	25	0
AL	Baldwin County	795	495	210	90	0
AL	Barbour County	165	90	65	(D)	(D)
AL	Bibb County	65	40	(D)	0	(D)
AL	Blount County	295	255	(D)	(D)	0
AL	Bullock County	105	80	(D)	(D)	0

State/ Area	Area Name	Total	Speak Spanish or Spanish Creole	Speak other Indo European language	Speak Asian or Pacific Island language	Speak other language
AL	Butler County	115	85	(D)	0	(D)
AL	Calhoun County	705	335	230	(D)	(D)
AL	Chambers County	150	80	65	0	0
AL	Cherokee County	20	10	10	0	0
AL	Chilton County	230	160	(D)	(D)	0
AL	Choctaw County	95	55	35	4	0
AL	Clarke County	90	50	(D)	(D)	0
AL	Clay County	85	70	15	0	0
AL	Cleburne County	50	40	10	0	0
AL	Coffee County	385	190	100	(D)	(D)
AL	Colbert County	220	145	(D)	45	(D)
AL	Conecuh County	65	30	(D)	(D)	0
AL	Coosa County	45	25	(D)	(D)	0
AL	Covington County	115	65	35	20	0
AL	Crenshaw County	20	20	0	0	0
AL	Cullman County	325	215	70	(D)	(D)
AL	Dale County	490	235	145	(D)	(D)
AL	Dallas County	145	65	60	(D)	(D)
AL	DeKalb County	450	350	(D)	(D)	0
AL	Elmore County	365	235	75	35	20
AL	Escambia County	120	75	25	(D)	(D)
AL	Etowah County	395	230	95	(D)	(D)
AL	Fayette County	45	25	20	0	0
AL	Franklin County	220	(D)	(D)	0	0
AL	Geneva County	130	70	45	(D)	(D)
AL	Greene County	45	30	(D)	(D)	0
AL	Hale County	45	(D)	20	(D)	0
AL	Henry County	70	45	(D)	(D)	0
AL	Houston County	325	135	105	(D)	(D)
AL	Jackson County	155	75	50	(D)	(D)
AL	Jefferson County	4555	2475	1210	650	220

State/ Area	Area Name	Total	Speak Spanish or Spanish Creole	Speak other Indo European language	Speak Asian or Pacific Island language	Speak other language
AL	Lamar County	50	(D)	25	(D)	0
AL	Lauderdale County	425	210	180	35	0
AL	Lawrence County	185	125	(D)	0	(D)
AL	Lee County	805	465	(D)	170	(D)
AL	Limestone County	505	335	(D)	90	(D)
AL	Lowndes County	35	15	15	(D)	(D)
AL	Macon County	210	185	25	0	0
AL	Madison County	2160	1040	530	520	70
AL	Marengo County	100	80	15	0	0
AL	Marion County	95	55	(D)	30	(D)
AL	Marshall County	555	460	(D)	(D)	0
AL	Mobile County	2770	1225	715	795	30
AL	Monroe County	130	110	(D)	(D)	0
AL	Montgomery County	1670	765	345	470	85
AL	Morgan County	975	730	150	(D)	(D)
AL	Perry County	45	30	(D)	(D)	0
AL	Pickens County	90	65	(D)	(D)	0
AL	Pike County	170	130	20	20	0
AL	Randolph County	110	50	(D)	0	(D)
AL	Russell County	285	160	70	55	0
AL	St. Clair County	275	190	50	(D)	(D)
AL	Shelby County	885	470	310	(D)	(D)
AL	Sumter County	85	60	25	0	0
AL	Talladega County	350	230	90	30	0
AL	Tallapoosa County	165	110	(D)	25	(D)
AL	Tuscaloosa County	1020	570	285	130	40
AL	Walker County	260	150	(D)	(D)	0
AL	Washington County	70	45	(D)	(D)	(D)
AL	Wilcox County	65	30	10	(D)	(D)
AL	Winston County	65	50	(D)	(D)	0
AK	Alaska	17525	3055	1685	5875	6910

State/ Area	Area Name	Total	Speak Spanish or Spanish Creole	Speak other Indo European language	Speak Asian or Pacific Island language	Speak other language
AK	Aleutians East Borough	410	85	0	310	15
AK	Aleutians West Census Area	590	165	(D)	335	(D)
AK	Anchorage Municipality	6580	1940	730	3310	600
AK	Bethel Census Area	2570	20	10	45	2495
AK	Bristol Bay Borough	4	0	0	(D)	(D)
AK	Denali Borough	25	(D)	(D)	10	(D)
AK	Dillingham Census Area	410	(D)	(D)	(D)	400
AK	Fairbanks North Star Borough	1205	365	230	360	250
AK	Haines Borough	0	0	0	0	0
AK	Juneau City and Borough	485	40	85	285	80
AK	Kenai Peninsula Borough	765	140	315	110	200
AK	Ketchikan Gateway Borough	285	20	25	220	15
AK	Kodiak Island Borough	700	50	30	565	50
AK	Lake and Peninsula Borough	50	(D)	(D)	0	40
AK	Matanuska-Susitna Borough	425	115	120	60	130
AK	Nome Census Area	435	15	10	15	395
AK	North Slope Borough	705	(D)	(D)	60	630
AK	Northwest Arctic Borough	490	(D)	(D)	4	480
AK	Prince of Wales-Outer Ketchikan Census Area	35	(D)	(D)	0	30

State/ Area	Area Name	Total	Speak Spanish or Spanish Creole	Speak other Indo European language	Speak Asian or Pacific Island language	Speak other language
AK	Sitka City and Borough	125	15	15	85	15
AK	Skagway-Hoonah-Angoon Census Area	30	(D)	4	(D)	15
AK	Southeast Fairbanks Census Area	110	15	25	10	60
AK	Valdez-Cordova Census Area	145	25	30	60	30
AK	Wade Hampton Census Area	700	0	0	0	700
AK	Wrangell-Petersburg Census Area	60	(D)	20	35	(D)
AK	Yakutat City and Borough	4	0	(D)	0	(D)
AK	Yukon-Koyukuk Census Area	190	(D)	(D)	0	180
AZ	Arizona	180665	118710	13820	11760	36375
AZ	Apache County	11635	250	(D)	(D)	11380
AZ	Cochise County	5640	4750	380	425	80
AZ	Coconino County	7140	1015	180	80	5870
AZ	Gila County	1955	850	75	20	1010
AZ	Graham County	1605	770	(D)	(D)	770
AZ	Greenlee County	340	(D)	0	0	(D)
AZ	La Paz County	510	410	15	20	70
AZ	Maricopa County	82965	61320	9985	8110	3550
AZ	Mohave County	2260	1415	390	95	355
AZ	Navajo County	10655	830	15	35	9780
AZ	Pima County	32905	26100	1900	2315	2590
AZ	Pinal County	6785	5720	190	180	690
AZ	Santa Cruz County	5885	5775	40	70	0
AZ	Yavapai County	1940	1300	430	115	95
AZ	Yuma County	8440	7865	165	280	125

State/ Area	Area Name	Total	Speak Spanish or Spanish Creole	Speak other Indo European language	Speak Asian or Pacific Island language	Speak other language
AR	Arkansas	18580	11845	3345	2810	580
AR	Arkansas County	140	85	30	(D)	(D)
AR	Ashley County	180	165	(D)	0	(D)
AR	Baxter County	255	85	135	35	0
AR	Benton County	1685	1265	140	255	25
AR	Boone County	135	105	(D)	0	(D)
AR	Bradley County	150	(D)	(D)	0	0
AR	Calhoun County	20	10	(D)	0	(D)
AR	Carroll County	345	300	30	20	0
AR	Chicot County	115	50	20	30	10
AR	Clark County	115	85	15	(D)	(D)
AR	Clay County	105	45	45	(D)	(D)
AR	Cleburne County	55	20	35	0	0
AR	Cleveland County	45	35	(D)	(D)	0
AR	Columbia County	135	105	15	(D)	(D)
AR	Conway County	65	35	10	(D)	(D)
AR	Craighead County	460	345	80	(D)	(D)
AR	Crawford County	425	265	40	95	20
AR	Crittenden County	475	315	70	90	0
AR	Cross County	90	80	(D)	(D)	(D)
AR	Dallas County	40	40	0	0	0
AR	Desha County	105	85	(D)	(D)	0
AR	Drew County	135	90	(D)	(D)	(D)
AR	Faulkner County	375	235	50	40	55
AR	Franklin County	45	30	(D)	(D)	0
AR	Fulton County	45	35	(D)	(D)	0
AR	Garland County	835	450	320	(D)	(D)
AR	Grant County	70	(D)	(D)	0	0
AR	Greene County	135	70	45	(D)	(D)
AR	Hempstead County	275	255	(D)	(D)	0
AR	Hot Spring County	100	65	10	(D)	(D)

State/ Area	Area Name	Total	Speak Spanish or Spanish Creole	Speak other Indo European language	Speak Asian or Pacific Island language	Speak other language
AR	Howard County	100	65	(D)	(D)	0
AR	Independence County	115	70	(D)	(D)	0
AR	Izard County	65	35	(D)	0	(D)
AR	Jackson County	35	35	0	0	0
AR	Jefferson County	550	365	145	(D)	(D)
AR	Johnson County	140	125	(D)	(D)	0
AR	Lafayette County	65	40	20	4	0
AR	Lawrence County	45	(D)	20	(D)	0
AR	Lee County	70	55	(D)	0	(D)
AR	Lincoln County	20	10	10	0	0
AR	Little River County	90	(D)	45	(D)	0
AR	Logan County	85	55	(D)	15	(D)
AR	Lonoke County	210	105	(D)	55	(D)
AR	Madison County	85	65	(D)	0	(D)
AR	Marion County	90	55	30	(D)	(D)
AR	Miller County	150	100	30	(D)	(D)
AR	Mississippi County	300	230	50	(D)	(D)
AR	Monroe County	35	25	10	0	0
AR	Montgomery County	15	(D)	4	(D)	0
AR	Nevada County	50	(D)	(D)	0	0
AR	Newton County	10	(D)	(D)	0	0
AR	Ouachita County	75	55	(D)	(D)	0
AR	Perry County	50	30	(D)	(D)	0
AR	Phillips County	110	65	20	25	0
AR	Pike County	30	20	(D)	(D)	0
AR	Poinsett County	95	(D)	0	(D)	0
AR	Polk County	45	30	(D)	0	(D)
AR	Pope County	305	185	(D)	70	(D)
AR	Prairie County	45	35	(D)	(D)	0
AR	Pulaski County	3205	1680	830	515	180
AR	Randolph County	75	55	20	0	0

State/ Area	Area Name	Total	Speak Spanish or Spanish Creole	Speak other Indo European language	Speak Asian or Pacific Island language	Speak other language
AR	St. Francis County	115	60	(D)	15	(D)
AR	Saline County	440	255	110	55	20
AR	Scott County	50	40	(D)	(D)	0
AR	Searcy County	30	15	10	(D)	(D)
AR	Sebastian County	1645	625	155	825	40
AR	Sevier County	365	355	(D)	(D)	0
AR	Sharp County	65	40	(D)	(D)	0
AR	Stone County	30	(D)	(D)	0	0
AR	Union County	155	95	45	(D)	(D)
AR	Van Buren County	80	45	(D)	0	(D)
AR	Washington County	1565	1140	170	240	10
AR	White County	245	140	60	50	0
AR	Woodruff County	25	20	(D)	(D)	0
AR	Yell County	275	235	20	(D)	(D)
CA	California	2030790	1071795	221430	701445	36125
CA	Alameda County	87865	24340	10855	51325	1345
CA	Alpine County	20	(D)	(D)	0	15
CA	Amador County	475	340	55	75	0
CA	Butte County	3595	2215	430	885	65
CA	Calaveras County	335	245	55	(D)	(D)
CA	Colusa County	960	840	75	40	0
CA	Contra Costa County	36975	14905	6030	15345	695
CA	Del Norte County	265	155	50	60	0
CA	El Dorado County	1820	1085	375	305	55
CA	Fresno County	44750	33470	3325	7625	330
CA	Glenn County	930	810	(D)	55	(D)
CA	Humboldt County	1630	850	480	180	120
CA	Imperial County	17225	16505	65	525	130
CA	Inyo County	310	220	25	50	20
CA	Kern County	30095	24680	1100	3995	315
CA	Kings County	6870	5220	410	1205	35

State/ Area	Area Name	Total	Speak Spanish or Spanish Creole	Speak other Indo European language	Speak Asian or Pacific Island language	Speak other language
CA	Lake County	905	615	200	(D)	(D)
CA	Lassen County	1015	750	(D)	165	(D)
CA	Los Angeles County	788775	448560	96690	229175	14355
CA	Madera County	5400	4700	440	195	60
CA	Marin County	5655	2195	1795	1565	100
CA	Mariposa County	95	65	(D)	(D)	0
CA	Mendocino County	1665	1250	245	130	40
CA	Merced County	12860	8800	2205	1805	50
CA	Modoc County	145	120	(D)	(D)	15
CA	Mono County	265	215	25	(D)	(D)
CA	Monterey County	23490	17640	1690	4010	155
CA	Napa County	3860	2705	560	475	120
CA	Nevada County	790	405	340	(D)	(D)
CA	Orange County	171255	69330	15110	83970	2845
CA	Placer County	3985	2190	840	870	90
CA	Plumas County	115	70	25	20	0
CA	Riverside County	67120	53215	4305	8445	1150
CA	Sacramento County	47610	15825	8130	22745	910
CA	San Benito County	2975	2710	(D)	155	(D)
CA	San Bernardino County	78250	59455	4635	12640	1520
CA	San Diego County	128010	72715	11395	40635	3270
CA	San Francisco County	102805	16025	10315	75190	1275
CA	San Joaquin County	29175	15680	3205	10010	280
CA	San Luis Obispo County	4560	2960	625	915	60
CA	San Mateo County	48695	16450	6395	24505	1345
CA	Santa Barbara County	15645	11760	1260	2550	80
CA	Santa Clara County	125290	35535	12830	74965	1955
CA	Santa Cruz County	8775	6505	1180	1010	80
CA	Shasta County	1415	675	265	410	65

State/ Area	Area Name	Total	Speak Spanish or Spanish Creole	Speak other Indo European language	Speak Asian or Pacific Island language	Speak other language
CA	Sierra County	35	25	(D)	(D)	0
CA	Siskiyou County	550	330	100	65	60
CA	Solano County	15285	6410	1490	7205	180
CA	Sonoma County	10495	6090	2000	2135	270
CA	Stanislaus County	20560	12765	3330	2590	1875
CA	Sutter County	3165	1825	1080	(D)	(D)
CA	Tehama County	1200	1125	(D)	(D)	0
CA	Trinity County	55	35	10	(D)	(D)
CA	Tulare County	19475	16100	1220	2050	105
CA	Tuolumne County	510	375	95	40	0
CA	Ventura County	35825	26145	2575	6645	455
CA	Yolo County	7085	4470	1055	1425	140
CA	Yuba County	1835	1095	95	645	0
CO	Colorado	86460	57405	13505	13300	2250
CO	Adams County	10205	7065	745	2230	165
CO	Alamosa County	720	665	30	(D)	(D)
CO	Arapahoe County	10365	4520	2375	3090	385
CO	Archuleta County	205	170	(D)	0	(D)
CO	Baca County	45	30	(D)	(D)	(D)
CO	Bent County	230	210	(D)	0	(D)
CO	Boulder County	4225	2415	920	740	150
CO	Chaffee County	440	340	(D)	(D)	0
CO	Cheyenne County	20	(D)	(D)	0	0
CO	Clear Creek County	50	45	(D)	(D)	0
CO	Conejos County	740	740	0	0	0
CO	Costilla County	525	505	10	(D)	(D)
CO	Crowley County	255	255	0	0	0
CO	Custer County	20	(D)	(D)	0	0
CO	Delta County	290	225	60	(D)	(D)
CO	Denver County	16935	12145	2470	1895	420
CO	Dolores County	25	(D)	(D)	0	15

State/ Area	Area Name	Total	Speak Spanish or Spanish Creole	Speak other Indo European language	Speak Asian or Pacific Island language	Speak other language
CO	Douglas County	1455	505	420	495	35
CO	Eagle County	1045	875	130	35	0
CO	Elbert County	130	95	35	0	0
CO	El Paso County	8095	4040	1825	2055	175
CO	Fremont County	795	625	125	(D)	(D)
CO	Garfield County	635	560	55	(D)	(D)
CO	Gilpin County	55	(D)	0	(D)	0
CO	Grand County	130	80	(D)	(D)	0
CO	Gunnison County	210	130	80	0	0
CO	Hinsdale County	15	(D)	(D)	0	(D)
CO	Huerfano County	230	215	15	0	0
CO	Jackson County	0	0	0	0	0
CO	Jefferson County	7180	3490	1695	1795	200
CO	Kiowa County	15	(D)	(D)	0	0
CO	Kit Carson County	130	115	(D)	(D)	0
CO	Lake County	230	220	15	0	0
CO	La Plata County	735	535	75	20	110
CO	Larimer County	2715	1725	625	330	30
CO	Las Animas County	490	460	30	(D)	(D)
CO	Lincoln County	50	(D)	25	(D)	0
CO	Logan County	360	270	(D)	(D)	0
CO	Mesa County	1400	1070	235	(D)	(D)
CO	Mineral County	4	(D)	(D)	0	0
CO	Moffat County	95	75	20	0	0
CO	Montezuma County	640	200	(D)	(D)	410
CO	Montrose County	470	420	35	0	15
CO	Morgan County	750	680	70	0	0
CO	Otero County	925	870	30	25	0
CO	Ouray County	15	(D)	(D)	0	0
CO	Park County	150	95	55	0	0
CO	Phillips County	40	30	(D)	(D)	0

State/Area	Area Name	Total	Speak Spanish or Spanish Creole	Speak other Indo European language	Speak Asian or Pacific Island language	Speak other language
CO	Pitkin County	190	125	40	(D)	(D)
CO	Prowers County	480	455	(D)	(D)	0
CO	Pueblo County	4385	3895	320	(D)	(D)
CO	Rio Blanco County	85	55	30	0	0
CO	Rio Grande County	610	590	(D)	0	(D)
CO	Routt County	135	55	55	25	0
CO	Saguache County	270	260	(D)	(D)	(D)
CO	San Juan County	10	(D)	0	0	(D)
CO	San Miguel County	65	55	(D)	0	(D)
CO	Sedgwick County	40	(D)	(D)	0	0
CO	Summit County	275	185	85	(D)	(D)
CO	Teller County	105	60	35	(D)	(D)
CO	Washington County	25	(D)	(D)	0	0
CO	Weld County	5215	4680	345	(D)	(D)
CO	Yuma County	90	80	10	0	0
CT	Connecticut	120895	61605	48455	8485	2350
CT	Fairfield County	34715	17325	13640	2785	970
CT	Hartford County	41915	21765	16995	2690	465
CT	Litchfield County	2590	500	1740	290	60
CT	Middlesex County	2700	720	1655	265	65
CT	New Haven County	29640	16750	10715	1615	560
CT	New London County	5035	2455	1945	530	110
CT	Tolland County	1835	695	880	215	45
CT	Windham County	2460	1400	890	95	75
DE	Delaware	12625	6965	3780	1645	235
DE	Kent County	2010	900	760	(D)	(D)
DE	New Castle County	9060	5110	2490	1255	210
DE	Sussex County	1555	955	530	55	15
DC	District of Columbia	11350	6975	2550	1305	520
FL	Florida	659465	508290	107370	32830	10970
FL	Alachua County	2855	1610	645	530	65

State/ Area	Area Name	Total	Speak Spanish or Spanish Creole	Speak other Indo European language	Speak Asian or Pacific Island language	Speak other language
FL	Baker County	145	105	(D)	(D)	0
FL	Bay County	1810	890	400	450	70
FL	Bradford County	265	140	70	(D)	(D)
FL	Brevard County	6935	3485	2310	980	160
FL	Broward County	65170	38990	20085	3910	2185
FL	Calhoun County	150	105	25	(D)	(D)
FL	Charlotte County	2235	620	1370	130	120
FL	Citrus County	2035	940	865	170	60
FL	Clay County	1380	785	215	330	50
FL	Collier County	8990	6490	2110	210	175
FL	Columbia County	645	440	135	(D)	(D)
FL	DeSoto County	780	665	95	(D)	(D)
FL	Dixie County	100	(D)	45	0	(D)
FL	Duval County	11445	5555	2305	2970	620
FL	Escambia County	3565	1465	1015	1035	50
FL	Flagler County	1125	510	495	85	40
FL	Franklin County	100	50	30	(D)	(D)
FL	Gadsden County	425	330	45	(D)	(D)
FL	Gilchrist County	55	30	25	0	0
FL	Glades County	325	240	(D)	(D)	40
FL	Gulf County	130	75	25	(D)	(D)
FL	Hamilton County	155	135	(D)	(D)	0
FL	Hardee County	1020	955	40	(D)	(D)
FL	Hendry County	1585	1485	50	25	25
FL	Hernando County	2885	1445	1145	150	150
FL	Highlands County	2280	1875	275	105	20
FL	Hillsborough County	36480	30120	3300	2570	490
FL	Holmes County	170	80	60	(D)	(D)
FL	Indian River County	1535	895	525	75	35
FL	Jackson County	405	305	(D)	40	(D)
FL	Jefferson County	150	100	(D)	(D)	0

State/ Area	Area Name	Total	Speak Spanish or Spanish Creole	Speak other Indo European language	Speak Asian or Pacific Island language	Speak other language
FL	Lafayette County	150	135	(D)	(D)	0
FL	Lake County	2650	1895	550	155	55
FL	Lee County	9005	6130	2315	425	135
FL	Leon County	2180	1190	570	360	65
FL	Levy County	410	345	45	(D)	(D)
FL	Liberty County	45	45	0	0	0
FL	Madison County	175	160	(D)	(D)	0
FL	Manatee County	5015	3035	1455	445	80
FL	Marion County	4455	3100	1075	195	90
FL	Martin County	1995	1140	645	110	105
FL	Miami-Dade County	307800	281235	21445	3415	1705
FL	Monroe County	2280	1835	375	70	0
FL	Nassau County	200	125	20	55	0
FL	Okaloosa County	2345	990	385	930	40
FL	Okeechobee County	770	625	115	(D)	(D)
FL	Orange County	42070	32870	5105	3525	570
FL	Osceola County	13165	11695	825	520	130
FL	Palm Beach County	37965	22315	12180	1920	1555
FL	Pasco County	6620	3085	2945	385	210
FL	Pinellas County	18540	7080	8100	2835	530
FL	Polk County	9725	7215	1565	820	125
FL	Putnam County	1040	795	(D)	(D)	0
FL	St. Johns County	1220	585	475	(D)	(D)
FL	St. Lucie County	3950	2220	1390	250	95
FL	Santa Rosa County	1120	605	255	240	25
FL	Sarasota County	5350	1885	2685	420	365
FL	Seminole County	9950	7505	1465	805	175
FL	Sumter County	735	495	170	40	30
FL	Suwannee County	325	225	75	(D)	(D)
FL	Taylor County	155	100	(D)	(D)	0
FL	Union County	160	125	(D)	0	(D)

State/ Area	Area Name	Total	Speak Spanish or Spanish Creole	Speak other Indo European language	Speak Asian or Pacific Island language	Speak other language
FL	Volusia County	9665	6060	2715	615	275
FL	Wakulla County	140	110	(D)	(D)	(D)
FL	Walton County	365	205	95	(D)	(D)
FL	Washington County	390	195	185	(D)	(D)
GA	Georgia	97850	51815	22250	20920	2865
GA	Appling County	120	110	(D)	(D)	0
GA	Atkinson County	125	110	0	15	0
GA	Bacon County	20	(D)	0	0	0
GA	Baker County	40	(D)	(D)	0	0
GA	Baldwin County	490	275	125	(D)	(D)
GA	Banks County	75	60	(D)	(D)	0
GA	Barrow County	460	170	(D)	165	(D)
GA	Bartow County	620	465	(D)	75	(D)
GA	Ben Hill County	125	(D)	(D)	0	0
GA	Berrien County	115	85	30	0	0
GA	Bibb County	1050	540	335	(D)	(D)
GA	Bleckley County	75	75	0	0	0
GA	Brantley County	60	50	(D)	(D)	0
GA	Brooks County	95	75	(D)	(D)	0
GA	Bryan County	140	95	25	(D)	(D)
GA	Bulloch County	560	325	130	65	35
GA	Burke County	155	(D)	85	(D)	0
GA	Butts County	205	140	(D)	(D)	0
GA	Calhoun County	20	(D)	15	(D)	0
GA	Camden County	455	265	105	50	35
GA	Candler County	150	(D)	0	(D)	0
GA	Carroll County	565	280	220	60	0
GA	Catoosa County	290	95	145	(D)	(D)
GA	Charlton County	60	30	25	0	0
GA	Chatham County	2535	1175	610	655	95

State/ Area	Area Name	Total	Speak Spanish or Spanish Creole	Speak other Indo European language	Speak Asian or Pacific Island language	Speak other language
GA	Chattahoochee County	280	180	60	(D)	(D)
GA	Chattooga County	110	65	(D)	20	(D)
GA	Cherokee County	1010	545	345	(D)	(D)
GA	Clarke County	1485	880	340	235	30
GA	Clay County	15	(D)	(D)	0	0
GA	Clayton County	4220	1915	630	1615	55
GA	Clinch County	50	(D)	(D)	0	0
GA	Cobb County	9345	4835	2145	2025	345
GA	Coffee County	460	405	40	15	0
GA	Colquitt County	335	290	25	(D)	(D)
GA	Columbia County	1055	350	310	395	0
GA	Cook County	120	75	10	(D)	(D)
GA	Coweta County	510	290	170	(D)	(D)
GA	Crawford County	75	35	(D)	(D)	0
GA	Crisp County	155	105	(D)	(D)	0
GA	Dade County	85	60	(D)	(D)	0
GA	Dawson County	85	65	20	0	0
GA	Decatur County	195	135	40	(D)	(D)
GA	DeKalb County	12075	5155	2840	3195	890
GA	Dodge County	90	75	(D)	(D)	0
GA	Dooly County	75	25	15	35	0
GA	Dougherty County	700	410	(D)	140	(D)
GA	Douglas County	720	495	155	(D)	(D)
GA	Early County	75	50	30	0	0
GA	Echols County	85	(D)	(D)	0	0
GA	Effingham County	290	135	75	80	0
GA	Elbert County	95	70	25	0	0
GA	Emanuel County	65	(D)	(D)	0	0
GA	Evans County	55	40	15	0	0
GA	Fannin County	85	35	45	(D)	(D)

State/ Area	Area Name	Total	Speak Spanish or Spanish Creole	Speak other Indo European language	Speak Asian or Pacific Island language	Speak other language
GA	Fayette County	980	405	310	(D)	(D)
GA	Floyd County	1005	615	200	110	85
GA	Forsyth County	875	490	220	105	60
GA	Franklin County	100	75	(D)	(D)	0
GA	Fulton County	12395	6720	3270	1990	415
GA	Gilmer County	150	125	15	(D)	(D)
GA	Glascock County	4	(D)	0	0	0
GA	Glynn County	590	335	150	(D)	(D)
GA	Gordon County	360	285	65	(D)	(D)
GA	Grady County	140	120	0	(D)	(D)
GA	Greene County	85	55	(D)	0	(D)
GA	Gwinnett County	14365	5720	3205	5190	250
GA	Habersham County	480	350	(D)	75	(D)
GA	Hall County	2145	1795	120	230	0
GA	Hancock County	15	(D)	(D)	0	0
GA	Haralson County	100	65	(D)	(D)	0
GA	Harris County	155	50	70	35	0
GA	Hart County	115	45	(D)	(D)	0
GA	Heard County	70	45	(D)	0	(D)
GA	Henry County	795	410	205	180	0
GA	Houston County	1095	545	(D)	320	(D)
GA	Irwin County	20	(D)	(D)	0	0
GA	Jackson County	325	195	65	(D)	(D)
GA	Jasper County	55	35	(D)	(D)	0
GA	Jeff Davis County	100	70	30	0	0
GA	Jefferson County	90	50	(D)	(D)	0
GA	Jenkins County	50	(D)	(D)	0	0
GA	Johnson County	20	(D)	(D)	0	0
GA	Jones County	120	80	15	25	0
GA	Lamar County	95	55	30	(D)	(D)
GA	Lanier County	30	20	0	(D)	(D)

State/ Area	Area Name	Total	Speak Spanish or Spanish Creole	Speak other Indo European language	Speak Asian or Pacific Island language	Speak other language
GA	Laurens County	205	115	70	20	0
GA	Lee County	85	50	(D)	(D)	0
GA	Liberty County	1285	675	315	(D)	(D)
GA	Lincoln County	15	(D)	(D)	0	0
GA	Long County	95	(D)	45	(D)	0
GA	Lowndes County	730	400	125	205	0
GA	Lumpkin County	180	85	45	55	0
GA	McDuffie County	50	25	(D)	0	(D)
GA	McIntosh County	15	(D)	(D)	0	0
GA	Macon County	100	45	60	0	0
GA	Madison County	155	125	(D)	15	(D)
GA	Marion County	30	(D)	(D)	0	0
GA	Meriwether County	75	45	30	0	0
GA	Miller County	40	25	(D)	(D)	0
GA	Mitchell County	110	80	(D)	(D)	0
GA	Monroe County	110	70	(D)	(D)	0
GA	Montgomery County	45	15	(D)	(D)	0
GA	Morgan County	20	(D)	(D)	0	0
GA	Murray County	365	330	15	(D)	(D)
GA	Muscogee County	2400	1180	740	(D)	(D)
GA	Newton County	370	130	170	(D)	(D)
GA	Oconee County	245	120	90	35	0
GA	Oglethorpe County	45	15	(D)	(D)	(D)
GA	Paulding County	495	245	225	(D)	(D)
GA	Peach County	190	135	15	35	0
GA	Pickens County	190	130	60	0	0
GA	Pierce County	95	80	15	0	0
GA	Pike County	80	60	20	0	0
GA	Polk County	410	365	(D)	(D)	0
GA	Pulaski County	60	40	0	(D)	(D)
GA	Putnam County	115	80	30	0	0

State/ Area	Area Name	Total	Speak Spanish or Spanish Creole	Speak other Indo European language	Speak Asian or Pacific Island language	Speak other language
GA	Quitman County	10	10	0	0	0
GA	Rabun County	175	100	45	30	0
GA	Randolph County	30	(D)	(D)	0	0
GA	Richmond County	2380	1115	640	565	60
GA	Rockdale County	650	440	(D)	110	(D)
GA	Schley County	20	(D)	(D)	0	0
GA	Screven County	110	30	25	55	0
GA	Seminole County	150	(D)	(D)	0	0
GA	Spalding County	310	170	95	(D)	(D)
GA	Stephens County	135	60	(D)	(D)	30
GA	Stewart County	40	30	10	0	0
GA	Sumter County	250	160	55	35	0
GA	Talbot County	25	15	(D)	(D)	0
GA	Taliaferro County	4	(D)	0	0	0
GA	Tattnall County	210	195	(D)	(D)	0
GA	Taylor County	30	25	(D)	(D)	0
GA	Telfair County	65	(D)	(D)	0	0
GA	Terrell County	95	60	(D)	0	(D)
GA	Thomas County	330	260	30	40	0
GA	Tift County	255	215	20	(D)	(D)
GA	Toombs County	270	250	(D)	(D)	0
GA	Towns County	55	30	(D)	(D)	0
GA	Treutlen County	115	55	(D)	(D)	0
GA	Troup County	335	245	(D)	(D)	0
GA	Turner County	145	(D)	(D)	0	0
GA	Twiggs County	40	(D)	0	(D)	0
GA	Union County	85	55	(D)	(D)	0
GA	Upson County	140	115	(D)	(D)	0
GA	Walker County	380	225	110	50	0
GA	Walton County	490	280	135	75	0
GA	Ware County	270	160	65	(D)	(D)

State/ Area	Area Name	Total	Speak Spanish or Spanish Creole	Speak other Indo European language	Speak Asian or Pacific Island language	Speak other language
GA	Warren County	60	35	(D)	(D)	0
GA	Washington County	65	35	(D)	(D)	0
GA	Wayne County	250	115	70	(D)	(D)
GA	Webster County	15	(D)	(D)	0	0
GA	Wheeler County	30	15	15	0	0
GA	White County	165	110	(D)	0	(D)
GA	Whitfield County	1595	1455	40	95	0
GA	Wilcox County	25	10	(D)	(D)	0
GA	Wilkes County	25	(D)	0	(D)	0
GA	Wilkinson County	45	15	15	(D)	(D)
GA	Worth County	40	(D)	0	(D)	0
HI	Hawaii	86590	3045	1860	81360	325
HI	Hawaii County	6620	385	245	5950	35
HI	Honolulu County	68665	2165	1350	64895	255
HI	Kalawao County	45	0	0	45	0
HI	Kauai County	2965	125	(D)	2775	(D)
HI	Maui County	8295	365	(D)	7695	(D)
ID	Idaho	15415	10540	2635	1600	645
ID	Ada County	3425	1540	990	785	110
ID	Adams County	25	10	10	0	0
ID	Bannock County	690	385	90	85	130
ID	Bear Lake County	35	30	(D)	0	(D)
ID	Benewah County	55	40	(D)	(D)	(D)
ID	Bingham County	655	460	65	25	105
ID	Blaine County	260	230	(D)	(D)	0
ID	Boise County	65	50	10	(D)	(D)
ID	Bonner County	210	100	70	30	10
ID	Bonneville County	770	530	150	90	0
ID	Boundary County	65	45	(D)	(D)	0
ID	Butte County	25	(D)	(D)	0	0
ID	Camas County	4	0	4	0	0

State/ Area	Area Name	Total	Speak Spanish or Spanish Creole	Speak other Indo European language	Speak Asian or Pacific Island language	Speak other language
ID	Canyon County	2950	2520	220	165	40
ID	Caribou County	55	30	25	0	0
ID	Cassia County	425	380	40	0	0
ID	Clark County	20	20	0	0	0
ID	Clearwater County	95	75	10	(D)	(D)
ID	Custer County	20	(D)	10	(D)	0
ID	Elmore County	415	315	65	(D)	(D)
ID	Franklin County	85	(D)	0	(D)	0
ID	Fremont County	120	115	(D)	0	(D)
ID	Gem County	165	85	45	(D)	(D)
ID	Gooding County	340	280	(D)	(D)	40
ID	Idaho County	55	25	25	0	0
ID	Jefferson County	190	165	4	20	0
ID	Jerome County	300	255	(D)	0	(D)
ID	Kootenai County	565	285	195	(D)	(D)
ID	Latah County	220	115	40	30	35
ID	Lemhi County	20	20	0	0	0
ID	Lewis County	40	20	10	(D)	(D)
ID	Lincoln County	50	(D)	0	(D)	0
ID	Madison County	265	190	50	30	0
ID	Minidoka County	495	440	30	(D)	(D)
ID	Nez Perce County	220	105	40	45	30
ID	Oneida County	30	30	0	0	0
ID	Owyhee County	295	255	(D)	(D)	20
ID	Payette County	345	300	35	(D)	(D)
ID	Power County	125	105	(D)	0	(D)
ID	Shoshone County	100	45	35	(D)	(D)
ID	Teton County	70	(D)	(D)	0	0
ID	Twin Falls County	920	600	215	85	20
ID	Valley County	45	25	(D)	0	(D)
ID	Washington County	100	(D)	(D)	0	0

State/ Area	Area Name	Total	Speak Spanish or Spanish Creole	Speak other Indo European language	Speak Asian or Pacific Island language	Speak other language
IL	Illinois	370945	193445	118910	47720	10870
IL	Adams County	270	150	90	30	0
IL	Alexander County	50	(D)	20	(D)	(D)
IL	Bond County	120	75	(D)	(D)	0
IL	Boone County	555	480	75	0	0
IL	Brown County	0	0	0	0	0
IL	Bureau County	270	190	45	(D)	(D)
IL	Calhoun County	30	25	(D)	(D)	0
IL	Carroll County	120	60	45	(D)	(D)
IL	Cass County	125	115	(D)	(D)	0
IL	Champaign County	2125	815	405	790	115
IL	Christian County	175	60	100	(D)	(D)
IL	Clark County	80	40	20	20	0
IL	Clay County	15	(D)	0	(D)	0
IL	Clinton County	110	35	60	15	0
IL	Coles County	350	230	90	(D)	(D)
IL	Cook County	271600	141830	87585	33405	8780
IL	Crawford County	135	85	(D)	(D)	0
IL	Cumberland County	25	15	10	0	0
IL	DeKalb County	1135	720	285	95	35
IL	De Witt County	40	30	(D)	(D)	(D)
IL	Douglas County	340	80	255	10	0
IL	DuPage County	25360	8690	11005	5240	425
IL	Edgar County	85	60	(D)	0	(D)
IL	Edwards County	20	4	10	0	0
IL	Effingham County	115	25	80	15	0
IL	Fayette County	100	70	30	0	0
IL	Ford County	50	25	(D)	(D)	0
IL	Franklin County	135	40	95	0	0
IL	Fulton County	180	115	45	25	0
IL	Gallatin County	30	10	10	(D)	(D)

State/ Area	Area Name	Total	Speak Spanish or Spanish Creole	Speak other Indo European language	Speak Asian or Pacific Island language	Speak other language
IL	Greene County	65	15	35	15	0
IL	Grundy County	250	140	(D)	(D)	0
IL	Hamilton County	20	(D)	(D)	0	0
IL	Hancock County	30	25	(D)	(D)	0
IL	Hardin County	4	(D)	(D)	0	0
IL	Henderson County	30	15	15	0	0
IL	Henry County	285	140	110	(D)	(D)
IL	Iroquois County	205	115	(D)	(D)	0
IL	Jackson County	610	305	175	95	35
IL	Jasper County	35	(D)	20	(D)	0
IL	Jefferson County	215	115	(D)	(D)	0
IL	Jersey County	105	(D)	50	(D)	0
IL	Jo Daviess County	90	55	35	0	0
IL	Johnson County	50	35	(D)	(D)	0
IL	Kane County	13470	10820	1510	945	195
IL	Kankakee County	905	520	245	(D)	(D)
IL	Kendall County	685	480	155	(D)	(D)
IL	Knox County	425	300	60	45	20
IL	Lake County	16805	8770	5070	2670	290
IL	La Salle County	935	580	255	95	10
IL	Lawrence County	80	45	40	0	0
IL	Lee County	165	100	25	45	0
IL	Livingston County	245	155	70	(D)	(D)
IL	Logan County	190	95	60	(D)	(D)
IL	McDonough County	320	165	105	(D)	(D)
IL	McHenry County	3470	1785	1355	230	100
IL	McLean County	1295	755	335	185	20
IL	Macon County	530	270	150	90	15
IL	Macoupin County	195	(D)	95	(D)	0
IL	Madison County	1425	620	665	(D)	(D)
IL	Marion County	235	120	90	(D)	(D)

State/ Area	Area Name	Total	Speak Spanish or Spanish Creole	Speak other Indo European language	Speak Asian or Pacific Island language	Speak other language
IL	Marshall County	60	(D)	40	(D)	0
IL	Mason County	80	45	(D)	(D)	0
IL	Massac County	55	(D)	(D)	(D)	(D)
IL	Menard County	80	65	(D)	(D)	0
IL	Mercer County	70	45	(D)	0	(D)
IL	Monroe County	165	(D)	95	(D)	0
IL	Montgomery County	115	(D)	60	(D)	0
IL	Morgan County	175	90	60	(D)	(D)
IL	Moultrie County	240	(D)	210	(D)	0
IL	Ogle County	575	430	(D)	(D)	0
IL	Peoria County	1700	700	525	290	180
IL	Perry County	115	45	45	25	0
IL	Piatt County	65	40	25	0	0
IL	Pike County	65	50	15	0	0
IL	Pope County	20	(D)	(D)	0	0
IL	Pulaski County	45	25	(D)	0	(D)
IL	Putnam County	80	45	(D)	(D)	0
IL	Randolph County	170	(D)	100	(D)	0
IL	Richland County	50	(D)	(D)	0	0
IL	Rock Island County	1875	1295	395	155	30
IL	St. Clair County	1930	855	605	390	80
IL	Saline County	125	65	25	(D)	(D)
IL	Sangamon County	990	315	425	225	25
IL	Schuyler County	25	20	(D)	(D)	0
IL	Scott County	4	(D)	(D)	0	0
IL	Shelby County	75	50	(D)	(D)	0
IL	Stark County	25	15	10	0	0
IL	Stephenson County	310	95	160	(D)	(D)
IL	Tazewell County	685	285	255	80	60
IL	Union County	85	40	35	(D)	(D)
IL	Vermilion County	670	435	155	60	20

State/ Area	Area Name	Total	Speak Spanish or Spanish Creole	Speak other Indo European language	Speak Asian or Pacific Island language	Speak other language
IL	Wabash County	55	25	30	0	0
IL	Warren County	160	125	(D)	(D)	0
IL	Washington County	145	45	95	0	0
IL	Wayne County	60	20	20	(D)	(D)
IL	White County	50	30	(D)	(D)	(D)
IL	Whiteside County	710	530	160	(D)	(D)
IL	Will County	7710	4410	2165	1015	120
IL	Williamson County	285	155	85	40	0
IL	Winnebago County	3770	1865	1225	615	65
IL	Woodford County	195	105	(D)	(D)	0
IN	Indiana	61515	31360	22655	5950	1550
IN	Adams County	1030	105	925	0	0
IN	Allen County	3300	1670	940	565	125
IN	Bartholomew County	470	190	165	115	0
IN	Benton County	45	30	(D)	(D)	0
IN	Blackford County	45	25	(D)	(D)	0
IN	Boone County	85	(D)	40	(D)	0
IN	Brown County	65	(D)	(D)	0	0
IN	Carroll County	125	105	(D)	(D)	0
IN	Cass County	430	325	(D)	(D)	0
IN	Clark County	405	275	75	(D)	(D)
IN	Clay County	70	40	(D)	0	(D)
IN	Clinton County	180	(D)	(D)	0	0
IN	Crawford County	25	20	4	0	0
IN	Daviess County	540	90	440	(D)	(D)
IN	Dearborn County	230	(D)	135	(D)	0
IN	Decatur County	50	(D)	(D)	0	0
IN	DeKalb County	135	50	35	(D)	(D)
IN	Delaware County	655	505	125	(D)	(D)
IN	Dubois County	360	(D)	235	0	(D)
IN	Elkhart County	3870	1560	2100	(D)	(D)

State/ Area	Area Name	Total	Speak Spanish or Spanish Creole	Speak other Indo European language	Speak Asian or Pacific Island language	Speak other language
IN	Fayette County	80	(D)	(D)	0	0
IN	Floyd County	390	130	215	20	20
IN	Fountain County	105	50	35	25	0
IN	Franklin County	145	(D)	75	(D)	0
IN	Fulton County	180	135	(D)	(D)	0
IN	Gibson County	135	90	25	20	0
IN	Grant County	640	375	155	(D)	(D)
IN	Greene County	145	75	65	(D)	(D)
IN	Hamilton County	1400	455	485	430	30
IN	Hancock County	240	115	80	40	0
IN	Harrison County	125	100	(D)	(D)	0
IN	Hendricks County	440	225	115	(D)	(D)
IN	Henry County	285	165	80	(D)	(D)
IN	Howard County	480	245	170	(D)	(D)
IN	Huntington County	250	160	75	20	0
IN	Jackson County	275	185	25	65	0
IN	Jasper County	210	125	75	(D)	(D)
IN	Jay County	100	40	60	0	0
IN	Jefferson County	145	115	(D)	(D)	0
IN	Jennings County	75	50	(D)	0	(D)
IN	Johnson County	440	225	120	(D)	(D)
IN	Knox County	160	100	40	(D)	(D)
IN	Kosciusko County	995	455	430	105	0
IN	LaGrange County	2630	230	2385	(D)	(D)
IN	Lake County	13000	8505	3740	505	245
IN	LaPorte County	1070	570	395	30	80
IN	Lawrence County	125	75	40	(D)	(D)
IN	Madison County	755	490	195	55	15
IN	Marion County	9465	4905	2840	1355	365
IN	Marshall County	730	290	405	(D)	(D)
IN	Martin County	15	(D)	(D)	0	0

State/ Area	Area Name	Total	Speak Spanish or Spanish Creole	Speak other Indo European language	Speak Asian or Pacific Island language	Speak other language
IN	Miami County	180	115	35	(D)	(D)
IN	Monroe County	1205	445	400	260	100
IN	Montgomery County	125	80	25	(D)	(D)
IN	Morgan County	190	130	60	0	0
IN	Newton County	105	40	45	(D)	(D)
IN	Noble County	680	420	200	60	0
IN	Ohio County	10	(D)	0	0	0
IN	Orange County	80	50	(D)	0	(D)
IN	Owen County	40	15	25	0	0
IN	Parke County	130	35	90	(D)	(D)
IN	Perry County	85	30	55	0	0
IN	Pike County	40	20	(D)	(D)	0
IN	Porter County	1335	660	470	175	30
IN	Posey County	100	65	35	0	0
IN	Pulaski County	55	30	25	0	0
IN	Putnam County	155	95	(D)	(D)	0
IN	Randolph County	95	55	40	0	0
IN	Ripley County	75	50	(D)	(D)	0
IN	Rush County	35	(D)	(D)	(D)	0
IN	St. Joseph County	3265	1665	1105	355	140
IN	Scott County	85	(D)	(D)	0	0
IN	Shelby County	185	110	(D)	(D)	0
IN	Spencer County	100	30	75	0	0
IN	Starke County	215	(D)	160	(D)	0
IN	Steuben County	220	130	(D)	(D)	0
IN	Sullivan County	135	115	(D)	(D)	0
IN	Switzerland County	30	20	10	0	0
IN	Tippecanoe County	1735	835	425	375	105
IN	Tipton County	60	45	(D)	10	(D)
IN	Union County	45	(D)	25	(D)	0
IN	Vanderburgh County	1185	490	465	(D)	(D)

State/ Area	Area Name	Total	Speak Spanish or Spanish Creole	Speak other Indo European language	Speak Asian or Pacific Island language	Speak other language
IN	Vermillion County	55	15	30	(D)	(D)
IN	Vigo County	445	230	135	(D)	(D)
IN	Wabash County	200	100	(D)	(D)	0
IN	Warren County	20	(D)	(D)	0	0
IN	Warrick County	315	205	75	35	0
IN	Washington County	125	(D)	90	(D)	0
IN	Wayne County	465	260	120	50	35
IN	Wells County	190	110	70	(D)	(D)
IN	White County	270	190	(D)	(D)	0
IN	Whitley County	120	60	45	(D)	(D)
IA	Iowa	23990	11890	7155	4435	510
IA	Adair County	30	(D)	15	(D)	0
IA	Adams County	20	(D)	(D)	(D)	0
IA	Allamakee County	85	45	40	0	0
IA	Appanoose County	35	35	(D)	(D)	0
IA	Audubon County	30	(D)	(D)	0	0
IA	Benton County	95	45	(D)	0	(D)
IA	Black Hawk County	1185	730	315	(D)	(D)
IA	Boone County	115	65	35	(D)	(D)
IA	Bremer County	165	120	45	0	0
IA	Buchanan County	405	(D)	335	(D)	0
IA	Buena Vista County	490	275	65	150	0
IA	Butler County	75	35	40	0	0
IA	Calhoun County	25	15	10	0	0
IA	Carroll County	110	70	25	(D)	(D)
IA	Cass County	50	35	(D)	(D)	0
IA	Cedar County	120	75	40	(D)	(D)
IA	Cerro Gordo County	355	205	100	50	0
IA	Cherokee County	50	20	15	(D)	(D)
IA	Chickasaw County	50	(D)	30	(D)	0
IA	Clarke County	25	(D)	(D)	0	0

State/ Area	Area Name	Total	Speak Spanish or Spanish Creole	Speak other Indo European language	Speak Asian or Pacific Island language	Speak other language
IA	Clay County	65	35	(D)	(D)	0
IA	Clayton County	90	25	55	(D)	(D)
IA	Clinton County	265	150	85	30	0
IA	Crawford County	150	130	(D)	(D)	0
IA	Dallas County	260	195	50	(D)	(D)
IA	Davis County	335	25	310	0	0
IA	Decatur County	85	45	45	0	0
IA	Delaware County	75	30	40	0	0
IA	Des Moines County	275	140	70	(D)	(D)
IA	Dickinson County	95	65	(D)	(D)	0
IA	Dubuque County	490	200	225	(D)	(D)
IA	Emmet County	85	65	15	0	0
IA	Fayette County	120	75	25	20	0
IA	Floyd County	85	40	35	(D)	(D)
IA	Franklin County	75	35	(D)	(D)	0
IA	Fremont County	30	15	(D)	(D)	0
IA	Greene County	50	25	20	0	0
IA	Grundy County	85	20	65	0	0
IA	Guthrie County	60	35	30	0	0
IA	Hamilton County	95	55	30	10	0
IA	Hancock County	35	20	(D)	0	(D)
IA	Hardin County	110	85	25	0	0
IA	Harrison County	80	45	(D)	(D)	0
IA	Henry County	180	75	20	85	0
IA	Howard County	115	(D)	105	0	(D)
IA	Humboldt County	55	30	(D)	(D)	0
IA	Ida County	40	20	20	0	0
IA	Iowa County	130	(D)	90	(D)	0
IA	Jackson County	100	(D)	60	(D)	0
IA	Jasper County	130	40	75	(D)	(D)
IA	Jefferson County	55	25	(D)	(D)	0

State/ Area	Area Name	Total	Speak Spanish or Spanish Creole	Speak other Indo European language	Speak Asian or Pacific Island language	Speak other language
IA	Johnson County	1225	595	345	270	20
IA	Jones County	120	70	(D)	(D)	0
IA	Keokuk County	10	(D)	(D)	0	0
IA	Kossuth County	65	(D)	30	(D)	0
IA	Lee County	230	175	35	20	0
IA	Linn County	1205	515	335	260	95
IA	Louisa County	290	270	(D)	(D)	0
IA	Lucas County	60	(D)	50	(D)	0
IA	Lyon County	70	(D)	(D)	0	0
IA	Madison County	25	15	(D)	(D)	0
IA	Mahaska County	130	55	60	15	0
IA	Marion County	245	95	80	70	0
IA	Marshall County	470	295	(D)	90	(D)
IA	Mills County	35	(D)	20	(D)	0
IA	Mitchell County	95	(D)	85	0	(D)
IA	Monona County	40	30	(D)	(D)	(D)
IA	Monroe County	40	(D)	(D)	0	0
IA	Montgomery County	15	(D)	10	(D)	0
IA	Muscatine County	830	705	70	(D)	(D)
IA	O'Brien County	105	65	35	(D)	(D)
IA	Osceola County	30	(D)	(D)	0	0
IA	Page County	60	30	(D)	(D)	0
IA	Palo Alto County	15	15	0	0	0
IA	Plymouth County	110	75	(D)	(D)	0
IA	Pocahontas County	35	15	(D)	(D)	0
IA	Polk County	4665	1850	980	1760	80
IA	Pottawattamie County	585	335	160	(D)	(D)
IA	Poweshiek County	100	(D)	50	(D)	0
IA	Ringgold County	55	(D)	35	0	(D)
IA	Sac County	65	20	45	0	0
IA	Scott County	1320	580	335	365	45

State/ Area	Area Name	Total	Speak Spanish or Spanish Creole	Speak other Indo European language	Speak Asian or Pacific Island language	Speak other language
IA	Shelby County	80	25	45	10	0
IA	Sioux County	200	90	105	4	0
IA	Story County	590	230	235	90	30
IA	Tama County	225	70	80	(D)	(D)
IA	Taylor County	55	55	0	0	0
IA	Union County	45	(D)	(D)	0	0
IA	Van Buren County	80	4	75	0	0
IA	Wapello County	215	140	(D)	45	(D)
IA	Warren County	220	105	90	(D)	(D)
IA	Washington County	190	(D)	125	(D)	0
IA	Wayne County	30	4	25	0	0
IA	Webster County	350	135	135	(D)	(D)
IA	Winnebago County	85	40	45	0	0
IA	Winneshiek County	140	70	50	20	0
IA	Woodbury County	1440	935	135	350	25
IA	Worth County	65	(D)	35	(D)	0
IA	Wright County	175	160	15	0	0
KS	Kansas	32850	18820	6090	7255	685
KS	Allen County	95	60	25	10	0
KS	Anderson County	60	(D)	40	(D)	0
KS	Atchison County	100	80	(D)	(D)	0
KS	Barber County	35	(D)	(D)	0	0
KS	Barton County	295	195	90	(D)	(D)
KS	Bourbon County	80	(D)	45	0	(D)
KS	Brown County	50	15	(D)	(D)	15
KS	Butler County	245	130	90	(D)	(D)
KS	Chase County	4	4	0	0	0
KS	Chautauqua County	10	10	0	0	0
KS	Cherokee County	115	65	(D)	(D)	0
KS	Cheyenne County	20	(D)	10	(D)	0
KS	Clark County	4	0	(D)	0	0

State/ Area	Area Name	Total	Speak Spanish or Spanish Creole	Speak other Indo European language	Speak Asian or Pacific Island language	Speak other language
KS	Clay County	40	(D)	25	(D)	0
KS	Cloud County	30	10	20	0	0
KS	Coffey County	35	(D)	15	(D)	0
KS	Comanche County	4	0	(D)	0	0
KS	Cowley County	295	140	(D)	140	(D)
KS	Crawford County	205	115	(D)	(D)	45
KS	Decatur County	10	(D)	(D)	0	0
KS	Dickinson County	95	70	25	0	0
KS	Doniphan County	30	(D)	15	(D)	0
KS	Douglas County	910	340	205	240	125
KS	Edwards County	40	20	(D)	(D)	0
KS	Elk County	25	20	(D)	(D)	0
KS	Ellis County	395	95	265	35	0
KS	Ellsworth County	80	30	40	(D)	(D)
KS	Finney County	1775	1495	60	220	0
KS	Ford County	1220	1045	(D)	95	(D)
KS	Franklin County	130	90	(D)	(D)	0
KS	Geary County	675	305	(D)	250	(D)
KS	Gove County	30	(D)	20	0	(D)
KS	Graham County	15	(D)	(D)	0	0
KS	Grant County	315	(D)	(D)	0	0
KS	Gray County	90	65	(D)	0	(D)
KS	Greeley County	15	15	0	0	0
KS	Greenwood County	30	(D)	(D)	0	0
KS	Hamilton County	50	40	(D)	(D)	0
KS	Harper County	10	(D)	(D)	0	0
KS	Harvey County	455	245	155	(D)	(D)
KS	Haskell County	160	145	15	0	0
KS	Hodgeman County	4	(D)	(D)	0	0
KS	Jackson County	45	35	(D)	0	(D)
KS	Jefferson County	90	60	20	10	0

State/ Area	Area Name	Total	Speak Spanish or Spanish Creole	Speak other Indo European language	Speak Asian or Pacific Island language	Speak other language
KS	Jewell County	10	(D)	(D)	0	0
KS	Johnson County	4835	1935	1360	1460	75
KS	Kearny County	150	140	15	0	0
KS	Kingman County	4	(D)	0	0	0
KS	Kiowa County	10	(D)	0	(D)	0
KS	Labette County	100	50	(D)	(D)	0
KS	Lane County	20	(D)	10	(D)	0
KS	Leavenworth County	735	265	280	185	0
KS	Lincoln County	25	4	20	0	0
KS	Linn County	40	25	(D)	(D)	0
KS	Logan County	30	(D)	(D)	0	0
KS	Lyon County	685	585	65	(D)	(D)
KS	McPherson County	210	70	130	10	0
KS	Marion County	120	40	80	0	0
KS	Marshall County	65	(D)	20	(D)	0
KS	Meade County	75	50	25	0	0
KS	Miami County	125	60	45	25	0
KS	Mitchell County	30	20	10	0	0
KS	Montgomery County	165	120	(D)	25	(D)
KS	Morris County	20	(D)	(D)	0	0
KS	Morton County	65	50	(D)	(D)	0
KS	Nemaha County	25	(D)	(D)	0	0
KS	Neosho County	70	40	(D)	(D)	0
KS	Ness County	15	10	(D)	(D)	0
KS	Norton County	50	(D)	(D)	0	0
KS	Osage County	80	35	35	(D)	(D)
KS	Osborne County	20	10	10	0	0
KS	Ottawa County	10	(D)	(D)	0	0
KS	Pawnee County	50	10	(D)	(D)	0
KS	Phillips County	20	10	(D)	(D)	0
KS	Pottawatomie County	55	35	15	(D)	(D)

State/ Area	Area Name	Total	Speak Spanish or Spanish Creole	Speak other Indo European language	Speak Asian or Pacific Island language	Speak other language
KS	Pratt County	85	(D)	(D)	0	0
KS	Rawlins County	25	(D)	10	0	(D)
KS	Reno County	630	340	250	(D)	(D)
KS	Republic County	65	25	25	15	0
KS	Rice County	75	55	(D)	(D)	0
KS	Riley County	685	380	(D)	160	(D)
KS	Rooks County	30	(D)	15	(D)	0
KS	Rush County	75	10	65	0	0
KS	Russell County	80	30	50	0	0
KS	Saline County	700	270	120	305	0
KS	Scott County	35	(D)	(D)	0	0
KS	Sedgwick County	7560	3520	840	3015	185
KS	Seward County	1260	1195	(D)	40	(D)
KS	Shawnee County	1560	1040	310	175	35
KS	Sheridan County	10	(D)	(D)	0	(D)
KS	Sherman County	75	75	0	0	0
KS	Smith County	25	(D)	10	(D)	0
KS	Stafford County	45	20	10	15	0
KS	Stanton County	40	(D)	(D)	0	0
KS	Stevens County	170	(D)	(D)	0	0
KS	Sumner County	190	115	55	(D)	(D)
KS	Thomas County	70	40	(D)	(D)	0
KS	Trego County	30	0	30	0	0
KS	Wabaunsee County	20	15	4	0	0
KS	Wallace County	15	(D)	(D)	0	0
KS	Washington County	40	(D)	(D)	0	0
KS	Wichita County	50	50	0	0	0
KS	Wilson County	25	(D)	15	0	(D)
KS	Woodson County	10	(D)	0	(D)	0
KS	Wyandotte County	2835	2180	225	385	45
KY	Kentucky	23735	12415	7280	3445	595

State/ Area	Area Name	Total	Speak Spanish or Spanish Creole	Speak other Indo European language	Speak Asian or Pacific Island language	Speak other language
KY	Adair County	175	45	130	0	0
KY	Allen County	95	30	65	0	0
KY	Anderson County	110	(D)	45	(D)	0
KY	Ballard County	15	(D)	(D)	0	0
KY	Barren County	185	65	95	25	0
KY	Bath County	35	15	15	0	0
KY	Bell County	120	65	(D)	(D)	0
KY	Boone County	590	345	110	100	30
KY	Bourbon County	95	70	25	0	0
KY	Boyd County	225	145	50	(D)	(D)
KY	Boyle County	135	105	(D)	(D)	0
KY	Bracken County	35	(D)	15	(D)	0
KY	Breathitt County	70	45	25	0	0
KY	Breckinridge County	120	45	65	15	0
KY	Bullitt County	220	110	95	10	0
KY	Butler County	75	40	(D)	(D)	0
KY	Caldwell County	30	0	(D)	(D)	0
KY	Calloway County	280	130	90	(D)	(D)
KY	Campbell County	505	325	135	45	0
KY	Carlisle County	10	(D)	(D)	0	0
KY	Carroll County	10	(D)	(D)	0	0
KY	Carter County	80	50	(D)	(D)	0
KY	Casey County	110	45	65	0	0
KY	Christian County	940	500	315	95	35
KY	Clark County	165	(D)	(D)	65	0
KY	Clay County	75	45	25	0	0
KY	Clinton County	150	135	20	0	0
KY	Crittenden County	185	(D)	155	(D)	0
KY	Cumberland County	20	(D)	10	(D)	0
KY	Daviess County	640	470	150	20	0
KY	Edmonson County	15	(D)	(D)	0	0

State/ Area	Area Name	Total	Speak Spanish or Spanish Creole	Speak other Indo European language	Speak Asian or Pacific Island language	Speak other language
KY	Elliott County	20	(D)	(D)	0	0
KY	Estill County	35	(D)	20	(D)	0
KY	Fayette County	2365	1255	580	440	90
KY	Fleming County	35	(D)	(D)	0	0
KY	Floyd County	135	85	(D)	(D)	0
KY	Franklin County	265	185	50	(D)	(D)
KY	Fulton County	4	(D)	0	0	0
KY	Gallatin County	25	(D)	(D)	0	0
KY	Garrard County	75	50	(D)	0	(D)
KY	Grant County	80	45	35	0	0
KY	Graves County	165	115	(D)	(D)	0
KY	Grayson County	70	45	25	0	0
KY	Green County	15	(D)	(D)	(D)	0
KY	Greenup County	90	50	(D)	20	(D)
KY	Hancock County	40	(D)	0	(D)	0
KY	Hardin County	1225	425	290	475	35
KY	Harlan County	95	30	45	(D)	(D)
KY	Harrison County	55	30	(D)	0	(D)
KY	Hart County	85	(D)	50	(D)	0
KY	Henderson County	160	(D)	80	(D)	0
KY	Henry County	70	40	(D)	10	(D)
KY	Hickman County	25	(D)	10	(D)	0
KY	Hopkins County	190	80	70	(D)	(D)
KY	Jackson County	80	50	(D)	(D)	0
KY	Jefferson County	5430	2500	1720	1025	185
KY	Jessamine County	170	100	25	45	0
KY	Johnson County	60	(D)	(D)	0	0
KY	Kenton County	955	480	380	(D)	(D)
KY	Knott County	25	(D)	0	0	(D)
KY	Knox County	90	65	25	0	0
KY	Larue County	45	(D)	0	(D)	0

State/ Area	Area Name	Total	Speak Spanish or Spanish Creole	Speak other Indo European language	Speak Asian or Pacific Island language	Speak other language
KY	Laurel County	245	135	80	(D)	(D)
KY	Lawrence County	45	30	(D)	(D)	0
KY	Lee County	10	(D)	(D)	0	0
KY	Leslie County	50	35	(D)	(D)	0
KY	Letcher County	120	60	40	(D)	(D)
KY	Lewis County	25	(D)	(D)	0	0
KY	Lincoln County	110	50	60	0	0
KY	Livingston County	60	35	25	0	0
KY	Logan County	115	90	(D)	(D)	0
KY	Lyon County	40	(D)	(D)	0	0
KY	McCracken County	220	115	80	25	0
KY	McCreary County	35	(D)	(D)	0	0
KY	McLean County	20	15	(D)	0	(D)
KY	Madison County	420	195	135	90	0
KY	Magoffin County	20	(D)	(D)	(D)	0
KY	Marion County	85	70	(D)	(D)	0
KY	Marshall County	135	65	50	15	0
KY	Martin County	20	(D)	(D)	(D)	0
KY	Mason County	70	40	(D)	(D)	0
KY	Meade County	160	35	65	65	0
KY	Menifee County	35	30	(D)	(D)	0
KY	Mercer County	75	50	(D)	(D)	0
KY	Metcalfe County	20	(D)	(D)	0	0
KY	Monroe County	80	50	30	0	0
KY	Montgomery County	55	40	10	0	0
KY	Morgan County	85	30	10	(D)	(D)
KY	Muhlenberg County	80	60	20	0	0
KY	Nelson County	185	110	45	30	0
KY	Nicholas County	10	(D)	0	0	0
KY	Ohio County	90	65	25	0	0
KY	Oldham County	215	105	(D)	50	(D)

State/ Area	Area Name	Total	Speak Spanish or Spanish Creole	Speak other Indo European language	Speak Asian or Pacific Island language	Speak other language
KY	Owen County	65	40	10	10	0
KY	Owsley County	20	(D)	(D)	0	0
KY	Pendleton County	20	(D)	(D)	0	0
KY	Perry County	105	85	(D)	(D)	0
KY	Pike County	190	95	60	(D)	(D)
KY	Powell County	15	(D)	(D)	0	0
KY	Pulaski County	270	170	(D)	55	(D)
KY	Robertson County	4	(D)	0	(D)	0
KY	Rockcastle County	75	25	35	(D)	(D)
KY	Rowan County	155	95	(D)	(D)	0
KY	Russell County	120	70	20	(D)	(D)
KY	Scott County	150	100	(D)	0	(D)
KY	Shelby County	165	120	(D)	(D)	0
KY	Simpson County	45	25	(D)	(D)	0
KY	Spencer County	85	35	50	0	0
KY	Taylor County	115	65	(D)	0	(D)
KY	Todd County	140	90	(D)	(D)	0
KY	Trigg County	125	70	(D)	(D)	0
KY	Trimble County	15	(D)	(D)	0	0
KY	Union County	105	55	35	(D)	(D)
KY	Warren County	730	445	165	(D)	(D)
KY	Washington County	75	45	(D)	(D)	0
KY	Wayne County	20	(D)	0	0	0
KY	Webster County	75	50	20	0	0
KY	Whitley County	150	85	65	0	0
KY	Wolfe County	15	(D)	(D)	0	0
KY	Woodford County	60	(D)	(D)	0	0
LA	Louisiana	76760	19975	45765	9805	1210
LA	Acadia Parish	2050	45	1960	(D)	(D)
LA	Allen Parish	635	300	260	(D)	(D)
LA	Ascension Parish	590	230	325	(D)	(D)

State/ Area	Area Name	Total	Speak Spanish or Spanish Creole	Speak other Indo European language	Speak Asian or Pacific Island language	Speak other language
LA	Assumption Parish	940	25	870	45	0
LA	Avoyelles Parish	1860	270	1545	(D)	(D)
LA	Beauregard Parish	200	55	110	30	0
LA	Bienville Parish	80	55	20	0	0
LA	Bossier Parish	915	505	(D)	270	(D)
LA	Caddo Parish	1415	675	520	185	35
LA	Calcasieu Parish	2625	370	2040	170	45
LA	Caldwell Parish	40	30	(D)	(D)	0
LA	Cameron Parish	250	(D)	210	(D)	0
LA	Catahoula Parish	50	15	35	0	0
LA	Claiborne Parish	75	45	20	(D)	(D)
LA	Concordia Parish	90	35	40	(D)	(D)
LA	De Soto Parish	210	110	(D)	(D)	0
LA	East Baton Rouge Parish	4755	1550	1870	1205	130
LA	East Carroll Parish	45	20	(D)	(D)	(D)
LA	East Feliciana Parish	280	120	120	40	0
LA	Evangeline Parish	2380	75	2295	10	0
LA	Franklin Parish	75	(D)	40	(D)	0
LA	Grant Parish	115	(D)	70	(D)	0
LA	Iberia Parish	2375	190	1870	320	0
LA	Iberville Parish	245	(D)	200	(D)	0
LA	Jackson Parish	75	(D)	55	(D)	(D)
LA	Jefferson Parish	10445	5035	2330	2770	310
LA	Jefferson Davis Parish	1010	75	890	35	10
LA	Lafayette Parish	5795	495	4945	270	80
LA	Lafourche Parish	4120	250	3750	120	0
LA	La Salle Parish	115	85	25	0	0
LA	Lincoln Parish	395	155	140	(D)	(D)
LA	Livingston Parish	675	285	355	25	10
LA	Madison Parish	20	(D)	(D)	0	0

State/ Area	Area Name	Total	Speak Spanish or Spanish Creole	Speak other Indo European language	Speak Asian or Pacific Island language	Speak other language
LA	Morehouse Parish	130	85	(D)	(D)	(D)
LA	Natchitoches Parish	320	140	120	60	0
LA	Orleans Parish	8245	4025	1990	2060	170
LA	Ouachita Parish	940	495	285	(D)	(D)
LA	Plaquemines Parish	360	50	205	100	0
LA	Pointe Coupee Parish	355	(D)	300	0	(D)
LA	Rapides Parish	1075	255	650	115	55
LA	Red River Parish	40	25	(D)	(D)	0
LA	Richland Parish	45	(D)	(D)	0	0
LA	Sabine Parish	105	50	40	(D)	(D)
LA	St. Bernard Parish	1105	490	260	280	70
LA	St. Charles Parish	630	180	385	60	0
LA	St. Helena Parish	15	(D)	0	(D)	0
LA	St. James Parish	305	(D)	290	0	(D)
LA	St. John the Baptist Parish	400	225	145	(D)	(D)
LA	St. Landry Parish	3660	60	3555	50	0
LA	St. Martin Parish	3220	65	3090	(D)	(D)
LA	St. Mary Parish	855	220	470	(D)	(D)
LA	St. Tammany Parish	1735	820	645	245	25
LA	Tangipahoa Parish	835	245	480	(D)	(D)
LA	Tensas Parish	15	(D)	(D)	0	0
LA	Terrebonne Parish	2575	260	2170	145	0
LA	Union Parish	75	60	(D)	(D)	0
LA	Vermilion Parish	3175	70	2890	215	0
LA	Vernon Parish	770	425	155	190	0
LA	Washington Parish	265	140	(D)	(D)	0
LA	Webster Parish	110	55	40	15	0
LA	West Baton Rouge Parish	230	(D)	165	0	(D)
LA	West Carroll Parish	115	(D)	60	0	(D)

State/ Area	Area Name	Total	Speak Spanish or Spanish Creole	Speak other Indo European language	Speak Asian or Pacific Island language	Speak other language
LA	West Feliciana Parish	75	(D)	50	(D)	0
LA	Winn Parish	30	20	15	0	0
ME	Maine	17605	1670	14580	1030	325
ME	Androscoggin County	3465	175	3255	35	0
ME	Aroostook County	3640	(D)	3495	65	(D)
ME	Cumberland County	2090	375	1315	355	45
ME	Franklin County	195	35	105	45	4
ME	Hancock County	250	70	150	(D)	(D)
ME	Kennebec County	1840	160	1580	105	0
ME	Knox County	135	50	80	(D)	(D)
ME	Lincoln County	125	15	105	4	0
ME	Oxford County	380	35	300	10	35
ME	Penobscot County	1145	195	720	175	55
ME	Piscataquis County	80	(D)	50	(D)	0
ME	Sagadahoc County	225	25	180	20	0
ME	Somerset County	360	60	265	(D)	(D)
ME	Waldo County	145	30	105	(D)	(D)
ME	Washington County	240	50	70	10	105
ME	York County	3285	310	2805	140	35
MD	Maryland	94995	32930	28970	29420	3670
MD	Allegany County	320	190	75	55	0
MD	Anne Arundel County	5595	2030	1570	1875	120
MD	Baltimore County	12445	2710	6190	3065	480
MD	Calvert County	380	185	140	(D)	(D)
MD	Caroline County	165	70	65	(D)	(D)
MD	Carroll County	1060	365	580	(D)	(D)
MD	Cecil County	515	285	210	(D)	(D)
MD	Charles County	1030	380	310	305	30
MD	Dorchester County	200	100	55	45	0
MD	Frederick County	1300	550	485	235	30
MD	Garrett County	180	(D)	145	(D)	0

State/ Area	Area Name	Total	Speak Spanish or Spanish Creole	Speak other Indo European language	Speak Asian or Pacific Island language	Speak other language
MD	Harford County	1990	645	810	500	35
MD	Howard County	4600	955	1200	2320	130
MD	Kent County	165	105	(D)	(D)	0
MD	Montgomery County	35895	11490	8515	14585	1305
MD	Prince George's County	15760	7785	2910	4160	910
MD	Queen Anne's County	290	110	135	45	0
MD	St. Mary's County	950	260	430	(D)	(D)
MD	Somerset County	210	75	100	(D)	(D)
MD	Talbot County	260	160	65	(D)	(D)
MD	Washington County	685	290	180	150	70
MD	Wicomico County	835	360	245	210	25
MD	Worcester County	385	115	205	50	20
MD	Baltimore city	9775	3700	4290	1330	455
MA	Massachusetts	205355	75295	92735	33280	4045
MA	Barnstable County	1910	445	1290	145	30
MA	Berkshire County	1445	315	1010	95	30
MA	Bristol County	24455	3650	19725	860	215
MA	Dukes County	85	(D)	(D)	0	0
MA	Essex County	22750	12165	7580	2495	510
MA	Franklin County	730	265	420	20	30
MA	Hampden County	23875	16020	6715	1010	135
MA	Hampshire County	2475	950	1150	(D)	(D)
MA	Middlesex County	42910	10225	22380	9520	790
MA	Nantucket County	130	85	(D)	(D)	0
MA	Norfolk County	16500	1870	7320	6740	570
MA	Plymouth County	7135	2165	4145	740	90
MA	Suffolk County	39885	16055	13785	8985	1060
MA	Worcester County	21065	11075	7115	2305	570
MI	Michigan	129340	41150	50170	15570	22450
MI	Alcona County	50	10	30	(D)	(D)

State/Area	Area Name	Total	Speak Spanish or Spanish Creole	Speak other Indo European language	Speak Asian or Pacific Island language	Speak other language
MI	Alger County	110	50	25	0	40
MI	Allegan County	1085	840	140	80	25
MI	Alpena County	255	30	205	0	20
MI	Antrim County	70	(D)	40	0	(D)
MI	Arenac County	100	40	35	15	10
MI	Baraga County	125	(D)	0	(D)	100
MI	Barry County	195	85	105	(D)	(D)
MI	Bay County	945	395	465	80	0
MI	Benzie County	100	60	(D)	0	(D)
MI	Berrien County	1695	815	745	105	25
MI	Branch County	335	140	130	20	45
MI	Calhoun County	965	655	210	100	0
MI	Cass County	285	135	105	(D)	(D)
MI	Charlevoix County	160	55	85	(D)	(D)
MI	Cheboygan County	150	50	55	(D)	(D)
MI	Chippewa County	330	130	95	45	55
MI	Clare County	220	65	140	(D)	(D)
MI	Clinton County	335	185	130	20	0
MI	Crawford County	70	(D)	40	(D)	0
MI	Delta County	130	10	65	10	45
MI	Dickinson County	175	35	125	(D)	(D)
MI	Eaton County	850	345	260	205	40
MI	Emmet County	210	85	100	(D)	(D)
MI	Genesee County	3015	1245	1045	310	415
MI	Gladwin County	230	35	180	10	4
MI	Gogebic County	150	(D)	65	(D)	55
MI	Grand Traverse County	425	170	175	15	60
MI	Gratiot County	365	230	70	50	15
MI	Hillsdale County	240	90	120	(D)	(D)
MI	Houghton County	415	45	70	35	265

State/ Area	Area Name	Total	Speak Spanish or Spanish Creole	Speak other Indo European language	Speak Asian or Pacific Island language	Speak other language
MI	Huron County	265	80	165	(D)	(D)
MI	Ingham County	3550	1665	965	705	215
MI	Ionia County	360	240	75	15	25
MI	Iosco County	160	60	85	(D)	(D)
MI	Iron County	85	20	40	4	20
MI	Isabella County	405	240	85	55	20
MI	Jackson County	995	590	290	100	20
MI	Kalamazoo County	2125	995	750	305	75
MI	Kalkaska County	20	10	10	0	0
MI	Kent County	7885	4495	1500	1610	280
MI	Keweenaw County	15	(D)	(D)	0	10
MI	Lake County	65	40	(D)	(D)	0
MI	Lapeer County	620	365	200	10	45
MI	Leelanau County	155	85	50	(D)	(D)
MI	Lenawee County	1005	765	140	70	30
MI	Livingston County	795	220	355	165	55
MI	Luce County	45	40	(D)	(D)	(D)
MI	Mackinac County	50	20	25	(D)	(D)
MI	Macomb County	17770	1365	11020	1975	3410
MI	Manistee County	185	70	90	(D)	(D)
MI	Marquette County	470	105	130	40	200
MI	Mason County	200	115	70	(D)	(D)
MI	Mecosta County	370	115	225	10	20
MI	Menominee County	110	25	70	(D)	(D)
MI	Midland County	485	205	150	(D)	(D)
MI	Missaukee County	60	30	25	4	0
MI	Monroe County	845	265	405	70	105
MI	Montcalm County	420	195	180	15	30
MI	Montmorency County	55	20	35	0	0
MI	Muskegon County	1395	690	535	105	60
MI	Newaygo County	295	185	95	(D)	(D)

State/ Area	Area Name	Total	Speak Spanish or Spanish Creole	Speak other Indo European language	Speak Asian or Pacific Island language	Speak other language
MI	Oakland County	23165	3960	9105	4175	5920
MI	Oceana County	295	265	(D)	0	(D)
MI	Ogemaw County	115	35	45	20	15
MI	Ontonagon County	95	(D)	(D)	0	80
MI	Osceola County	130	(D)	95	(D)	0
MI	Oscoda County	125	(D)	(D)	0	0
MI	Otsego County	125	35	75	4	10
MI	Ottawa County	2990	1705	450	755	85
MI	Presque Isle County	130	4	125	0	0
MI	Roscommon County	140	60	65	(D)	(D)
MI	Saginaw County	2115	1225	660	125	105
MI	St. Clair County	1275	500	575	65	130
MI	St. Joseph County	830	315	460	(D)	(D)
MI	Sanilac County	445	165	250	(D)	(D)
MI	Schoolcraft County	55	(D)	30	0	(D)
MI	Shiawassee County	340	195	130	(D)	(D)
MI	Tuscola County	525	195	275	40	15
MI	Van Buren County	1185	850	270	30	40
MI	Washtenaw County	3930	1160	1290	1050	425
MI	Wayne County	36105	10975	13095	2515	9520
MI	Wexford County	180	25	120	15	20
MN	Minnesota	56475	18135	16800	17395	4150
MN	Aitkin County	105	(D)	35	(D)	40
MN	Anoka County	2500	790	825	715	170
MN	Becker County	235	50	60	15	110
MN	Beltrami County	370	85	90	60	135
MN	Benton County	285	165	100	(D)	(D)
MN	Big Stone County	85	(D)	70	(D)	0
MN	Blue Earth County	405	220	90	85	15
MN	Brown County	300	85	215	(D)	(D)
MN	Carlton County	280	50	70	20	135

State/ Area	Area Name	Total	Speak Spanish or Spanish Creole	Speak other Indo European language	Speak Asian or Pacific Island language	Speak other language
MN	Carver County	590	190	240	160	0
MN	Cass County	155	65	45	10	35
MN	Chippewa County	65	30	30	(D)	(D)
MN	Chisago County	180	50	75	20	40
MN	Clay County	735	355	310	70	0
MN	Clearwater County	45	10	30	(D)	(D)
MN	Cook County	35	10	10	0	15
MN	Cottonwood County	150	10	115	25	0
MN	Crow Wing County	275	145	90	25	15
MN	Dakota County	4065	1090	1260	1455	255
MN	Dodge County	115	90	(D)	(D)	0
MN	Douglas County	210	70	90	30	20
MN	Faribault County	80	50	25	(D)	(D)
MN	Fillmore County	315	(D)	270	(D)	0
MN	Freeborn County	410	275	(D)	(D)	0
MN	Goodhue County	220	110	80	20	10
MN	Grant County	40	(D)	25	0	(D)
MN	Hennepin County	17435	4485	4780	6710	1460
MN	Houston County	100	40	45	15	0
MN	Hubbard County	105	30	35	15	20
MN	Isanti County	150	70	65	(D)	(D)
MN	Itasca County	230	35	95	25	75
MN	Jackson County	40	20	(D)	(D)	0
MN	Kanabec County	85	(D)	50	20	(D)
MN	Kandiyohi County	525	420	95	(D)	(D)
MN	Kittson County	40	10	30	0	0
MN	Koochiching County	70	40	(D)	(D)	20
MN	Lac qui Parle County	45	15	30	0	0
MN	Lake County	70	(D)	30	(D)	30
MN	Lake of the Woods County	25	(D)	(D)	0	0

State/ Area	Area Name	Total	Speak Spanish or Spanish Creole	Speak other Indo European language	Speak Asian or Pacific Island language	Speak other language
MN	Le Sueur County	255	115	125	(D)	(D)
MN	Lincoln County	40	(D)	25	(D)	(D)
MN	Lyon County	235	120	40	30	45
MN	McLeod County	460	230	170	(D)	(D)
MN	Mahnomen County	35	(D)	(D)	10	15
MN	Marshall County	135	(D)	105	(D)	0
MN	Martin County	105	50	40	(D)	(D)
MN	Meeker County	115	40	55	(D)	(D)
MN	Mille Lacs County	170	85	60	(D)	(D)
MN	Morrison County	270	110	135	30	0
MN	Mower County	415	265	90	(D)	(D)
MN	Murray County	80	25	45	(D)	(D)
MN	Nicollet County	220	120	75	30	0
MN	Nobles County	360	230	(D)	70	(D)
MN	Norman County	65	25	40	(D)	(D)
MN	Olmsted County	1345	380	275	605	85
MN	Otter Tail County	485	210	195	(D)	(D)
MN	Pennington County	80	15	60	(D)	(D)
MN	Pine County	235	155	50	(D)	(D)
MN	Pipestone County	75	(D)	45	15	(D)
MN	Polk County	360	160	185	(D)	(D)
MN	Pope County	55	(D)	40	0	(D)
MN	Ramsey County	9755	2620	1605	5090	440
MN	Red Lake County	60	(D)	40	(D)	20
MN	Redwood County	65	40	20	(D)	(D)
MN	Renville County	175	115	(D)	(D)	0
MN	Rice County	600	300	165	90	45
MN	Rock County	70	(D)	45	(D)	0
MN	Roseau County	155	(D)	75	60	(D)
MN	St. Louis County	1590	425	610	215	340
MN	Scott County	825	265	285	230	45

State/ Area	Area Name	Total	Speak Spanish or Spanish Creole	Speak other Indo European language	Speak Asian or Pacific Island language	Speak other language
MN	Sherburne County	450	200	170	(D)	(D)
MN	Sibley County	285	(D)	155	(D)	0
MN	Stearns County	1345	455	685	190	15
MN	Steele County	285	195	50	35	0
MN	Stevens County	60	40	20	0	0
MN	Swift County	190	(D)	65	(D)	0
MN	Todd County	180	95	(D)	0	(D)
MN	Traverse County	25	15	10	0	0
MN	Wabasha County	85	55	20	(D)	(D)
MN	Wadena County	200	20	25	15	135
MN	Waseca County	115	(D)	55	0	(D)
MN	Washington County	1825	540	515	720	50
MN	Watonwan County	220	190	25	4	0
MN	Wilkin County	50	35	15	0	0
MN	Winona County	485	260	175	(D)	(D)
MN	Wright County	540	290	200	25	25
MN	Yellow Medicine County	80	50	20	(D)	(D)
MS	Mississippi	18180	9810	3905	2660	1805
MS	Adams County	415	305	45	65	0
MS	Alcorn County	165	115	35	(D)	(D)
MS	Amite County	55	35	10	10	0
MS	Attala County	95	65	(D)	0	(D)
MS	Benton County	35	(D)	(D)	0	0
MS	Bolivar County	345	220	70	30	25
MS	Calhoun County	60	(D)	(D)	0	0
MS	Carroll County	35	10	(D)	(D)	0
MS	Chickasaw County	70	40	30	0	0
MS	Choctaw County	55	35	(D)	0	(D)
MS	Claiborne County	70	55	15	0	0
MS	Clarke County	60	35	(D)	(D)	0

State/ Area	Area Name	Total	Speak Spanish or Spanish Creole	Speak other Indo European language	Speak Asian or Pacific Island language	Speak other language
MS	Clay County	95	65	(D)	(D)	0
MS	Coahoma County	125	45	50	(D)	(D)
MS	Copiah County	125	(D)	60	0	(D)
MS	Covington County	70	60	0	(D)	(D)
MS	DeSoto County	745	425	155	(D)	(D)
MS	Forrest County	405	240	120	45	0
MS	Franklin County	65	50	(D)	(D)	0
MS	George County	100	65	(D)	(D)	0
MS	Greene County	105	80	25	0	0
MS	Grenada County	70	40	(D)	(D)	0
MS	Hancock County	280	135	95	(D)	(D)
MS	Harrison County	2230	845	320	1025	35
MS	Hinds County	1610	950	440	120	100
MS	Holmes County	100	55	(D)	0	(D)
MS	Humphreys County	70	(D)	35	(D)	0
MS	Issaquena County	0	0	0	0	0
MS	Itawamba County	80	50	(D)	(D)	0
MS	Jackson County	1110	530	(D)	285	(D)
MS	Jasper County	90	(D)	(D)	0	0
MS	Jefferson County	65	35	(D)	(D)	0
MS	Jefferson Davis County	30	10	10	(D)	(D)
MS	Jones County	295	190	55	(D)	(D)
MS	Kemper County	140	40	(D)	(D)	70
MS	Lafayette County	360	280	40	(D)	(D)
MS	Lamar County	240	110	90	40	0
MS	Lauderdale County	270	170	60	(D)	(D)
MS	Lawrence County	30	15	(D)	0	(D)
MS	Leake County	290	120	(D)	(D)	150
MS	Lee County	365	230	110	20	0
MS	Leflore County	140	95	(D)	(D)	(D)

State/ Area	Area Name	Total	Speak Spanish or Spanish Creole	Speak other Indo European language	Speak Asian or Pacific Island language	Speak other language
MS	Lincoln County	70	(D)	(D)	0	0
MS	Lowndes County	210	145	35	(D)	(D)
MS	Madison County	590	330	(D)	125	(D)
MS	Marion County	105	65	20	(D)	(D)
MS	Marshall County	160	125	(D)	20	(D)
MS	Monroe County	110	(D)	55	(D)	0
MS	Montgomery County	90	65	25	0	0
MS	Neshoba County	890	35	(D)	(D)	810
MS	Newton County	200	30	(D)	(D)	145
MS	Noxubee County	65	20	45	0	0
MS	Oktibbeha County	290	145	80	(D)	(D)
MS	Panola County	185	125	30	(D)	(D)
MS	Pearl River County	335	160	150	(D)	(D)
MS	Perry County	45	40	(D)	(D)	0
MS	Pike County	295	180	(D)	0	(D)
MS	Pontotoc County	110	80	(D)	(D)	0
MS	Prentiss County	100	60	20	20	0
MS	Quitman County	30	20	(D)	(D)	0
MS	Rankin County	560	345	95	90	30
MS	Scott County	280	180	10	(D)	(D)
MS	Sharkey County	35	20	(D)	(D)	0
MS	Simpson County	100	55	(D)	0	(D)
MS	Smith County	60	50	(D)	0	(D)
MS	Stone County	135	80	55	0	0
MS	Sunflower County	170	130	25	(D)	(D)
MS	Tallahatchie County	65	(D)	35	(D)	0
MS	Tate County	120	95	(D)	(D)	0
MS	Tippah County	75	(D)	(D)	0	0
MS	Tishomingo County	100	55	10	(D)	(D)
MS	Tunica County	35	(D)	(D)	0	0
MS	Union County	195	170	(D)	(D)	0

State/Area	Area Name	Total	Speak Spanish or Spanish Creole	Speak other Indo European language	Speak Asian or Pacific Island language	Speak other language
MS	Walthall County	70	55	15	0	0
MS	Warren County	200	100	50	(D)	(D)
MS	Washington County	355	180	100	(D)	(D)
MS	Wayne County	55	(D)	30	(D)	0
MS	Webster County	80	55	(D)	(D)	0
MS	Wilkinson County	105	75	(D)	0	(D)
MS	Winston County	130	75	20	0	35
MS	Yalobusha County	50	30	15	(D)	(D)
MS	Yazoo County	175	125	25	(D)	(D)
MO	Missouri	44510	18870	16290	7930	1420
MO	Adair County	225	140	65	25	0
MO	Andrew County	25	(D)	(D)	0	0
MO	Atchison County	10	(D)	(D)	0	0
MO	Audrain County	320	55	235	(D)	(D)
MO	Barry County	260	200	45	(D)	(D)
MO	Barton County	65	20	15	10	15
MO	Bates County	65	(D)	35	(D)	0
MO	Benton County	75	40	25	(D)	(D)
MO	Bollinger County	15	15	(D)	0	(D)
MO	Boone County	955	305	325	275	45
MO	Buchanan County	695	455	180	60	0
MO	Butler County	285	105	110	(D)	(D)
MO	Caldwell County	20	15	(D)	(D)	0
MO	Callaway County	170	65	(D)	50	(D)
MO	Camden County	165	100	60	4	0
MO	Cape Girardeau County	300	155	120	20	4
MO	Carroll County	75	(D)	70	(D)	0
MO	Carter County	20	(D)	10	(D)	0
MO	Cass County	385	225	110	(D)	(D)
MO	Cedar County	130	45	(D)	35	(D)

State/ Area	Area Name	Total	Speak Spanish or Spanish Creole	Speak other Indo European language	Speak Asian or Pacific Island language	Speak other language
MO	Chariton County	25	10	(D)	(D)	(D)
MO	Christian County	175	95	45	(D)	(D)
MO	Clark County	70	(D)	50	(D)	0
MO	Clay County	1225	550	445	(D)	(D)
MO	Clinton County	80	45	20	15	0
MO	Cole County	555	305	145	55	45
MO	Cooper County	100	55	30	(D)	(D)
MO	Crawford County	50	40	(D)	(D)	0
MO	Dade County	25	20	(D)	(D)	0
MO	Dallas County	135	20	115	0	0
MO	Daviess County	195	(D)	190	(D)	0
MO	DeKalb County	105	60	(D)	(D)	0
MO	Dent County	85	40	40	0	0
MO	Douglas County	90	45	25	(D)	(D)
MO	Dunklin County	190	100	(D)	(D)	0
MO	Franklin County	490	250	135	(D)	(D)
MO	Gasconade County	135	(D)	100	(D)	0
MO	Gentry County	4	(D)	(D)	0	0
MO	Greene County	1680	875	410	345	45
MO	Grundy County	100	45	35	15	0
MO	Harrison County	30	(D)	25	(D)	0
MO	Henry County	95	40	45	10	0
MO	Hickory County	45	25	20	0	0
MO	Holt County	15	15	(D)	(D)	0
MO	Howard County	55	40	(D)	(D)	0
MO	Howell County	150	70	(D)	50	(D)
MO	Iron County	35	15	10	10	0
MO	Jackson County	8005	4595	1885	1300	225
MO	Jasper County	760	470	110	160	20
MO	Jefferson County	1055	485	415	115	40
MO	Johnson County	310	125	100	85	0

State/ Area	Area Name	Total	Speak Spanish or Spanish Creole	Speak other Indo European language	Speak Asian or Pacific Island language	Speak other language
MO	Knox County	15	(D)	(D)	0	0
MO	Laclede County	145	75	55	15	0
MO	Lafayette County	155	75	70	10	0
MO	Lawrence County	230	130	(D)	(D)	0
MO	Lewis County	100	(D)	80	(D)	0
MO	Lincoln County	145	70	65	(D)	(D)
MO	Linn County	55	(D)	20	(D)	0
MO	Livingston County	50	(D)	20	0	(D)
MO	McDonald County	245	215	(D)	10	(D)
MO	Macon County	105	(D)	65	(D)	0
MO	Madison County	35	30	10	0	0
MO	Maries County	35	15	20	0	0
MO	Marion County	75	50	(D)	(D)	0
MO	Mercer County	15	(D)	(D)	0	0
MO	Miller County	190	75	85	(D)	(D)
MO	Mississippi County	10	(D)	0	(D)	0
MO	Moniteau County	190	(D)	145	(D)	0
MO	Monroe County	100	(D)	90	(D)	0
MO	Montgomery County	85	15	25	45	0
MO	Morgan County	340	45	290	(D)	(D)
MO	New Madrid County	55	25	30	0	0
MO	Newton County	285	175	75	35	0
MO	Nodaway County	195	115	60	(D)	(D)
MO	Oregon County	15	(D)	10	(D)	0
MO	Osage County	75	(D)	55	(D)	0
MO	Ozark County	40	10	10	15	0
MO	Pemiscot County	120	105	(D)	(D)	(D)
MO	Perry County	225	65	135	25	0
MO	Pettis County	355	210	130	15	0
MO	Phelps County	215	85	90	(D)	(D)
MO	Pike County	155	60	95	0	0

State/ Area	Area Name	Total	Speak Spanish or Spanish Creole	Speak other Indo European language	Speak Asian or Pacific Island language	Speak other language
MO	Platte County	680	255	(D)	245	(D)
MO	Polk County	200	(D)	120	(D)	0
MO	Pulaski County	635	235	145	240	15
MO	Putnam County	25	20	(D)	(D)	0
MO	Ralls County	35	(D)	10	(D)	0
MO	Randolph County	160	115	(D)	(D)	0
MO	Ray County	100	75	(D)	0	(D)
MO	Reynolds County	15	4	(D)	(D)	0
MO	Ripley County	65	35	(D)	(D)	0
MO	St. Charles County	1605	740	635	185	45
MO	St. Clair County	15	15	(D)	(D)	0
MO	Ste. Genevieve County	75	(D)	55	0	(D)
MO	St. Francois County	340	135	170	20	20
MO	St. Louis County	9850	2770	4330	2340	410
MO	Saline County	130	85	20	20	0
MO	Schuyler County	4	(D)	0	0	0
MO	Scotland County	45	(D)	(D)	0	0
MO	Scott County	115	(D)	80	(D)	0
MO	Shannon County	25	(D)	(D)	0	0
MO	Shelby County	15	(D)	10	(D)	0
MO	Stoddard County	115	(D)	50	(D)	0
MO	Stone County	140	50	40	(D)	(D)
MO	Sullivan County	95	90	4	0	0
MO	Taney County	330	175	115	(D)	(D)
MO	Texas County	80	25	40	15	0
MO	Vernon County	95	20	25	50	0
MO	Warren County	140	90	40	(D)	(D)
MO	Washington County	100	45	35	(D)	(D)
MO	Wayne County	35	30	4	0	0
MO	Webster County	365	40	310	(D)	(D)

State/ Area	Area Name	Total	Speak Spanish or Spanish Creole	Speak other Indo European language	Speak Asian or Pacific Island language	Speak other language
MO	Worth County	4	(D)	0	0	0
MO	Wright County	65	40	(D)	(D)	0
MO	St. Louis city	4420	1240	1795	1100	285
MT	Montana	8545	2260	3510	600	2180
MT	Beaverhead County	35	20	15	0	0
MT	Big Horn County	915	40	(D)	(D)	845
MT	Blaine County	95	10	50	0	40
MT	Broadwater County	35	(D)	25	(D)	(D)
MT	Carbon County	60	15	35	0	10
MT	Carter County	4	(D)	(D)	(D)	0
MT	Cascade County	725	185	390	70	80
MT	Chouteau County	60	(D)	10	(D)	30
MT	Custer County	90	25	20	15	30
MT	Daniels County	10	(D)	(D)	0	0
MT	Dawson County	100	(D)	75	0	(D)
MT	Deer Lodge County	95	40	50	(D)	(D)
MT	Fallon County	10	(D)	(D)	0	0
MT	Fergus County	45	30	15	0	0
MT	Flathead County	315	75	170	40	30
MT	Gallatin County	540	330	110	(D)	(D)
MT	Garfield County	4	0	4	0	0
MT	Glacier County	415	0	250	15	150
MT	Golden Valley County	4	0	(D)	(D)	0
MT	Granite County	10	(D)	(D)	(D)	0
MT	Hill County	340	10	135	15	180
MT	Jefferson County	55	35	15	(D)	(D)
MT	Judith Basin County	20	(D)	(D)	0	0
MT	Lake County	190	20	30	25	120
MT	Lewis and Clark County	325	115	200	(D)	(D)
MT	Liberty County	120	0	(D)	(D)	0

State/ Area	Area Name	Total	Speak Spanish or Spanish Creole	Speak other Indo European language	Speak Asian or Pacific Island language	Speak other language
MT	Lincoln County	150	(D)	85	0	(D)
MT	McCone County	4	0	(D)	0	0
MT	Madison County	45	30	15	0	0
MT	Meagher County	4	0	(D)	0	(D)
MT	Mineral County	30	(D)	15	(D)	(D)
MT	Missoula County	780	300	265	165	50
MT	Musselshell County	25	(D)	15	0	(D)
MT	Park County	45	30	(D)	(D)	0
MT	Petroleum County	0	0	0	0	0
MT	Phillips County	4	0	(D)	0	(D)
MT	Pondera County	130	(D)	105	(D)	10
MT	Powder River County	4	0	0	(D)	(D)
MT	Powell County	35	(D)	(D)	0	0
MT	Prairie County	10	0	10	0	0
MT	Ravalli County	170	55	85	(D)	(D)
MT	Richland County	60	20	40	0	0
MT	Roosevelt County	95	(D)	35	(D)	55
MT	Rosebud County	260	35	(D)	(D)	210
MT	Sanders County	80	25	30	15	10
MT	Sheridan County	40	15	25	0	0
MT	Silver Bow County	260	55	140	(D)	(D)
MT	Stillwater County	60	20	30	(D)	(D)
MT	Sweet Grass County	25	(D)	15	(D)	0
MT	Teton County	180	(D)	165	0	(D)
MT	Toole County	130	(D)	110	(D)	10
MT	Treasure County	4	(D)	0	0	0
MT	Valley County	20	(D)	(D)	0	10
MT	Wheatland County	65	(D)	(D)	0	0
MT	Wibaux County	4	0	(D)	0	0
MT	Yellowstone County	1190	535	425	65	165
NE	Nebraska	18860	11265	4110	3000	485

State/ Area	Area Name	Total	Speak Spanish or Spanish Creole	Speak other Indo European language	Speak Asian or Pacific Island language	Speak other language
NE	Adams County	245	115	80	50	0
NE	Antelope County	40	30	(D)	(D)	0
NE	Arthur County	0	0	0	0	0
NE	Banner County	4	4	0	0	0
NE	Blaine County	4	(D)	0	0	0
NE	Boone County	15	(D)	(D)	0	0
NE	Box Butte County	95	80	(D)	(D)	0
NE	Boyd County	20	15	(D)	(D)	0
NE	Brown County	10	4	(D)	(D)	0
NE	Buffalo County	400	305	70	(D)	(D)
NE	Burt County	20	(D)	(D)	0	0
NE	Butler County	110	15	90	0	0
NE	Cass County	115	85	20	4	0
NE	Cedar County	40	25	(D)	0	(D)
NE	Chase County	20	(D)	(D)	0	0
NE	Cherry County	40	15	(D)	(D)	10
NE	Cheyenne County	50	35	(D)	0	(D)
NE	Clay County	85	30	50	0	0
NE	Colfax County	475	400	(D)	(D)	0
NE	Cuming County	95	(D)	(D)	0	0
NE	Custer County	65	35	(D)	(D)	(D)
NE	Dakota County	590	475	15	95	0
NE	Dawes County	85	60	(D)	0	(D)
NE	Dawson County	670	610	(D)	50	(D)
NE	Deuel County	10	(D)	(D)	0	0
NE	Dixon County	65	55	(D)	(D)	0
NE	Dodge County	295	230	60	(D)	(D)
NE	Douglas County	5470	3190	1325	805	150
NE	Dundy County	4	(D)	0	0	(D)
NE	Fillmore County	40	25	15	0	0
NE	Franklin County	4	(D)	(D)	0	0

State/ Area	Area Name	Total	Speak Spanish or Spanish Creole	Speak other Indo European language	Speak Asian or Pacific Island language	Speak other language
NE	Frontier County	4	(D)	o	(D)	o
NE	Furnas County	30	25	(D)	(D)	o
NE	Gage County	135	35	100	o	o
NE	Garden County	10	(D)	o	(D)	o
NE	Garfield County	4	(D)	(D)	o	o
NE	Gosper County	4	o	(D)	o	o
NE	Grant County	o	o	o	o	o
NE	Greeley County	15	(D)	(D)	o	o
NE	Hall County	835	690	(D)	110	(D)
NE	Hamilton County	40	(D)	20	(D)	o
NE	Harlan County	10	10	o	o	o
NE	Hayes County	15	(D)	(D)	o	o
NE	Hitchcock County	20	(D)	(D)	o	o
NE	Holt County	40	(D)	o	(D)	o
NE	Hooker County	o	o	o	o	o
NE	Howard County	15	(D)	10	(D)	o
NE	Jefferson County	25	o	25	o	o
NE	Johnson County	65	30	(D)	20	(D)
NE	Kearney County	30	30	o	o	o
NE	Keith County	55	15	(D)	20	(D)
NE	Keya Paha County	20	(D)	(D)	o	o
NE	Kimball County	25	(D)	o	(D)	(D)
NE	Knox County	90	(D)	70	(D)	o
NE	Lancaster County	3070	1195	665	1085	120
NE	Lincoln County	240	205	10	(D)	(D)
NE	Logan County	4	(D)	o	o	o
NE	Loup County	4	(D)	o	o	o
NE	McPherson County	o	o	o	o	o
NE	Madison County	600	530	45	(D)	(D)
NE	Merrick County	60	35	(D)	(D)	o
NE	Morrill County	100	70	(D)	(D)	o

State/ Area	Area Name	Total	Speak Spanish or Spanish Creole	Speak other Indo European language	Speak Asian or Pacific Island language	Speak other language
NE	Nance County	45	20	25	0	0
NE	Nemaha County	65	(D)	30	(D)	0
NE	Nuckolls County	15	(D)	(D)	0	0
NE	Otoe County	65	50	15	0	0
NE	Pawnee County	10	(D)	(D)	(D)	0
NE	Perkins County	10	(D)	(D)	0	0
NE	Phelps County	75	50	25	0	0
NE	Pierce County	20	(D)	(D)	0	0
NE	Platte County	345	255	65	(D)	(D)
NE	Polk County	25	10	15	0	0
NE	Red Willow County	55	(D)	0	(D)	0
NE	Richardson County	40	(D)	(D)	0	0
NE	Rock County	4	(D)	0	0	0
NE	Saline County	290	115	115	(D)	(D)
NE	Sarpy County	1355	545	(D)	445	(D)
NE	Saunders County	200	50	145	(D)	(D)
NE	Scotts Bluff County	880	785	50	30	20
NE	Seward County	80	30	45	0	0
NE	Sheridan County	35	15	(D)	(D)	10
NE	Sherman County	30	10	20	0	0
NE	Sioux County	4	(D)	(D)	0	0
NE	Stanton County	30	15	(D)	(D)	0
NE	Thayer County	30	15	10	(D)	(D)
NE	Thomas County	10	10	0	0	0
NE	Thurston County	45	10	15	0	20
NE	Valley County	35	4	25	0	0
NE	Washington County	95	50	10	35	0
NE	Wayne County	80	40	35	(D)	(D)
NE	Webster County	20	10	(D)	(D)	0
NE	Wheeler County	10	10	0	0	0
NE	York County	115	(D)	60	(D)	0

State/ Area	Area Name	Total	Speak Spanish or Spanish Creole	Speak other Indo European language	Speak Asian or Pacific Island language	Speak other language
NV	Nevada	63085	40130	6500	14395	2060
NV	Churchill County	320	145	50	95	35
NV	Clark County	48520	30540	4735	11840	1410
NV	Douglas County	575	425	85	(D)	(D)
NV	Elko County	1200	890	45	40	225
NV	Esmeralda County	20	(D)	0	0	(D)
NV	Eureka County	20	10	(D)	(D)	(D)
NV	Humboldt County	575	455	(D)	(D)	105
NV	Lander County	195	165	0	(D)	(D)
NV	Lincoln County	15	15	0	0	0
NV	Lyon County	560	450	80	(D)	(D)
NV	Mineral County	45	30	0	0	15
NV	Nye County	330	185	110	(D)	(D)
NV	Pershing County	165	150	(D)	0	(D)
NV	Storey County	35	(D)	(D)	(D)	0
NV	Washoe County	9430	5890	1175	2185	180
NV	White Pine County	150	70	55	(D)	(D)
NV	Carson City	920	670	(D)	125	(D)
NV	New Hampshire	15575	3365	10250	1505	450
NH	Belknap County	605	125	430	(D)	(D)
NH	Carroll County	220	30	170	(D)	(D)
NH	Cheshire County	545	135	330	40	40
NH	Coos County	1035	(D)	995	(D)	0
NH	Grafton County	520	125	290	(D)	(D)
NH	Hillsborough County	7080	1695	4585	625	175
NH	Merrimack County	1405	275	990	95	50
NH	Rockingham County	2685	700	1510	405	70
NH	Strafford County	1235	215	785	205	30
NH	Sullivan County	240	(D)	175	(D)	30
NJ	New Jersey	377190	196955	119665	47305	13265
NJ	Atlantic County	10025	5250	2605	1965	210

State/ Area	Area Name	Total	Speak Spanish or Spanish Creole	Speak other Indo European language	Speak Asian or Pacific Island language	Speak other language
NJ	Bergen County	48050	13955	20670	11410	2010
NJ	Burlington County	8075	3245	2835	1685	315
NJ	Camden County	17025	10140	3660	2985	240
NJ	Cape May County	1640	830	660	80	65
NJ	Cumberland County	7135	6025	855	190	65
NJ	Essex County	42710	24590	14585	2725	815
NJ	Gloucester County	3020	1020	1400	510	95
NJ	Hudson County	66595	48775	11250	4455	2115
NJ	Hunterdon County	1345	425	725	165	35
NJ	Mercer County	11355	5580	3850	1525	400
NJ	Middlesex County	37580	15255	13100	7005	2220
NJ	Monmouth County	13780	4815	5550	2880	540
NJ	Morris County	14055	5000	5490	3245	325
NJ	Ocean County	10020	3980	5055	595	395
NJ	Passaic County	38440	25240	9420	1670	2115
NJ	Salem County	975	635	275	(D)	(D)
NJ	Somerset County	9225	3075	3500	2045	605
NJ	Sussex County	1755	525	950	170	110
NJ	Union County	33330	18230	12655	1895	555
NJ	Warren County	1050	365	585	55	45
NM	New Mexico	108925	79605	2685	2205	24430
NM	Bernalillo County	23275	19330	1170	1350	1420
NM	Catron County	115	90	(D)	(D)	20
NM	Chaves County	3615	3470	60	55	30
NM	Cibola County	2185	790	(D)	(D)	1365
NM	Colfax County	590	545	(D)	0	(D)
NM	Curry County	1760	1515	(D)	155	(D)
NM	De Baca County	175	(D)	0	0	(D)
NM	Dona Ana County	14640	14325	150	105	60
NM	Eddy County	3010	2895	85	(D)	(D)
NM	Grant County	2205	2150	(D)	(D)	25

State/ Area	Area Name	Total	Speak Spanish or Spanish Creole	Speak other Indo European language	Speak Asian or Pacific Island language	Speak other language
NM	Guadalupe County	485	(D)	0	0	(D)
NM	Harding County	65	65	0	0	0
NM	Hidalgo County	495	(D)	(D)	0	0
NM	Lea County	2455	2415	(D)	0	(D)
NM	Lincoln County	695	655	25	(D)	(D)
NM	Los Alamos County	290	165	(D)	65	(D)
NM	Luna County	1715	1705	(D)	(D)	(D)
NM	McKinley County	10835	720	45	30	10040
NM	Mora County	1010	(D)	0	0	(D)
NM	Otero County	2580	2140	150	110	180
NM	Quay County	425	395	(D)	(D)	(D)
NM	Rio Arriba County	4405	4130	15	0	260
NM	Roosevelt County	860	825	(D)	(D)	0
NM	Sandoval County	4715	1605	190	80	2840
NM	San Juan County	8210	1220	45	25	6925
NM	San Miguel County	3100	3020	(D)	0	(D)
NM	Santa Fe County	5990	5455	305	100	135
NM	Sierra County	310	285	15	(D)	(D)
NM	Socorro County	1555	945	(D)	0	(D)
NM	Taos County	2755	2545	(D)	(D)	195
NM	Torrance County	690	660	(D)	(D)	15
NM	Union County	205	205	0	0	0
NM	Valencia County	3505	3210	90	35	175
NY	New York	1000175	488250	328230	153960	29735
NY	Albany County	5075	1365	2725	770	215
NY	Allegany County	320	100	190	(D)	(D)
NY	Bronx County	142620	123180	13085	3990	2365
NY	Broome County	2960	570	1695	565	125
NY	Cattaraugus County	955	215	635	45	60
NY	Cayuga County	705	260	420	(D)	(D)
NY	Chautauqua County	2460	1535	840	45	40

State/ Area	Area Name	Total	Speak Spanish or Spanish Creole	Speak other Indo European language	Speak Asian or Pacific Island language	Speak other language
NY	Chemung County	580	185	315	(D)	(D)
NY	Chenango County	330	100	195	(D)	(D)
NY	Clinton County	810	225	495	90	0
NY	Columbia County	665	215	420	15	15
NY	Cortland County	355	(D)	210	0	(D)
NY	Delaware County	505	120	345	25	15
NY	Dutchess County	4760	1980	1920	580	285
NY	Erie County	16695	6290	8270	1200	935
NY	Essex County	440	275	135	30	0
NY	Franklin County	500	305	180	(D)	(D)
NY	Fulton County	500	155	320	25	0
NY	Genesee County	385	100	210	65	15
NY	Greene County	895	255	595	30	20
NY	Hamilton County	20	10	10	(D)	(D)
NY	Herkimer County	650	125	510	(D)	(D)
NY	Jefferson County	1285	735	365	150	35
NY	Kings County	239625	88425	102455	38515	10225
NY	Lewis County	150	40	85	(D)	(D)
NY	Livingston County	490	255	135	(D)	(D)
NY	Madison County	500	200	200	60	40
NY	Monroe County	18105	7925	6950	2670	565
NY	Montgomery County	1285	800	460	(D)	(D)
NY	Nassau County	49135	17035	23215	7125	1755
NY	New York County	124230	83935	14205	23845	2240
NY	Niagara County	2620	650	1765	120	90
NY	Oneida County	3685	1290	1880	465	50
NY	Onondaga County	6945	2015	3385	1245	300
NY	Ontario County	830	455	310	(D)	(D)
NY	Orange County	12115	4730	6390	635	365
NY	Orleans County	325	205	95	(D)	(D)
NY	Oswego County	835	325	450	40	20

State/ Area	Area Name	Total	Speak Spanish or Spanish Creole	Speak other Indo European language	Speak Asian or Pacific Island language	Speak other language
NY	Otsego County	510	165	320	15	10
NY	Putnam County	1865	615	1100	85	65
NY	Queens County	225530	88035	75340	56450	5705
NY	Rensselaer County	1795	585	860	210	140
NY	Richmond County	21290	6310	9270	4595	1115
NY	Rockland County	13035	3620	7340	1520	560
NY	St. Lawrence County	985	345	550	50	35
NY	Saratoga County	1540	440	960	(D)	(D)
NY	Schenectady County	2730	660	1690	190	195
NY	Schoharie County	250	(D)	195	0	(D)
NY	Schuyler County	120	30	80	(D)	(D)
NY	Seneca County	360	80	250	30	0
NY	Steuben County	665	175	430	45	15
NY	Suffolk County	37565	18825	14390	3615	730
NY	Sullivan County	2235	1165	930	95	45
NY	Tioga County	270	(D)	115	80	(D)
NY	Tompkins County	1250	350	420	455	25
NY	Ulster County	2980	1235	1480	205	60
NY	Warren County	545	165	275	75	30
NY	Washington County	360	190	140	(D)	(D)
NY	Wayne County	740	335	320	(D)	(D)
NY	Westchester County	37590	17895	15275	3340	1080
NY	Wyoming County	205	135	(D)	(D)	0
NY	Yates County	420	40	370	(D)	(D)
NC	North Carolina	80300	48210	16200	13395	2495
NC	Alamance County	1390	970	250	140	30
NC	Alexander County	195	125	(D)	(D)	0
NC	Alleghany County	65	25	(D)	(D)	0
NC	Anson County	180	115	45	(D)	(D)
NC	Ashe County	125	65	40	15	0
NC	Avery County	165	100	35	30	0

State/ Area	Area Name	Total	Speak Spanish or Spanish Creole	Speak other Indo European language	Speak Asian or Pacific Island language	Speak other language
NC	Beaufort County	255	210	(D)	(D)	(D)
NC	Bertie County	70	45	15	(D)	(D)
NC	Bladen County	280	235	(D)	(D)	20
NC	Brunswick County	475	275	180	(D)	(D)
NC	Buncombe County	1595	970	470	110	40
NC	Burke County	815	340	(D)	390	(D)
NC	Cabarrus County	1195	795	260	(D)	(D)
NC	Caldwell County	445	360	65	20	0
NC	Camden County	0	0	0	0	0
NC	Carteret County	330	160	(D)	85	(D)
NC	Caswell County	135	110	25	0	0
NC	Catawba County	1795	900	(D)	495	(D)
NC	Chatham County	390	250	(D)	(D)	0
NC	Cherokee County	140	55	(D)	(D)	35
NC	Chowan County	90	(D)	(D)	0	0
NC	Clay County	50	30	20	0	0
NC	Cleveland County	645	335	240	(D)	(D)
NC	Columbus County	325	265	40	(D)	(D)
NC	Craven County	735	320	(D)	245	(D)
NC	Cumberland County	5555	2950	1160	1345	100
NC	Currituck County	120	65	30	25	0
NC	Dare County	145	90	(D)	(D)	0
NC	Davidson County	1190	805	255	(D)	(D)
NC	Davie County	215	135	60	0	25
NC	Duplin County	600	545	15	40	0
NC	Durham County	2815	1690	685	370	70
NC	Edgecombe County	415	330	65	(D)	(D)
NC	Forsyth County	3080	2050	545	470	15
NC	Franklin County	275	185	55	30	0
NC	Gaston County	1495	875	315	280	25
NC	Gates County	40	(D)	15	(D)	0

State/ Area	Area Name	Total	Speak Spanish or Spanish Creole	Speak other Indo European language	Speak Asian or Pacific Island language	Speak other language
NC	Graham County	55	(D)	(D)	0	45
NC	Granville County	480	355	40	45	40
NC	Greene County	125	120	4	0	0
NC	Guilford County	4990	2660	1135	995	200
NC	Halifax County	230	165	35	(D)	(D)
NC	Harnett County	915	675	165	(D)	(D)
NC	Haywood County	285	(D)	150	(D)	0
NC	Henderson County	1045	725	210	95	20
NC	Hertford County	170	110	30	25	0
NC	Hoke County	460	270	80	110	0
NC	Hyde County	20	(D)	0	0	(D)
NC	Iredell County	1125	720	215	165	30
NC	Jackson County	340	135	30	30	140
NC	Johnston County	1455	1235	125	80	15
NC	Jones County	45	20	(D)	(D)	0
NC	Lee County	590	485	55	45	0
NC	Lenoir County	405	285	60	(D)	(D)
NC	Lincoln County	590	445	110	(D)	(D)
NC	McDowell County	235	130	(D)	65	(D)
NC	Macon County	145	(D)	70	(D)	0
NC	Madison County	145	75	40	30	0
NC	Martin County	130	100	(D)	(D)	0
NC	Mecklenburg County	11670	5940	2575	2785	365
NC	Mitchell County	80	60	25	0	0
NC	Montgomery County	415	310	40	65	0
NC	Moore County	460	300	155	4	0
NC	Nash County	660	455	95	55	55
NC	New Hanover County	1240	685	325	160	70
NC	Northampton County	105	(D)	70	(D)	0
NC	Onslow County	2110	1415	270	405	25
NC	Orange County	1230	620	255	295	60

State/Area	Area Name	Total	Speak Spanish or Spanish Creole	Speak other Indo European language	Speak Asian or Pacific Island language	Speak other language
NC	Pamlico County	145	70	45	(D)	(D)
NC	Pasquotank County	290	170	70	50	0
NC	Pender County	375	255	85	(D)	(D)
NC	Perquimans County	60	(D)	(D)	0	0
NC	Person County	200	135	30	(D)	(D)
NC	Pitt County	1055	725	180	110	35
NC	Polk County	165	145	(D)	0	(D)
NC	Randolph County	925	680	120	(D)	(D)
NC	Richmond County	335	200	95	40	0
NC	Robeson County	975	735	155	(D)	(D)
NC	Rockingham County	665	425	165	75	0
NC	Rowan County	750	450	160	(D)	(D)
NC	Rutherford County	380	250	110	(D)	(D)
NC	Sampson County	680	555	65	(D)	(D)
NC	Scotland County	280	180	55	(D)	(D)
NC	Stanly County	300	185	(D)	60	(D)
NC	Stokes County	210	135	(D)	0	(D)
NC	Surry County	565	445	65	30	25
NC	Swain County	85	(D)	(D)	0	65
NC	Transylvania County	145	(D)	90	(D)	0
NC	Tyrrell County	10	(D)	(D)	(D)	0
NC	Union County	1205	910	135	100	60
NC	Vance County	305	265	45	0	0
NC	Wake County	7460	3470	1590	1905	495
NC	Warren County	110	70	25	(D)	(D)
NC	Washington County	80	40	(D)	(D)	0
NC	Watauga County	200	105	(D)	(D)	0
NC	Wayne County	1075	710	165	160	40
NC	Wilkes County	375	275	55	50	0
NC	Wilson County	810	655	110	(D)	(D)
NC	Yadkin County	275	270	(D)	(D)	0

State/ Area	Area Name	Total	Speak Spanish or Spanish Creole	Speak other Indo European language	Speak Asian or Pacific Island language	Speak other language
NC	Yancey County	50	25	(D)	(D)	0
ND	North Dakota	7700	1810	5155	275	460
ND	Adams County	15	0	15	0	0
ND	Barnes County	65	(D)	45	(D)	0
ND	Benson County	70	(D)	(D)	0	40
ND	Billings County	10	0	(D)	0	0
ND	Bottineau County	35	15	20	0	0
ND	Bowman County	20	(D)	10	0	(D)
ND	Burke County	10	(D)	(D)	0	0
ND	Burleigh County	1280	280	850	70	80
ND	Cass County	815	365	305	75	70
ND	Cavalier County	25	(D)	(D)	0	0
ND	Dickey County	100	4	90	0	0
ND	Divide County	20	(D)	(D)	0	0
ND	Dunn County	65	4	45	0	15
ND	Eddy County	15	0	15	0	0
ND	Emmons County	205	0	205	0	0
ND	Foster County	50	(D)	(D)	0	0
ND	Golden Valley County	0	0	0	0	0
ND	Grand Forks County	725	390	270	45	20
ND	Grant County	70	0	(D)	0	(D)
ND	Griggs County	15	(D)	(D)	0	0
ND	Hettinger County	35	0	35	0	0
ND	Kidder County	55	(D)	(D)	0	0
ND	LaMoure County	125	(D)	(D)	0	0
ND	Logan County	185	(D)	(D)	0	0
ND	McHenry County	70	(D)	65	(D)	0
ND	McIntosh County	425	(D)	420	(D)	0
ND	McKenzie County	80	(D)	15	(D)	45
ND	McLean County	80	(D)	70	(D)	0
ND	Mercer County	175	(D)	(D)	0	0

State/ Area	Area Name	Total	Speak Spanish or Spanish Creole	Speak other Indo European language	Speak Asian or Pacific Island language	Speak other language
ND	Morton County	275	50	230	0	0
ND	Mountrail County	70	(D)	30	(D)	35
ND	Nelson County	20	0	(D)	0	(D)
ND	Oliver County	20	0	(D)	0	(D)
ND	Pembina County	65	35	(D)	(D)	0
ND	Pierce County	105	0	105	0	0
ND	Ramsey County	70	(D)	50	0	(D)
ND	Ransom County	60	(D)	55	0	(D)
ND	Renville County	10	0	10	0	0
ND	Richland County	120	(D)	80	(D)	0
ND	Rolette County	85	(D)	25	(D)	50
ND	Sargent County	25	15	10	0	0
ND	Sheridan County	60	(D)	(D)	0	0
ND	Sioux County	25	0	0	0	25
ND	Slope County	0	0	0	0	0
ND	Stark County	405	(D)	330	0	(D)
ND	Steele County	20	(D)	(D)	0	0
ND	Stutsman County	300	15	285	0	0
ND	Towner County	10	(D)	(D)	0	(D)
ND	Traill County	55	(D)	35	0	(D)
ND	Walsh County	250	100	150	0	0
ND	Ward County	535	195	260	45	35
ND	Wells County	100	(D)	(D)	0	0
ND	Williams County	150	65	75	0	10
OH	Ohio	125425	44510	59020	14545	7350
OH	Adams County	225	(D)	185	(D)	0
OH	Allen County	580	315	225	(D)	(D)
OH	Ashland County	375	85	265	(D)	(D)
OH	Ashtabula County	1200	570	515	35	80
OH	Athens County	465	260	195	(D)	(D)
OH	Auglaize County	190	115	40	35	0

State/ Area	Area Name	Total	Speak Spanish or Spanish Creole	Speak other Indo European language	Speak Asian or Pacific Island language	Speak other language
OH	Belmont County	440	160	220	35	20
OH	Brown County	130	95	20	(D)	(D)
OH	Butler County	2655	1150	765	655	90
OH	Carroll County	135	70	(D)	(D)	0
OH	Champaign County	130	100	25	0	0
OH	Clark County	805	540	180	70	15
OH	Clermont County	765	250	345	155	15
OH	Clinton County	210	135	65	(D)	(D)
OH	Columbiana County	565	285	175	75	30
OH	Coshocton County	605	25	505	80	0
OH	Crawford County	185	45	90	(D)	(D)
OH	Cuyahoga County	32450	10480	16135	2965	2875
OH	Darke County	155	85	40	(D)	(D)
OH	Defiance County	405	275	100	25	0
OH	Delaware County	605	230	235	105	35
OH	Erie County	655	330	260	30	35
OH	Fairfield County	645	290	245	(D)	(D)
OH	Fayette County	215	115	(D)	50	(D)
OH	Franklin County	12450	4800	3760	3165	720
OH	Fulton County	510	350	95	65	0
OH	Gallia County	210	85	110	(D)	(D)
OH	Geauga County	2180	160	1895	60	65
OH	Greene County	1355	530	395	380	55
OH	Guernsey County	295	95	185	(D)	(D)
OH	Hamilton County	6890	2450	2900	1300	240
OH	Hancock County	560	320	150	60	30
OH	Hardin County	265	75	180	4	0
OH	Harrison County	65	(D)	40	(D)	0
OH	Henry County	255	140	(D)	(D)	0
OH	Highland County	85	(D)	35	(D)	0
OH	Hocking County	130	70	(D)	(D)	0

State/ Area	Area Name	Total	Speak Spanish or Spanish Creole	Speak other Indo European language	Speak Asian or Pacific Island language	Speak other language
OH	Holmes County	5085	45	5040	0	0
OH	Huron County	460	230	(D)	0	(D)
OH	Jackson County	120	65	(D)	(D)	0
OH	Jefferson County	565	210	330	(D)	(D)
OH	Knox County	470	(D)	345	(D)	0
OH	Lake County	2660	555	1705	195	205
OH	Lawrence County	165	90	55	(D)	(D)
OH	Licking County	640	280	250	35	75
OH	Logan County	370	105	200	(D)	(D)
OH	Lorain County	4975	3550	1010	120	295
OH	Lucas County	5325	2575	1600	635	520
OH	Madison County	295	115	115	(D)	(D)
OH	Mahoning County	4225	1695	2155	140	235
OH	Marion County	415	185	135	(D)	(D)
OH	Medina County	1395	265	930	110	95
OH	Meigs County	70	40	30	0	0
OH	Mercer County	155	80	(D)	(D)	0
OH	Miami County	455	170	215	(D)	(D)
OH	Monroe County	135	(D)	120	(D)	0
OH	Montgomery County	4365	1505	1635	1005	220
OH	Morgan County	60	30	(D)	(D)	0
OH	Morrow County	235	(D)	165	(D)	0
OH	Muskingum County	495	195	215	85	0
OH	Noble County	115	60	50	0	0
OH	Ottawa County	295	210	65	(D)	(D)
OH	Paulding County	170	105	35	(D)	(D)
OH	Perry County	130	(D)	70	(D)	0
OH	Pickaway County	425	210	(D)	85	(D)
OH	Pike County	130	40	80	(D)	(D)
OH	Portage County	1035	315	475	110	130
OH	Preble County	195	95	80	(D)	(D)

State/ Area	Area Name	Total	Speak Spanish or Spanish Creole	Speak other Indo European language	Speak Asian or Pacific Island language	Speak other language
OH	Putnam County	290	195	60	(D)	(D)
OH	Richland County	1190	200	805	115	70
OH	Ross County	415	180	175	(D)	(D)
OH	Sandusky County	790	655	115	(D)	(D)
OH	Scioto County	310	120	80	25	90
OH	Seneca County	340	225	90	(D)	(D)
OH	Shelby County	275	150	90	(D)	(D)
OH	Stark County	2695	920	1430	220	120
OH	Summit County	5015	1095	2655	795	475
OH	Trumbull County	2595	440	1850	150	160
OH	Tuscarawas County	880	190	675	(D)	(D)
OH	Union County	115	65	(D)	(D)	0
OH	Van Wert County	80	50	(D)	(D)	0
OH	Vinton County	35	20	(D)	(D)	0
OH	Warren County	900	375	(D)	275	(D)
OH	Washington County	300	170	115	(D)	(D)
OH	Wayne County	2165	205	1875	55	30
OH	Williams County	245	125	60	(D)	(D)
OH	Wood County	980	635	250	65	30
OH	Wyandot County	145	105	(D)	(D)	0
OK	Oklahoma	36875	20235	4910	7225	4505
OK	Adair County	520	85	(D)	(D)	425
OK	Alfalfa County	55	20	(D)	0	(D)
OK	Atoka County	45	35	(D)	0	(D)
OK	Beaver County	95	(D)	(D)	0	0
OK	Beckham County	105	80	(D)	(D)	0
OK	Blaine County	235	155	(D)	(D)	40
OK	Bryan County	200	130	45	0	25
OK	Caddo County	310	165	(D)	(D)	125
OK	Canadian County	975	405	170	385	15
OK	Carter County	385	205	(D)	(D)	125

State/ Area	Area Name	Total	Speak Spanish or Spanish Creole	Speak other Indo European language	Speak Asian or Pacific Island language	Speak other language
OK	Cherokee County	515	180	45	0	290
OK	Choctaw County	75	30	(D)	(D)	45
OK	Cimarron County	80	(D)	(D)	0	0
OK	Cleveland County	2390	1000	395	900	90
OK	Coal County	65	30	(D)	(D)	15
OK	Comanche County	2275	1255	385	570	65
OK	Cotton County	50	45	(D)	0	(D)
OK	Craig County	70	35	(D)	(D)	(D)
OK	Creek County	330	190	75	15	50
OK	Custer County	465	350	50	55	10
OK	Delaware County	425	95	(D)	(D)	310
OK	Dewey County	40	30	0	(D)	(D)
OK	Ellis County	40	15	25	0	0
OK	Garfield County	485	230	75	155	30
OK	Garvin County	175	135	(D)	(D)	(D)
OK	Grady County	270	200	35	(D)	(D)
OK	Grant County	25	15	(D)	(D)	0
OK	Greer County	115	70	(D)	(D)	40
OK	Harmon County	160	(D)	(D)	0	0
OK	Harper County	45	35	(D)	(D)	0
OK	Haskell County	60	45	(D)	0	(D)
OK	Hughes County	160	(D)	0	(D)	120
OK	Jackson County	585	510	45	35	0
OK	Jefferson County	60	(D)	0	(D)	0
OK	Johnston County	40	25	(D)	0	(D)
OK	Kay County	340	230	50	35	25
OK	Kingfisher County	130	115	15	0	0
OK	Kiowa County	130	90	(D)	0	(D)
OK	Latimer County	45	20	(D)	(D)	15
OK	Le Flore County	320	210	40	10	60
OK	Lincoln County	255	135	65	35	20

State/ Area	Area Name	Total	Speak Spanish or Spanish Creole	Speak other Indo European language	Speak Asian or Pacific Island language	Speak other language
OK	Logan County	230	145	60	(D)	(D)
OK	Love County	100	100	0	0	0
OK	McClain County	310	230	65	(D)	(D)
OK	McCurtain County	230	95	0	10	125
OK	McIntosh County	165	30	15	30	95
OK	Major County	85	45	(D)	0	(D)
OK	Marshall County	165	130	15	(D)	(D)
OK	Mayes County	390	95	65	30	200
OK	Murray County	85	55	0	(D)	(D)
OK	Muskogee County	400	160	60	70	110
OK	Noble County	55	30	(D)	(D)	(D)
OK	Nowata County	45	45	0	0	0
OK	Okfuskee County	185	(D)	50	(D)	95
OK	Oklahoma County	10140	5435	1175	3050	480
OK	Okmulgee County	320	140	(D)	(D)	105
OK	Osage County	235	130	65	20	25
OK	Ottawa County	215	200	0	15	0
OK	Pawnee County	85	50	(D)	(D)	20
OK	Payne County	480	205	(D)	155	(D)
OK	Pittsburg County	255	160	30	35	30
OK	Pontotoc County	215	105	(D)	(D)	70
OK	Pottawatomie County	375	150	65	25	140
OK	Pushmataha County	100	30	(D)	(D)	55
OK	Roger Mills County	15	(D)	(D)	0	10
OK	Rogers County	270	130	65	55	20
OK	Seminole County	205	45	30	10	125
OK	Sequoyah County	310	70	(D)	(D)	220
OK	Stephens County	370	330	30	(D)	(D)
OK	Texas County	840	785	45	(D)	(D)
OK	Tillman County	185	185	0	0	0
OK	Tulsa County	5610	3250	855	1190	320

State/ Area	Area Name	Total	Speak Spanish or Spanish Creole	Speak other Indo European language	Speak Asian or Pacific Island language	Speak other language
OK	Wagoner County	360	160	85	55	60
OK	Washington County	375	220	75	35	40
OK	Washita County	105	75	(D)	0	(D)
OK	Woods County	75	75	0	0	0
OK	Woodward County	145	120	(D)	(D)	0
OR	Oregon	51470	23045	10520	16500	1410
OR	Baker County	130	105	(D)	(D)	0
OR	Benton County	935	510	(D)	290	(D)
OR	Clackamas County	3975	1340	1230	1250	160
OR	Clatsop County	315	180	40	65	30
OR	Columbia County	250	145	35	40	35
OR	Coos County	315	175	90	(D)	(D)
OR	Crook County	165	(D)	0	(D)	0
OR	Curry County	135	(D)	70	(D)	0
OR	Deschutes County	955	685	170	(D)	(D)
OR	Douglas County	585	355	105	85	45
OR	Gilliam County	10	(D)	(D)	(D)	0
OR	Grant County	35	25	(D)	0	(D)
OR	Harney County	50	15	(D)	(D)	10
OR	Hood River County	480	385	25	70	0
OR	Jackson County	1685	1090	290	270	35
OR	Jefferson County	250	180	(D)	(D)	30
OR	Josephine County	580	365	145	45	25
OR	Klamath County	570	395	100	60	15
OR	Lake County	75	55	(D)	(D)	0
OR	Lane County	2995	1595	760	555	80
OR	Lincoln County	390	255	70	40	25
OR	Linn County	875	505	190	(D)	(D)
OR	Malheur County	940	815	(D)	80	(D)
OR	Marion County	6070	3915	1150	930	75
OR	Morrow County	200	185	(D)	(D)	(D)

State/ Area	Area Name	Total	Speak Spanish or Spanish Creole	Speak other Indo European language	Speak Asian or Pacific Island language	Speak other language
OR	Multnomah County	15350	3625	3705	7525	490
OR	Polk County	550	260	190	(D)	(D)
OR	Sherman County	10	(D)	(D)	0	0
OR	Tillamook County	150	125	15	(D)	(D)
OR	Umatilla County	1380	1165	70	110	35
OR	Union County	175	120	(D)	35	(D)
OR	Wallowa County	35	25	(D)	0	(D)
OR	Wasco County	345	275	25	20	20
OR	Washington County	9535	3295	1595	4445	195
OR	Wheeler County	4	(D)	(D)	0	0
OR	Yamhill County	970	655	175	(D)	(D)
PA	Pennsylvania	202560	83385	84120	29035	6020
PA	Adams County	745	435	220	85	0
PA	Allegheny County	13400	2770	8525	1580	525
PA	Armstrong County	335	95	170	35	30
PA	Beaver County	1575	360	1050	105	65
PA	Bedford County	265	75	160	30	0
PA	Berks County	10095	6910	2495	630	55
PA	Blair County	755	225	460	(D)	(D)
PA	Bradford County	340	115	200	(D)	(D)
PA	Bucks County	9520	2630	5275	1325	290
PA	Butler County	705	205	390	(D)	(D)
PA	Cambria County	1235	515	595	75	50
PA	Cameron County	4	0	(D)	0	0
PA	Carbon County	735	195	500	(D)	(D)
PA	Centre County	1315	385	675	235	20
PA	Chester County	5985	2835	2080	905	160
PA	Clarion County	220	70	120	20	10
PA	Clearfield County	380	120	205	(D)	(D)
PA	Clinton County	340	100	215	(D)	(D)
PA	Columbia County	470	170	250	30	25

State/ Area	Area Name	Total	Speak Spanish or Spanish Creole	Speak other Indo European language	Speak Asian or Pacific Island language	Speak other language
PA	Crawford County	1065	180	855	20	10
PA	Cumberland County	2345	785	1110	410	40
PA	Dauphin County	4245	2235	1110	710	195
PA	Delaware County	9695	2015	4465	2700	515
PA	Elk County	180	55	95	(D)	(D)
PA	Erie County	2830	1125	1450	200	50
PA	Fayette County	790	270	470	20	30
PA	Forest County	15	(D)	10	(D)	0
PA	Franklin County	850	400	400	50	0
PA	Fulton County	60	20	35	(D)	(D)
PA	Greene County	295	190	90	(D)	(D)
PA	Huntingdon County	280	145	120	15	0
PA	Indiana County	850	175	600	60	15
PA	Jefferson County	280	75	180	10	10
PA	Juniata County	255	75	170	10	0
PA	Lackawanna County	2250	590	1395	230	35
PA	Lancaster County	13715	5725	6530	1335	120
PA	Lawrence County	975	130	795	25	25
PA	Lebanon County	2185	1240	740	175	35
PA	Lehigh County	9430	5785	1980	760	900
PA	Luzerne County	2930	870	1765	185	110
PA	Lycoming County	665	265	295	65	45
PA	McKean County	230	90	100	(D)	(D)
PA	Mercer County	1295	295	885	75	40
PA	Mifflin County	1030	65	945	20	0
PA	Monroe County	1955	745	1000	150	60
PA	Montgomery County	11665	2430	4545	4320	370
PA	Montour County	170	(D)	105	40	(D)
PA	Northampton County	5695	3550	1535	405	200
PA	Northumberland County	775	260	440	75	0

State/ Area	Area Name	Total	Speak Spanish or Spanish Creole	Speak other Indo European language	Speak Asian or Pacific Island language	Speak other language
PA	Perry County	215	65	120	30	0
PA	Philadelphia County	60365	29655	18595	10495	1620
PA	Pike County	730	250	415	55	10
PA	Potter County	140	35	65	(D)	(D)
PA	Schuylkill County	1465	605	790	(D)	(D)
PA	Snyder County	785	(D)	705	(D)	0
PA	Somerset County	700	140	505	20	30
PA	Sullivan County	30	(D)	30	(D)	0
PA	Susquehanna County	215	60	135	(D)	(D)
PA	Tioga County	225	80	135	(D)	(D)
PA	Union County	590	165	385	(D)	(D)
PA	Venango County	340	130	195	(D)	(D)
PA	Warren County	230	75	125	35	0
PA	Washington County	1410	300	1020	70	20
PA	Wayne County	615	170	385	60	0
PA	Westmoreland County	2620	835	1515	190	85
PA	Wyoming County	130	50	75	(D)	(D)
PA	York County	4330	2680	1125	470	55
RI	Rhode Island	38765	14195	20235	3660	675
RI	Bristol County	1805	95	1645	(D)	(D)
RI	Kent County	2690	470	1710	385	125
RI	Newport County	1410	405	770	215	20
RI	Providence County	31685	12955	15495	2760	470
RI	Washington County	1180	275	615	245	45
SC	South Carolina	32745	18170	8770	5090	715
SC	Abbeville County	195	145	40	(D)	(D)
SC	Aiken County	850	505	195	(D)	(D)
SC	Allendale County	40	30	(D)	(D)	0
SC	Anderson County	935	570	265	(D)	(D)
SC	Bamberg County	35	(D)	(D)	0	0

State/ Area	Area Name	Total	Speak Spanish or Spanish Creole	Speak other Indo European language	Speak Asian or Pacific Island language	Speak other language
SC	Barnwell County	145	85	(D)	(D)	0
SC	Beaufort County	1320	955	240	(D)	(D)
SC	Berkeley County	1675	700	325	590	60
SC	Calhoun County	55	35	(D)	10	(D)
SC	Charleston County	2860	1440	950	445	25
SC	Cherokee County	305	240	(D)	(D)	0
SC	Chester County	180	100	(D)	(D)	0
SC	Chesterfield County	275	185	50	(D)	(D)
SC	Clarendon County	125	75	25	(D)	(D)
SC	Colleton County	195	155	(D)	(D)	0
SC	Darlington County	515	315	170	(D)	(D)
SC	Dillon County	230	195	(D)	(D)	0
SC	Dorchester County	665	325	190	(D)	(D)
SC	Edgefield County	280	175	80	(D)	(D)
SC	Fairfield County	115	90	(D)	0	(D)
SC	Florence County	980	450	395	(D)	(D)
SC	Georgetown County	320	195	(D)	(D)	0
SC	Greenville County	3455	1935	780	615	125
SC	Greenwood County	535	365	85	(D)	(D)
SC	Hampton County	125	95	10	15	0
SC	Horry County	2005	950	735	250	65
SC	Jasper County	110	60	(D)	(D)	0
SC	Kershaw County	325	165	115	50	0
SC	Lancaster County	260	145	90	(D)	(D)
SC	Laurens County	310	230	(D)	(D)	0
SC	Lee County	200	100	45	(D)	(D)
SC	Lexington County	1540	850	405	250	35
SC	McCormick County	90	65	30	0	0
SC	Marion County	245	150	80	(D)	(D)
SC	Marlboro County	135	75	25	40	0
SC	Newberry County	205	130	75	0	0

State/ Area	Area Name	Total	Speak Spanish or Spanish Creole	Speak other Indo European language	Speak Asian or Pacific Island language	Speak other language
SC	Oconee County	415	260	120	(D)	(D)
SC	Orangeburg County	540	255	240	15	30
SC	Pickens County	655	385	185	45	35
SC	Richland County	4180	2320	1055	755	50
SC	Saluda County	95	(D)	(D)	0	0
SC	Spartanburg County	2720	1345	610	700	65
SC	Sumter County	765	400	180	(D)	(D)
SC	Union County	100	60	(D)	(D)	0
SC	Williamsburg County	230	80	130	20	0
SC	York County	1205	685	310	185	30
SD	South Dakota	9280	1730	4875	635	2045
SD	Aurora County	25	15	(D)	(D)	0
SD	Beadle County	240	50	170	(D)	(D)
SD	Bennett County	85	(D)	(D)	0	75
SD	Bon Homme County	180	(D)	155	0	(D)
SD	Brookings County	280	75	155	(D)	(D)
SD	Brown County	475	105	320	(D)	(D)
SD	Brule County	145	(D)	135	0	(D)
SD	Buffalo County	20	0	0	0	20
SD	Butte County	50	(D)	(D)	0	0
SD	Campbell County	20	0	20	0	0
SD	Charles Mix County	190	10	130	0	50
SD	Clark County	120	0	120	0	0
SD	Clay County	105	40	(D)	(D)	30
SD	Codington County	135	25	80	30	0
SD	Corson County	130	0	(D)	(D)	115
SD	Custer County	20	(D)	10	(D)	(D)
SD	Davison County	90	0	70	(D)	(D)
SD	Day County	70	(D)	35	0	(D)
SD	Deuel County	40	10	30	0	0
SD	Dewey County	150	(D)	10	(D)	130

State/ Area	Area Name	Total	Speak Spanish or Spanish Creole	Speak other Indo European language	Speak Asian or Pacific Island language	Speak other language
SD	Douglas County	100	(D)	(D)	0	0
SD	Edmunds County	185	(D)	(D)	0	0
SD	Fall River County	45	(D)	30	0	(D)
SD	Faulk County	150	0	150	0	0
SD	Grant County	55	(D)	45	0	(D)
SD	Gregory County	15	(D)	(D)	0	4
SD	Haakon County	10	(D)	10	(D)	(D)
SD	Hamlin County	60	(D)	50	(D)	(D)
SD	Hand County	80	(D)	75	(D)	0
SD	Hanson County	130	(D)	(D)	0	0
SD	Harding County	4	0	0	0	(D)
SD	Hughes County	140	35	75	(D)	(D)
SD	Hutchinson County	410	(D)	405	(D)	0
SD	Hyde County	35	10	25	0	0
SD	Jackson County	35	(D)	0	0	(D)
SD	Jerauld County	20	(D)	10	0	(D)
SD	Jones County	0	0	0	0	0
SD	Kingsbury County	35	15	15	(D)	(D)
SD	Lake County	185	(D)	135	(D)	0
SD	Lawrence County	170	55	95	(D)	(D)
SD	Lincoln County	120	40	60	(D)	(D)
SD	Lyman County	25	(D)	(D)	(D)	20
SD	McCook County	15	(D)	15	(D)	0
SD	McPherson County	330	0	330	0	0
SD	Marshall County	95	4	70	0	20
SD	Meade County	155	50	65	(D)	(D)
SD	Mellette County	65	0	0	0	65
SD	Miner County	45	15	30	0	0
SD	Minnehaha County	1245	540	355	200	145
SD	Moody County	105	(D)	65	(D)	15
SD	Pennington County	805	240	215	170	180

State/ Area	Area Name	Total	Speak Spanish or Spanish Creole	Speak other Indo European language	Speak Asian or Pacific Island language	Speak other language
SD	Perkins County	25	15	(D)	(D)	0
SD	Potter County	10	(D)	4	(D)	0
SD	Roberts County	115	(D)	20	(D)	80
SD	Sanborn County	55	4	45	0	0
SD	Shannon County	450	(D)	(D)	0	430
SD	Spink County	230	(D)	210	0	(D)
SD	Stanley County	20	4	15	0	0
SD	Sully County	15	4	10	0	0
SD	Todd County	265	(D)	0	0	(D)
SD	Tripp County	20	(D)	0	(D)	(D)
SD	Turner County	55	(D)	50	(D)	(D)
SD	Union County	85	55	15	(D)	(D)
SD	Walworth County	125	(D)	95	0	(D)
SD	Yankton County	270	65	170	(D)	(D)
SD	Ziebach County	110	0	0	(D)	(D)
TN	Tennessee	39525	21055	9840	7200	1425
TN	Anderson County	535	225	200	110	0
TN	Bedford County	250	175	55	25	0
TN	Benton County	15	(D)	(D)	0	0
TN	Bledsoe County	80	65	0	(D)	(D)
TN	Blount County	490	220	150	105	20
TN	Bradley County	615	390	180	45	0
TN	Campbell County	150	105	(D)	(D)	0
TN	Cannon County	50	30	(D)	(D)	0
TN	Carroll County	115	(D)	60	(D)	0
TN	Carter County	225	135	45	45	0
TN	Cheatham County	180	130	35	(D)	(D)
TN	Chester County	90	55	(D)	(D)	0
TN	Claiborne County	130	50	45	(D)	(D)
TN	Clay County	35	(D)	(D)	20	0
TN	Cocke County	130	70	(D)	(D)	0

State/ Area	Area Name	Total	Speak Spanish or Spanish Creole	Speak other Indo European language	Speak Asian or Pacific Island language	Speak other language
TN	Coffee County	155	110	(D)	35	(D)
TN	Crockett County	95	85	(D)	(D)	0
TN	Cumberland County	285	140	100	(D)	(D)
TN	Davidson County	6485	3230	1640	1180	430
TN	Decatur County	65	(D)	(D)	0	0
TN	DeKalb County	40	25	(D)	(D)	0
TN	Dickson County	270	210	(D)	(D)	0
TN	Dyer County	165	55	80	30	0
TN	Fayette County	110	45	35	(D)	(D)
TN	Fentress County	80	(D)	(D)	40	0
TN	Franklin County	270	160	95	(D)	(D)
TN	Gibson County	205	85	100	20	0
TN	Giles County	115	55	(D)	30	(D)
TN	Grainger County	100	55	(D)	(D)	0
TN	Greene County	330	125	155	(D)	(D)
TN	Grundy County	70	50	(D)	0	(D)
TN	Hamblen County	395	235	75	(D)	(D)
TN	Hamilton County	2320	1035	690	555	35
TN	Hancock County	20	(D)	(D)	0	0
TN	Hardeman County	165	(D)	55	(D)	0
TN	Hardin County	120	65	(D)	30	(D)
TN	Hawkins County	210	105	50	55	0
TN	Haywood County	105	105	0	0	0
TN	Henderson County	95	45	35	15	0
TN	Henry County	135	90	(D)	(D)	0
TN	Hickman County	125	115	(D)	(D)	0
TN	Houston County	15	(D)	(D)	0	0
TN	Humphreys County	65	35	30	0	0
TN	Jackson County	55	(D)	(D)	0	0
TN	Jefferson County	210	120	60	(D)	(D)
TN	Johnson County	90	60	(D)	(D)	0

State/ Area	Area Name	Total	Speak Spanish or Spanish Creole	Speak other Indo European language	Speak Asian or Pacific Island language	Speak other language
TN	Knox County	2355	1165	690	345	155
TN	Lake County	70	50	(D)	0	(D)
TN	Lauderdale County	170	105	20	(D)	(D)
TN	Lawrence County	370	50	305	15	0
TN	Lewis County	20	(D)	(D)	0	0
TN	Lincoln County	220	100	100	(D)	(D)
TN	Loudon County	140	100	15	30	0
TN	McMinn County	160	110	(D)	35	(D)
TN	McNairy County	125	75	(D)	(D)	0
TN	Macon County	75	(D)	(D)	0	0
TN	Madison County	535	290	155	(D)	(D)
TN	Marion County	105	55	30	(D)	(D)
TN	Marshall County	75	50	(D)	(D)	0
TN	Maury County	355	290	65	0	0
TN	Meigs County	60	35	25	0	0
TN	Monroe County	150	110	(D)	(D)	0
TN	Montgomery County	1670	900	325	420	25
TN	Moore County	4	0	0	(D)	0
TN	Morgan County	35	15	(D)	(D)	0
TN	Obion County	135	85	(D)	(D)	0
TN	Overton County	130	80	(D)	0	(D)
TN	Perry County	30	(D)	(D)	0	0
TN	Pickett County	25	(D)	15	0	(D)
TN	Polk County	60	30	(D)	(D)	0
TN	Putnam County	575	395	(D)	80	(D)
TN	Rhea County	140	100	25	15	0
TN	Roane County	265	140	65	60	0
TN	Robertson County	265	195	35	35	0
TN	Rutherford County	1600	685	225	675	25
TN	Scott County	45	35	(D)	0	(D)
TN	Sequatchie County	35	35	0	0	0

State/ Area	Area Name	Total	Speak Spanish or Spanish Creole	Speak other Indo European language	Speak Asian or Pacific Island language	Speak other language
TN	Sevier County	485	245	170	(D)	(D)
TN	Shelby County	8610	4550	1740	1920	400
TN	Smith County	45	30	(D)	(D)	0
TN	Stewart County	50	(D)	0	25	(D)
TN	Sullivan County	605	285	195	(D)	(D)
TN	Sumner County	735	355	230	(D)	(D)
TN	Tipton County	270	200	40	(D)	(D)
TN	Trousdale County	25	(D)	(D)	0	0
TN	Unicoi County	100	(D)	(D)	0	0
TN	Union County	20	10	(D)	(D)	(D)
TN	Van Buren County	4	(D)	0	0	0
TN	Warren County	310	270	(D)	20	(D)
TN	Washington County	495	305	155	35	0
TN	Wayne County	45	(D)	(D)	0	0
TN	Weakley County	220	170	25	(D)	(D)
TN	White County	110	(D)	45	(D)	0
TN	Williamson County	885	430	290	(D)	(D)
TN	Wilson County	435	270	100	(D)	(D)
TX	Texas	1005865	877715	42450	78700	7000
TX	Anderson County	500	470	(D)	(D)	0
TX	Andrews County	600	600	0	0	0
TX	Angelina County	1630	1450	70	(D)	(D)
TX	Aransas County	765	535	(D)	190	(D)
TX	Archer County	70	50	(D)	0	(D)
TX	Armstrong County	10	10	0	0	0
TX	Atascosa County	4260	4215	50	0	0
TX	Austin County	640	445	(D)	(D)	0
TX	Bailey County	335	335	0	0	0
TX	Bandera County	385	325	(D)	(D)	0
TX	Bastrop County	1690	1445	155	(D)	(D)
TX	Baylor County	55	(D)	(D)	0	0

State/ Area	Area Name	Total	Speak Spanish or Spanish Creole	Speak other Indo European language	Speak Asian or Pacific Island language	Speak other language
TX	Bee County	3570	3515	(D)	(D)	o
TX	Bell County	6600	4590	800	1145	65
TX	Bexar County	108830	102390	2595	3460	380
TX	Blanco County	235	205	25	o	o
TX	Borden County	35	35	o	o	o
TX	Bosque County	315	300	(D)	(D)	o
TX	Bowie County	705	510	165	(D)	(D)
TX	Brazoria County	7160	6065	270	765	55
TX	Brazos County	3530	2955	275	275	20
TX	Brewster County	735	715	(D)	(D)	o
TX	Briscoe County	65	65	o	o	o
TX	Brooks County	1555	1555	o	o	o
TX	Brown County	730	665	30	(D)	(D)
TX	Burleson County	545	430	100	(D)	(D)
TX	Burnet County	625	590	(D)	(D)	o
TX	Caldwell County	1910	1870	15	25	o
TX	Calhoun County	1180	1010	(D)	(D)	o
TX	Callahan County	100	(D)	(D)	o	o
TX	Cameron County	48355	48080	65	150	60
TX	Camp County	140	140	o	o	o
TX	Carson County	90	90	o	o	o
TX	Cass County	170	135	(D)	(D)	o
TX	Castro County	630	(D)	o	(D)	o
TX	Chambers County	465	340	(D)	(D)	o
TX	Cherokee County	720	685	(D)	(D)	o
TX	Childress County	160	145	(D)	(D)	o
TX	Clay County	50	30	20	o	o
TX	Cochran County	320	(D)	(D)	o	o
TX	Coke County	85	(D)	(D)	o	o
TX	Coleman County	150	140	(D)	(D)	o
TX	Collin County	9770	4330	1640	3665	135

State/ Area	Area Name	Total	Speak Spanish or Spanish Creole	Speak other Indo European language	Speak Asian or Pacific Island language	Speak other language
TX	Collingsworth County	120	(D)	(D)	0	0
TX	Colorado County	605	435	140	(D)	(D)
TX	Comal County	2610	2210	335	65	0
TX	Comanche County	270	(D)	0	(D)	0
TX	Concho County	285	265	(D)	(D)	0
TX	Cooke County	480	385	60	(D)	(D)
TX	Coryell County	1465	920	(D)	280	(D)
TX	Cottle County	60	60	0	0	0
TX	Crane County	215	(D)	(D)	0	0
TX	Crockett County	455	(D)	(D)	0	0
TX	Crosby County	605	(D)	0	(D)	0
TX	Culberson County	460	(D)	(D)	0	0
TX	Dallam County	170	(D)	0	0	(D)
TX	Dallas County	76755	59380	5015	10955	1410
TX	Dawson County	1370	1335	(D)	(D)	0
TX	Deaf Smith County	1670	(D)	0	(D)	0
TX	Delta County	15	15	0	0	0
TX	Denton County	8130	4975	945	2085	125
TX	DeWitt County	1070	950	120	0	0
TX	Dickens County	65	65	0	0	0
TX	Dimmit County	2015	(D)	(D)	0	0
TX	Donley County	50	40	0	(D)	(D)
TX	Duval County	2580	(D)	(D)	0	0
TX	Eastland County	320	310	(D)	0	(D)
TX	Ector County	7240	7010	80	110	40
TX	Edwards County	240	240	0	0	0
TX	Ellis County	2310	2100	165	(D)	(D)
TX	El Paso County	89945	88005	730	1020	190
TX	Erath County	740	690	(D)	(D)	0
TX	Falls County	575	540	(D)	(D)	0
TX	Fannin County	260	245	(D)	(D)	0

State/ Area	Area Name	Total	Speak Spanish or Spanish Creole	Speak other Indo European language	Speak Asian or Pacific Island language	Speak other language
TX	Fayette County	925	400	525	0	0
TX	Fisher County	205	(D)	0	(D)	0
TX	Floyd County	580	580	0	0	0
TX	Foard County	40	(D)	0	(D)	0
TX	Fort Bend County	16435	9305	2035	4790	305
TX	Franklin County	130	115	15	0	0
TX	Freestone County	195	160	15	20	0
TX	Frio County	2415	(D)	0	(D)	0
TX	Gaines County	1200	945	(D)	(D)	0
TX	Galveston County	6595	5155	680	735	25
TX	Garza County	365	365	0	0	0
TX	Gillespie County	860	435	400	(D)	(D)
TX	Glasscock County	50	(D)	(D)	0	0
TX	Goliad County	395	360	35	0	0
TX	Gonzales County	1140	1130	(D)	(D)	0
TX	Gray County	455	370	(D)	(D)	(D)
TX	Grayson County	905	695	140	50	25
TX	Gregg County	1410	1240	130	(D)	(D)
TX	Grimes County	535	470	(D)	(D)	0
TX	Guadalupe County	4175	3730	240	(D)	(D)
TX	Hale County	2755	2710	(D)	(D)	0
TX	Hall County	145	(D)	0	(D)	0
TX	Hamilton County	100	80	15	0	0
TX	Hansford County	200	200	0	0	0
TX	Hardeman County	80	(D)	0	0	(D)
TX	Hardin County	235	130	(D)	(D)	0
TX	Harris County	157310	117450	9275	28550	2030
TX	Harrison County	555	470	30	55	0
TX	Hartley County	40	40	0	0	0
TX	Haskell County	220	(D)	(D)	0	0
TX	Hays County	3595	3355	170	(D)	(D)

State/ Area	Area Name	Total	Speak Spanish or Spanish Creole	Speak other Indo European language	Speak Asian or Pacific Island language	Speak other language
TX	Hemphill County	70	(D)	(D)	0	0
TX	Henderson County	720	630	45	(D)	(D)
TX	Hidalgo County	77330	76815	240	250	25
TX	Hill County	645	590	35	20	0
TX	Hockley County	1390	1365	25	0	0
TX	Hood County	495	405	55	35	0
TX	Hopkins County	460	415	(D)	(D)	0
TX	Houston County	275	245	(D)	(D)	0
TX	Howard County	2005	1975	(D)	(D)	0
TX	Hudspeth County	375	370	(D)	(D)	0
TX	Hunt County	930	835	60	35	0
TX	Hutchinson County	250	240	(D)	(D)	(D)
TX	Irion County	85	85	0	0	0
TX	Jack County	110	(D)	(D)	0	0
TX	Jackson County	550	505	50	0	0
TX	Jasper County	290	225	(D)	(D)	0
TX	Jeff Davis County	180	180	0	0	0
TX	Jefferson County	5400	2970	1135	1225	70
TX	Jim Hogg County	1040	1040	0	0	0
TX	Jim Wells County	5830	5790	(D)	0	(D)
TX	Johnson County	2400	2135	125	140	0
TX	Jones County	535	505	(D)	(D)	0
TX	Karnes County	1725	1570	155	0	0
TX	Kaufman County	1165	950	(D)	145	(D)
TX	Kendall County	740	690	(D)	(D)	0
TX	Kenedy County	90	90	0	0	0
TX	Kent County	25	25	0	0	0
TX	Kerr County	1440	1235	175	30	0
TX	Kimble County	140	115	25	0	0
TX	King County	4	(D)	0	0	0
TX	Kinney County	385	385	0	0	0

State/ Area	Area Name	Total	Speak Spanish or Spanish Creole	Speak other Indo European language	Speak Asian or Pacific Island language	Speak other language
TX	Kleberg County	3720	3575	(D)	125	(D)
TX	Knox County	230	(D)	(D)	0	0
TX	Lamar County	330	255	(D)	35	(D)
TX	Lamb County	1160	1155	(D)	(D)	0
TX	Lampasas County	465	375	55	35	0
TX	La Salle County	1190	1190	0	0	0
TX	Lavaca County	500	255	230	(D)	(D)
TX	Lee County	415	255	(D)	(D)	0
TX	Leon County	110	105	(D)	(D)	0
TX	Liberty County	940	815	65	45	15
TX	Limestone County	340	310	15	15	0
TX	Lipscomb County	60	60	0	0	0
TX	Live Oak County	860	835	(D)	(D)	0
TX	Llano County	235	200	(D)	(D)	0
TX	Loving County	10	10	0	0	0
TX	Lubbock County	10445	9945	180	300	20
TX	Lynn County	510	505	4	0	0
TX	McCulloch County	295	295	0	0	0
TX	McLennan County	5020	4360	425	190	45
TX	McMullen County	60	60	(D)	0	(D)
TX	Madison County	600	(D)	(D)	0	0
TX	Marion County	30	(D)	(D)	0	0
TX	Martin County	365	350	15	0	0
TX	Mason County	115	100	15	0	0
TX	Matagorda County	1600	1460	30	110	0
TX	Maverick County	8795	8600	0	30	160
TX	Medina County	3160	3045	80	(D)	(D)
TX	Menard County	145	145	0	0	0
TX	Midland County	4830	4575	185	75	0
TX	Milam County	495	425	(D)	(D)	0
TX	Mills County	105	90	15	0	0

State/ Area	Area Name	Total	Speak Spanish or Spanish Creole	Speak other Indo European language	Speak Asian or Pacific Island language	Speak other language
TX	Mitchell County	780	780	0	0	0
TX	Montague County	130	115	(D)	(D)	0
TX	Montgomery County	4215	3515	420	265	20
TX	Moore County	1000	970	(D)	(D)	0
TX	Morris County	105	90	(D)	(D)	(D)
TX	Motley County	45	45	0	0	0
TX	Nacogdoches County	830	720	90	20	0
TX	Navarro County	865	770	30	35	30
TX	Newton County	80	70	(D)	(D)	0
TX	Nolan County	740	705	(D)	(D)	0
TX	Nueces County	28135	27255	(D)	445	(D)
TX	Ochiltree County	255	240	(D)	(D)	0
TX	Oldham County	45	45	0	0	0
TX	Orange County	945	405	250	260	30
TX	Palo Pinto County	660	600	25	40	0
TX	Panola County	135	95	(D)	(D)	0
TX	Parker County	985	870	65	(D)	(D)
TX	Parmer County	695	680	(D)	(D)	(D)
TX	Pecos County	2030	1990	(D)	(D)	0
TX	Polk County	870	720	(D)	(D)	105
TX	Potter County	4185	3480	(D)	665	(D)
TX	Presidio County	1005	1000	(D)	(D)	0
TX	Rains County	80	(D)	0	(D)	0
TX	Randall County	1260	940	120	170	25
TX	Reagan County	200	200	0	0	0
TX	Real County	125	125	0	0	0
TX	Red River County	105	95	(D)	0	(D)
TX	Reeves County	2175	2155	(D)	(D)	0
TX	Refugio County	595	580	(D)	(D)	0
TX	Roberts County	4	(D)	0	(D)	0
TX	Robertson County	250	210	40	0	0

State/ Area	Area Name	Total	Speak Spanish or Spanish Creole	Speak other Indo European language	Speak Asian or Pacific Island language	Speak other language
TX	Rockwall County	705	570	(D)	85	(D)
TX	Runnels County	565	550	15	0	0
TX	Rusk County	600	540	(D)	40	(D)
TX	Sabine County	100	65	20	10	0
TX	San Augustine County	60	(D)	0	(D)	0
TX	San Jacinto County	200	175	(D)	(D)	(D)
TX	San Patricio County	6085	5975	80	30	0
TX	San Saba County	190	(D)	(D)	0	0
TX	Schleicher County	260	(D)	0	(D)	0
TX	Scurry County	715	(D)	(D)	0	0
TX	Shackelford County	60	(D)	(D)	0	0
TX	Shelby County	275	230	(D)	(D)	0
TX	Sherman County	105	100	(D)	(D)	0
TX	Smith County	2620	2280	175	145	15
TX	Somervell County	145	130	0	15	0
TX	Starr County	10170	(D)	(D)	0	0
TX	Stephens County	225	200	(D)	0	(D)
TX	Sterling County	85	(D)	0	0	(D)
TX	Stonewall County	25	25	0	0	0
TX	Sutton County	410	390	(D)	0	(D)
TX	Swisher County	460	(D)	(D)	0	0
TX	Tarrant County	40825	29200	2830	8100	690
TX	Taylor County	2880	2580	150	150	0
TX	Terrell County	95	95	0	0	0
TX	Terry County	930	(D)	(D)	0	0
TX	Throckmorton County	20	(D)	(D)	0	0
TX	Titus County	1105	1090	(D)	(D)	0
TX	Tom Green County	4920	4630	175	(D)	(D)
TX	Travis County	27865	21925	1885	3690	360
TX	Trinity County	115	90	(D)	(D)	0

State/ Area	Area Name	Total	Speak Spanish or Spanish Creole	Speak other Indo European language	Speak Asian or Pacific Island language	Speak other language
TX	Tyler County	345	300	(D)	(D)	0
TX	Upshur County	270	235	25	(D)	(D)
TX	Upton County	275	(D)	(D)	0	0
TX	Uvalde County	3385	3365	(D)	(D)	0
TX	Val Verde County	6005	5905	60	40	0
TX	Van Zandt County	575	505	35	35	0
TX	Victoria County	4480	4175	170	(D)	(D)
TX	Walker County	1910	1785	75	(D)	(D)
TX	Waller County	875	780	80	15	0
TX	Ward County	805	(D)	(D)	0	0
TX	Washington County	745	410	235	100	0
TX	Webb County	33975	33845	(D)	80	(D)
TX	Wharton County	1835	1655	(D)	(D)	0
TX	Wheeler County	70	(D)	(D)	0	0
TX	Wichita County	2765	2005	(D)	525	(D)
TX	Wilbarger County	420	335	(D)	45	(D)
TX	Willacy County	3970	3970	0	0	0
TX	Williamson County	5655	4260	610	745	40
TX	Wilson County	1970	1790	150	30	0
TX	Winkler County	495	485	(D)	(D)	0
TX	Wise County	660	570	50	(D)	(D)
TX	Wood County	430	390	(D)	20	(D)
TX	Yoakum County	420	390	30	0	0
TX	Young County	225	(D)	(D)	0	0
TX	Zapata County	1970	1945	(D)	0	(D)
TX	Zavala County	2905	(D)	0	(D)	0
UT	Utah	31150	15650	6060	6505	2930
UT	Beaver County	95	45	(D)	(D)	30
UT	Box Elder County	380	220	120	(D)	(D)
UT	Cache County	780	450	125	185	20
UT	Carbon County	170	75	65	25	0

State/ Area	Area Name	Total	Speak Spanish or Spanish Creole	Speak other Indo European language	Speak Asian or Pacific Island language	Speak other language
UT	Daggett County	10	(D)	(D)	0	0
UT	Davis County	2300	1190	520	475	115
UT	Duchesne County	60	30	10	4	15
UT	Emery County	90	70	15	(D)	(D)
UT	Garfield County	35	4	(D)	(D)	15
UT	Grand County	105	45	(D)	(D)	45
UT	Iron County	305	185	70	20	30
UT	Juab County	25	15	0	0	15
UT	Kane County	55	30	10	0	15
UT	Millard County	105	70	15	(D)	(D)
UT	Morgan County	75	40	25	10	0
UT	Piute County	4	(D)	0	0	0
UT	Rich County	4	0	(D)	0	0
UT	Salt Lake County	15910	7360	3405	4525	620
UT	San Juan County	1770	70	0	0	1700
UT	Sanpete County	295	205	55	(D)	(D)
UT	Sevier County	100	60	(D)	20	(D)
UT	Summit County	265	175	40	45	0
UT	Tooele County	430	295	70	45	15
UT	Uintah County	225	125	15	25	65
UT	Utah County	3820	2280	840	610	80
UT	Wasatch County	110	90	15	(D)	(D)
UT	Washington County	700	485	110	40	65
UT	Wayne County	15	(D)	(D)	0	0
UT	Weber County	2920	2020	485	375	40
VT	Vermont	5370	835	3925	510	100
VT	Addison County	230	40	180	(D)	(D)
VT	Bennington County	210	60	150	0	0
VT	Caledonia County	250	20	215	(D)	(D)
VT	Chittenden County	1575	305	945	305	25
VT	Essex County	110	(D)	105	(D)	(D)

State/ Area	Area Name	Total	Speak Spanish or Spanish Creole	Speak other Indo European language	Speak Asian or Pacific Island language	Speak other language
VT	Franklin County	470	35	415	(D)	(D)
VT	Grand Isle County	60	(D)	50	(D)	0
VT	Lamoille County	195	(D)	150	(D)	0
VT	Orange County	160	35	120	(D)	(D)
VT	Orleans County	400	(D)	360	30	(D)
VT	Rutland County	515	100	380	(D)	(D)
VT	Washington County	555	75	435	40	4
VT	Windham County	280	65	165	(D)	(D)
VT	Windsor County	360	55	255	35	15
VA	Virginia	105440	40855	23355	37035	4195
VA	Accomack County	275	185	70	(D)	(D)
VA	Albemarle County	690	270	265	115	35
VA	Alleghany County	45	35	(D)	(D)	0
VA	Amelia County	75	40	35	0	0
VA	Amherst County	120	70	35	20	0
VA	Appomattox County	80	25	30	(D)	(D)
VA	Arlington County	6480	3120	1380	1550	430
VA	Augusta County	280	105	135	40	0
VA	Bath County	30	(D)	(D)	0	0
VA	Bedford County	230	115	40	75	0
VA	Bland County	35	(D)	(D)	0	0
VA	Botetourt County	160	115	(D)	0	(D)
VA	Brunswick County	30	(D)	(D)	0	0
VA	Buchanan County	60	25	35	0	0
VA	Buckingham County	45	20	(D)	(D)	0
VA	Campbell County	295	170	75	55	0
VA	Caroline County	35	(D)	0	(D)	0
VA	Carroll County	110	55	(D)	(D)	0
VA	Charles City County	25	0	(D)	(D)	0
VA	Charlotte County	80	(D)	50	(D)	0
VA	Chesterfield County	2560	860	745	870	85

State/Area	Area Name	Total	Speak Spanish or Spanish Creole	Speak other Indo European language	Speak Asian or Pacific Island language	Speak other language
VA	Clarke County	40	(D)	(D)	(D)	0
VA	Craig County	25	(D)	(D)	0	0
VA	Culpeper County	145	85	(D)	(D)	0
VA	Cumberland County	75	(D)	45	0	(D)
VA	Dickenson County	55	20	20	(D)	(D)
VA	Dinwiddie County	190	115	55	(D)	(D)
VA	Essex County	65	40	20	(D)	(D)
VA	Fairfax County	37735	10210	6620	19155	1755
VA	Fauquier County	365	175	105	(D)	(D)
VA	Floyd County	45	20	25	0	0
VA	Fluvanna County	80	50	30	0	0
VA	Franklin County	175	115	(D)	0	(D)
VA	Frederick County	500	275	120	105	0
VA	Giles County	40	20	20	0	0
VA	Gloucester County	250	85	130	35	0
VA	Goochland County	115	35	60	(D)	(D)
VA	Grayson County	100	75	25	0	0
VA	Greene County	30	0	(D)	(D)	0
VA	Greensville County	15	15	0	0	0
VA	Halifax County	160	85	(D)	(D)	0
VA	Hanover County	460	220	155	(D)	(D)
VA	Henrico County	3640	1085	1045	1400	115
VA	Henry County	330	165	135	(D)	(D)
VA	Highland County	15	(D)	(D)	0	0
VA	Isle of Wight County	105	55	25	(D)	(D)
VA	James City County	440	150	200	95	0
VA	King and Queen County	30	(D)	(D)	0	0
VA	King George County	70	40	(D)	(D)	0
VA	King William County	55	30	(D)	(D)	0
VA	Lancaster County	65	(D)	40	(D)	0

State/ Area	Area Name	Total	Speak Spanish or Spanish Creole	Speak other Indo European language	Speak Asian or Pacific Island language	Speak other language
VA	Lee County	65	(D)	35	(D)	0
VA	Loudoun County	2830	980	630	1115	105
VA	Louisa County	140	(D)	70	(D)	0
VA	Lunenburg County	25	15	10	0	0
VA	Madison County	80	45	(D)	(D)	0
VA	Mathews County	80	(D)	45	(D)	0
VA	Mecklenburg County	200	120	70	15	0
VA	Middlesex County	50	50	0	0	0
VA	Montgomery County	665	325	(D)	175	(D)
VA	Nelson County	95	(D)	50	(D)	0
VA	New Kent County	65	45	(D)	(D)	0
VA	Northampton County	90	70	20	0	0
VA	Northumberland County	90	55	(D)	(D)	0
VA	Nottoway County	85	(D)	40	(D)	0
VA	Orange County	70	50	(D)	(D)	0
VA	Page County	165	110	(D)	(D)	0
VA	Patrick County	150	100	20	30	0
VA	Pittsylvania County	275	185	(D)	(D)	0
VA	Powhatan County	120	(D)	55	0	(D)
VA	Prince Edward County	205	140	(D)	(D)	0
VA	Prince George County	475	230	(D)	130	(D)
VA	Prince William County	5370	2870	1175	1145	180
VA	Pulaski County	275	100	110	(D)	(D)
VA	Rappahannock County	30	(D)	0	(D)	0
VA	Richmond County	135	125	(D)	0	(D)
VA	Roanoke County	505	220	145	(D)	(D)
VA	Rockbridge County	75	40	(D)	(D)	0

State/ Area	Area Name	Total	Speak Spanish or Spanish Creole	Speak other Indo European language	Speak Asian or Pacific Island language	Speak other language
VA	Rockingham County	460	340	(D)	(D)	0
VA	Russell County	25	(D)	0	(D)	0
VA	Scott County	30	20	(D)	(D)	0
VA	Shenandoah County	255	200	35	(D)	(D)
VA	Smyth County	155	80	30	(D)	(D)
VA	Southampton County	60	60	0	0	0
VA	Spotsylvania County	695	280	205	175	40
VA	Stafford County	855	305	(D)	280	(D)
VA	Surry County	35	(D)	25	(D)	0
VA	Sussex County	60	30	25	0	0
VA	Tazewell County	125	65	45	20	0
VA	Warren County	180	105	35	(D)	(D)
VA	Washington County	220	135	(D)	45	(D)
VA	Westmoreland County	185	130	(D)	(D)	0
VA	Wise County	130	100	25	(D)	(D)
VA	Wythe County	90	50	45	0	0
VA	York County	495	155	100	240	0
VA	Alexandria city	3890	1835	745	825	485
VA	Bedford city	45	(D)	20	(D)	0
VA	Bristol city	80	(D)	(D)	30	0
VA	Buena Vista city	25	(D)	(D)	0	0
VA	Charlottesville city	435	205	(D)	140	(D)
VA	Chesapeake city	1720	745	450	485	45
VA	Clifton Forge city	20	(D)	(D)	0	0
VA	Colonial Heights city	190	45	45	100	0
VA	Covington city	30	(D)	(D)	(D)	0
VA	Danville city	240	150	70	20	0
VA	Emporia city	20	(D)	(D)	0	0
VA	Fairfax city	820	255	165	370	30
VA	Falls Church city	240	85	45	110	0

State/ Area	Area Name	Total	Speak Spanish or Spanish Creole	Speak other Indo European language	Speak Asian or Pacific Island language	Speak other language
VA	Franklin city	35	15	(D)	o	(D)
VA	Fredericksburg city	280	175	(D)	(D)	o
VA	Galax city	45	(D)	(D)	o	o
VA	Hampton city	1790	775	435	545	35
VA	Harrisonburg city	665	390	170	85	20
VA	Hopewell city	235	165	30	40	o
VA	Lexington city	45	(D)	(D)	o	o
VA	Lynchburg city	540	235	160	110	35
VA	Manassas city	615	290	(D)	235	(D)
VA	Manassas Park city	165	115	(D)	(D)	o
VA	Martinsville city	40	20	(D)	(D)	o
VA	Newport News city	2395	1085	430	845	35
VA	Norfolk city	3755	1845	750	1080	80
VA	Norton city	25	(D)	(D)	o	o
VA	Petersburg city	305	145	110	(D)	(D)
VA	Poquoson city	105	25	40	40	o
VA	Portsmouth city	1200	610	340	195	60
VA	Radford city	140	70	65	o	o
VA	Richmond city	2140	1180	675	240	45
VA	Roanoke city	750	380	205	110	55
VA	Salem city	180	(D)	55	60	(D)
VA	Staunton city	190	105	45	(D)	(D)
VA	Suffolk city	525	255	140	(D)	(D)
VA	Virginia Beach city	7355	2390	1450	3365	150
VA	Waynesboro city	145	(D)	(D)	o	o
VA	Williamsburg city	135	15	50	70	o
VA	Winchester city	255	140	40	75	o
WA	Washington	120930	41080	20370	56295	3185
WA	Adams County	775	745	(D)	o	(D)
WA	Asotin County	140	70	(D)	(D)	o
WA	Benton County	2620	1780	305	535	o

State/ Area	Area Name	Total	Speak Spanish or Spanish Creole	Speak other Indo European language	Speak Asian or Pacific Island language	Speak other language
WA	Chelan County	1490	1315	100	75	0
WA	Clallam County	710	395	180	95	40
WA	Clark County	4720	1395	1340	1795	195
WA	Columbia County	65	(D)	(D)	0	0
WA	Cowlitz County	885	445	120	300	20
WA	Douglas County	640	565	45	30	0
WA	Ferry County	25	15	(D)	0	(D)
WA	Franklin County	2150	1930	35	185	0
WA	Garfield County	10	(D)	0	(D)	0
WA	Grant County	2035	1810	180	50	0
WA	Grays Harbor County	635	265	185	165	15
WA	Island County	930	255	225	420	30
WA	Jefferson County	225	(D)	70	75	(D)
WA	King County	51605	8495	9020	32465	1625
WA	Kitsap County	3070	850	470	1690	65
WA	Kittitas County	310	145	125	(D)	(D)
WA	Klickitat County	235	185	(D)	(D)	30
WA	Lewis County	720	460	160	(D)	(D)
WA	Lincoln County	40	20	(D)	(D)	0
WA	Mason County	490	250	80	120	40
WA	Okanogan County	490	415	30	15	25
WA	Pacific County	255	105	25	105	20
WA	Pend Oreille County	70	15	40	(D)	(D)
WA	Pierce County	13025	3255	2270	7240	260
WA	San Juan County	115	50	55	(D)	(D)
WA	Skagit County	1520	1165	175	155	20
WA	Skamania County	45	40	(D)	(D)	0
WA	Snohomish County	11470	2705	2100	6355	310
WA	Spokane County	4010	1325	1330	1275	75
WA	Stevens County	160	85	65	15	0
WA	Thurston County	3485	910	550	1955	65

State/ Area	Area Name	Total	Speak Spanish or Spanish Creole	Speak other Indo European language	Speak Asian or Pacific Island language	Speak other language
WA	Wahkiakum County	20	10	0	0	10
WA	Walla Walla County	1135	970	(D)	85	(D)
WA	Whatcom County	1840	805	505	435	100
WA	Whitman County	420	190	(D)	150	(D)
WA	Yakima County	8335	7500	330	360	145
WV	West Virginia	8310	3555	3575	835	345
WV	Barbour County	40	20	20	0	0
WV	Berkeley County	395	220	100	40	35
WV	Boone County	55	30	20	0	0
WV	Braxton County	15	(D)	0	(D)	(D)
WV	Brooke County	160	(D)	135	(D)	0
WV	Cabell County	465	210	135	75	50
WV	Calhoun County	15	(D)	(D)	0	0
WV	Clay County	40	(D)	15	0	(D)
WV	Doddridge County	40	(D)	25	(D)	0
WV	Fayette County	210	90	105	(D)	(D)
WV	Gilmer County	25	(D)	(D)	(D)	0
WV	Grant County	15	(D)	(D)	0	0
WV	Greenbrier County	105	50	45	(D)	(D)
WV	Hampshire County	50	(D)	(D)	0	0
WV	Hancock County	500	100	380	(D)	(D)
WV	Hardy County	50	25	25	0	0
WV	Harrison County	320	135	135	(D)	(D)
WV	Jackson County	100	60	(D)	(D)	0
WV	Jefferson County	315	150	140	25	0
WV	Kanawha County	1055	465	380	125	90
WV	Lewis County	10	0	10	0	0
WV	Lincoln County	60	20	40	0	0
WV	Logan County	145	40	80	10	15
WV	McDowell County	90	30	40	(D)	(D)
WV	Marion County	235	115	85	(D)	(D)

State/ Area	Area Name	Total	Speak Spanish or Spanish Creole	Speak other Indo European language	Speak Asian or Pacific Island language	Speak other language
WV	Marshall County	195	105	70	20	0
WV	Mason County	45	(D)	35	(D)	0
WV	Mercer County	225	110	90	(D)	(D)
WV	Mineral County	80	35	20	20	0
WV	Mingo County	95	40	40	10	0
WV	Monongalia County	755	275	305	145	30
WV	Monroe County	65	(D)	40	15	(D)
WV	Morgan County	60	30	20	(D)	(D)
WV	Nicholas County	110	25	75	(D)	(D)
WV	Ohio County	320	140	150	(D)	(D)
WV	Pendleton County	65	45	(D)	(D)	0
WV	Pleasants County	20	15	10	0	0
WV	Pocahontas County	65	25	25	(D)	(D)
WV	Preston County	105	50	55	0	0
WV	Putnam County	135	60	45	20	10
WV	Raleigh County	535	290	175	(D)	(D)
WV	Randolph County	85	(D)	55	0	(D)
WV	Ritchie County	10	(D)	0	(D)	0
WV	Roane County	25	(D)	(D)	0	0
WV	Summers County	20	0	(D)	0	0
WV	Taylor County	85	15	65	0	0
WV	Tucker County	45	15	30	0	0
WV	Tyler County	25	(D)	(D)	0	0
WV	Upshur County	55	15	40	0	0
WV	Wayne County	160	85	65	(D)	(D)
WV	Webster County	35	25	10	0	0
WV	Wetzel County	60	30	(D)	(D)	0
WV	Wirt County	4	(D)	0	0	0
WV	Wood County	230	130	45	55	0
WV	Wyoming County	100	70	(D)	0	(D)
WI	Wisconsin	60000	27510	22325	8320	1845

State/ Area	Area Name	Total	Speak Spanish or Spanish Creole	Speak other Indo European language	Speak Asian or Pacific Island language	Speak other language
WI	Adams County	170	75	80	(D)	(D)
WI	Ashland County	85	(D)	35	(D)	30
WI	Barron County	270	75	185	(D)	(D)
WI	Bayfield County	45	(D)	25	0	(D)
WI	Brown County	1835	970	360	450	55
WI	Buffalo County	120	50	60	(D)	(D)
WI	Burnett County	75	20	35	(D)	(D)
WI	Calumet County	245	(D)	110	65	(D)
WI	Chippewa County	210	95	65	(D)	(D)
WI	Clark County	615	(D)	560	0	(D)
WI	Columbia County	415	150	230	4	30
WI	Crawford County	115	55	40	(D)	(D)
WI	Dane County	4645	2245	1245	1070	80
WI	Dodge County	725	380	310	10	25
WI	Door County	230	95	105	(D)	(D)
WI	Douglas County	275	50	100	20	110
WI	Dunn County	205	100	50	50	0
WI	Eau Claire County	980	315	355	260	50
WI	Florence County	45	20	30	0	0
WI	Fond du Lac County	665	275	370	(D)	(D)
WI	Forest County	110	25	30	4	45
WI	Grant County	370	190	170	(D)	(D)
WI	Green County	170	50	110	10	0
WI	Green Lake County	235	(D)	145	(D)	0
WI	Iowa County	130	65	45	(D)	(D)
WI	Iron County	45	10	30	(D)	(D)
WI	Jackson County	190	65	70	20	40
WI	Jefferson County	595	400	180	(D)	(D)
WI	Juneau County	160	50	65	(D)	(D)
WI	Kenosha County	2270	1100	915	160	100
WI	Kewaunee County	140	(D)	80	(D)	0

State/ Area	Area Name	Total	Speak Spanish or Spanish Creole	Speak other Indo European language	Speak Asian or Pacific Island language	Speak other language
WI	La Crosse County	930	330	220	330	50
WI	Lafayette County	70	40	30	0	0
WI	Langlade County	75	30	40	(D)	(D)
WI	Lincoln County	175	50	95	(D)	(D)
WI	Manitowoc County	545	190	260	95	0
WI	Marathon County	1385	(D)	610	500	(D)
WI	Marinette County	265	75	175	(D)	(D)
WI	Marquette County	215	105	90	(D)	(D)
WI	Menominee County	60	20	(D)	25	(D)
WI	Milwaukee County	19850	10965	5730	2650	505
WI	Monroe County	670	115	510	30	15
WI	Oconto County	200	95	95	(D)	(D)
WI	Oneida County	275	105	130	(D)	(D)
WI	Outagamie County	1300	700	240	345	15
WI	Ozaukee County	620	150	400	(D)	(D)
WI	Pepin County	70	(D)	55	(D)	0
WI	Pierce County	175	90	70	(D)	(D)
WI	Polk County	175	65	85	(D)	(D)
WI	Portage County	860	220	535	105	0
WI	Price County	100	30	45	(D)	(D)
WI	Racine County	2910	1785	815	220	90
WI	Richland County	105	(D)	70	0	(D)
WI	Rock County	1270	635	355	255	20
WI	Rusk County	95	20	60	(D)	(D)
WI	St. Croix County	270	110	135	10	20
WI	Sauk County	510	140	325	15	25
WI	Sawyer County	130	40	35	20	40
WI	Shawano County	225	60	130	(D)	(D)
WI	Sheboygan County	1230	445	445	(D)	(D)
WI	Taylor County	190	25	140	(D)	(D)
WI	Trempealeau County	290	100	190	0	0

State/ Area	Area Name	Total	Speak Spanish or Spanish Creole	Speak other Indo European language	Speak Asian or Pacific Island language	Speak other language
WI	Vernon County	650	30	605	15	0
WI	Vilas County	150	25	75	30	20
WI	Walworth County	1295	750	390	145	15
WI	Washburn County	80	35	35	(D)	(D)
WI	Washington County	880	275	540	(D)	(D)
WI	Waukesha County	3190	1240	1515	375	65
WI	Waupaca County	340	(D)	175	(D)	0
WI	Waushara County	240	(D)	140	(D)	0
WI	Winnebago County	1200	545	400	235	25
WI	Wood County	355	155	130	(D)	(D)
WY	Wyoming	4855	3190	960	385	315
WY	Albany County	305	195	55	(D)	(D)
WY	Big Horn County	80	65	15	0	0
WY	Campbell County	275	160	85	(D)	(D)
WY	Carbon County	200	145	(D)	0	(D)
WY	Converse County	135	(D)	0	(D)	0
WY	Crook County	15	0	(D)	(D)	0
WY	Fremont County	480	180	25	50	230
WY	Goshen County	225	165	60	0	0
WY	Hot Springs County	50	30	(D)	(D)	(D)
WY	Johnson County	50	(D)	(D)	0	0
WY	Laramie County	1260	935	205	(D)	(D)
WY	Lincoln County	70	55	10	4	0
WY	Natrona County	450	240	140	25	40
WY	Niobrara County	15	4	4	0	0
WY	Park County	240	90	(D)	(D)	0
WY	Platte County	75	50	25	0	0
WY	Sheridan County	195	135	45	(D)	(D)
WY	Sublette County	40	15	(D)	(D)	0
WY	Sweetwater County	435	340	75	(D)	(D)
WY	Teton County	75	(D)	(D)	0	0

State/ Area	Area Name	Total	Speak Spanish or Spanish Creole	Speak other Indo European language	Speak Asian or Pacific Island language	Speak other language
WY	Uinta County	105	90	15	0	0
WY	Washakie County	65	(D)	(D)	0	0
WY	Weston County	25	15	4	0	0

Source: Census 2000 Special Tabulation 194.

Note: Data are based on a sample and are rounded. (D) indicates suppression for disclosure concerns.

Index

About the Contributors

Casey Cobb is assistant professor of Educational Leadership and director of the Center for Education Policy Analysis at the University of Connecticut. He studies education policies that raise questions about equity and fairness. Casey is currently researching policies related to accountability, school choice, and bilingual education, and is co-writing a forthcoming book on school policy. He also serves as president of the New England Educational Research Organization. Casey lives in Tolland, Connecticut, with his wife, Sheri, and their two children, Caden and Sedona.

Wanda DeLeón is a doctoral student in the Department of Curriculum and Instruction, Neag School of Education, at the University of Connecticut.

David Gerwin is assistant professor of Secondary Education and Youth Services and co-coordinator of the Program in Social Studies at Queens College, City University of New York. He received his Ph.D. in American History from the Graduate School of Arts and Sciences, Columbia University in 1998 and his M.A. in The Teaching of Social Studies from Teachers College, Columbia University in 1995. His research interests include the lifetime career development of social studies teachers, the creation and development of professional practice networks, and ways that faculty and students experience the "methods" course. He is also interested in the use of oral history in the classroom and in historical research. As a historian he has written about community organizing during the 1960s in Newark, New Jersey.

Mileidis Gort is assistant professor of Bilingual Education and coordinator of Bilingual Education Programs in the Department of Curriculum and Instruction at the Neag School of Education, University of Connecticut. She is principal investigator of a five-year, $1.3 million U.S. Department of Education Title III National Professional Development Program Training Grant. Her current research examines the early bilingual and biliteracy development of English- and Spanish-dominant learners in Two-Way Bilingual Programs, as well as developmental, authentic assessment of biliteracy. Dr. Gort's work has been nationally recognized by the American Educational Research Association, the National Association for Bilingual Education, and the National Reading Conference. She has taught at the elementary and secondary levels and has collaborated with teachers, administrators, and parents in teacher-research, curriculum development, and professional development contexts. Her publications include book chapters, K–3 literature-based reading series, and peer-reviewed journals.

Cara Mulcahy is currently a doctoral candidate in the department of Curriculum and Instruction in the Neag School of Education at the University of Connecticut. Her field of study is English Education with special attention toward critical literacy and the teaching of reading. Prior to this Cara taught language arts, reading, and social studies at the middle school level. The focus of her dissertation is a close analysis of current models of language arts instruction to determine if they empower students and move them toward critical literacy. Future areas of research interest include adolescent literature, adolescent literacy, critical literacy, policy issues, social justice, issues of diversity, and critical theory.

Dina C. Osborn is a doctoral student in the Department of Educational Leadership, Neag School of Education, University of Connecticut.

Terry A. Osborn specializes in Educational Linguistics and Second Language Education in the Department of Curriculum and Instruction, Neag School of Education, University of Connecticut. Dr. Osborn taught public school German for six years at the high school level, including one year also at the middle school level. He received an M.A. in German from the University of

Tennessee-Knoxville and the Ph.D. from the University of Connecticut. He was on the faculty of Queens College, City University of New York, for three years. Dr. Osborn is co-editor, with Timothy Reagan, of *Critical Inquiry in Language Studies: An International Journal* (Lawrence Erlbaum Associates) and series editor of five series related to language, education and research. He co-authored, with Timothy Reagan, *The Foreign Language Educator in Society: Toward a Critical Pedagogy* and edited *The Future of Foreign Language Education in the United States.* He also authored *Critical Reflection and the Foreign Language Classroom*, winner of the 2001 American Educational Studies Association Critics' Choice Award. He received the Stephen A. Freeman Award from the Northeast Conference on the Teaching of Foreign Languages for the best published article on research in teaching techniques.

Sharon F. Rallis is professor of Educational Leadership in the Neag School of Education at the University of Connecticut. Her interests lie in qualitative methodology, program evaluation, and policy implementation. She has published extensively; her books include *Learning in the Field* (Sage, 2003), widely used as an introductory qualitative text, and *Principals of Dynamic Schools* (Corwin, 2000), offering an alternative perspective on school leadership. Rallis is the 2005 president of the American Evaluation Association.

Timothy Reagan is currently dean of the School of Education and professor of Linguistics and Education at Roger Williams University in Bristol, Rhode Island. His areas of research include foreign language education, teaching English to speakers of other languages, applied and educational linguistics, and the linguistics of natural sign languages. He is the author of *Language, Education and Ideology: Mapping the Linguistic Landscape of US Schools* (2002), the co-author, with Terry A. Osborn, of *The Foreign Language Educator in Society: Toward a Critical Pedagogy* (2002), and the co-editor, with Humphrey Tonkin, of *Language in the 21st Century* (2003).

Xaé Alicia Reyes is associate professor of Education and Puerto Rican and Latino Studies. She has been on the University of Connecticut faculty since fall 1999. Her areas of interest include educational ethnography, teacher education, school reform, and migration and schooling. She has previously taught at Rhode Island College, Brown University, and the University of Puerto Rico.